The Subwhative?

The Subjunctive in Spanish:
A Step-by-Step Workbook & Guide

Leslie Hayertz

Sassy Crow Books
Oregon
sassycrow.com

Acknowledgements are on page 269.

Cover illustration by Brian Jelgerhuis
Cover design by Brian Jelgerhuis

ISBN 13: 978-0-9997718-0-8

Table of Contents

Introduction...1

Nuts & Bolts: Grammar Terms..3

Part I

The Present Subjunctive

A. How to Form the Subjunctive:

Regular Verbs 9
Stem-Change Verbs...12
Irregular Verbs 14
Spelling Adjustments...16

B. How to Use the Subjunctive:

#1 Influence / Volition 21
    Decir...26
#2 Emotion 29
#3 Impersonal Expressions 37
#4 Doubt and Negation 41
    "The Fact That" & "It's Hard to Believe" 45
    "Creer" & "No Creer": The Speaker's Doubt or Certainty 46
#5 Compound Verbs 47
    What Is a Compound Verb?...47
    Present Participles & Progressive Tenses 48
    Past Participles & Perfect Tenses..49
    FYI—Other Uses of Participles 53
#6 Intended Purpose..59
#7 Contingencies 63
#8 Cuando...69
#9 Aunque 75
#10 Non-Existent People & Objects 81
    Negatives..85
#11 Hypothetical People & Objects...87
#12 "Si" Clauses 95
#13 Verbs of Influence: A Shortcut 97
#14 Indirect Commands 99
#15 The "-Evers" 103
#16 Expressions of Possibility (Single Clause) 107

Part II

The Past Subjunctive

A. How to Form the Subjunctive:

How to Form the Past Subjunctive 111
    Review of the "Ellos" Form of the Preterite 112
    The Other Past Subjunctive 115
    Courtesy Expressions 118

B. How to Use the Past Subjunctive:

Coordinating Tenses 121
    Verb Endings for the Preterite 122
    Verb Endings for the Imperfect 122
    A Summary of Preterite vs. Imperfect 123
#1 Influence / Volition 125
#2 Emotion 125
#3 Impersonal Expressions 125
#4 Doubt and Negation 125
    Ojalá 133
#5 Compound Verbs 135
#6 Intended Purpose 141
#7 Contingencies 145
#8 Cuando 145
    Future & Conditional 146
    "Ir a" + Infinitive 146
    Preterite & Imperfect 146
    Notes on Present Tense Indicative 150
#9 Aunque 163
#10 Non-Existent People & Objects 169
#11 Hypothetical People & Objects 169
#12 "Si" Clauses 177
    The Future & the Conditional 178
#13 Verbs of Influence: A Shortcut 187
#14 Indirect Commands 189
Como Si 190
#15 The "-Evers" 191
#16 Expressions of Possibility (Single Clause) 193
Review Crossword 194

Answer Key 197

Index 265

Acknowledgements 270

Introduction

Question: *Can't I get by without the subjunctive? Isn't it a very formal usage?*

Answer: Not at all.
The subjunctive is not fancy or highfalutin.
On the contrary, the subjunctive is used everywhere and by all speakers.
It is an intrinsic part of everyday Spanish.

Question: *But I haven't used the subjunctive, and I haven't missed it.*
If it's so common, how can that be?

Answer: When you start learning Spanish, you tend to speak in simple sentences.
Since the subjunctive is found only in dependent clauses (see p.3), it's a while
before you bump up against the need for the subjunctive.

So, congratulations!
Now that you're using more complex sentences, you are ready for the subjunctive.

This workbook will take you step by step through the various uses of the subjunctive.
Part I deals with the subjunctive in the present tense.
Part II covers the subjunctive in the past tense.

Note: The subjunctive is not a tense.
It's called a mode or mood, that is to say, a type of communication.

Spanish has three modes: the indicative, the imperative and the subjunctive.

1. **The indicative** is what you have mostly been using.
   It has a number of tenses: present, future, preterite, imperfect, etc.
   It's called the indicative because it indicates; it informs.

2. **The imperative** is used to command, instruct and direct.

3. **The subjunctive** is not a direct command and it is not information.
   It's used in many ways: for example, for situations tinged by emotion, for future
   contingencies, for things that are not factual or real, or are hypothetical or
   contrary to reality.

Nuts & Bolts: Grammar Terms

Subject   The actor in a sentence or clause.
(If there's no action, the subject is the topic of a sentence.)

examples:

María maneja un taxi.   **Mary** *drives a taxi.*
El árbol es verde.   *The* **tree** *is green.*
La paciencia es una virtud.   **Patience** *is a virtue.*

Verb   The action, or a word that expresses a state (to be, seem, etc.).

Juan **trabaja** aquí.   John **works** *here.*
Están en Guatemala.   *They* **are** *in Guatemala.*

Conjunction   A linking word that connects two or more parts of a sentence.

Comemos pan **y** mantequilla.   *We eat bread* **and** *butter.*
Lo mandó **adonde** ellos viven ahora.   *He sent it to* **where** *they live now.*
Compré el libro **que** leíste.   *I bought the book* **that** *you read.*

Note: "que" is the linking word most often used with the subjunctive.

Sentence   A statement, question or command that includes a conjugated verb and a subject.
(In Spanish the subject doesn't need to be stated if it is understood.)

Sonia estudia español.   *Sonia studies Spanish.*
Viajamos mucho.   *We travel a lot.*

Phrase   A group of words that has no conjugated verb.

un buen restaurante   *a good restaurant*
hacia el centro   *towards downtown*

Clause   A group of words within a sentence that includes a conjugated verb and a subject.
(The subject may be understood.)

There are main clauses and dependent clauses.

Main Clause: Sometimes called an independent clause, it can stand alone.

Dependent Clause: Sometimes called a subordinate clause, it cannot stand alone.
     A conjunction is needed to link it to the main clause.

<u>Vive en una casa</u> que <u>él mismo construyó.</u>   <u>*He lives in a house*</u> *that* <u>*he built himself.*</u>
  (main clause)   (dependent clause)   (main clause)   (dependent clause)

Infinitive   The basic form of a verb, ending in -ar, -er- or -ir.
It is "infinite" because it is not limited by time or person or mode/mood.
For example, the infinitive "hablar" is "to speak" (at any time, by any person, in any mood).
But "hablo" is conjugated—it is specific to "yo" and to the present time, indicative.

Conjugate   To make changes to a verb to show person, time (tense) and mode.

Mode / Mood   See the note on p.1.

Stem Change   A vowel change that takes place in a word stem. The stem is the root of a word, the part that you can add things to (ex.: con**ten**er). Stem-change verbs are not irregular— the vowel shifts follow a set pattern.

A. Are the following groups of words phrases or clauses?
   Write "P" for phrase and "C" for clause.

   _____1. que me gusta   _____5. una película de horror

   _____2. si quieres   _____6. cuando vengan

   _____3. llegar tarde   _____7. más despacio

   _____4. por favor   _____8. muy caro

B. In the following paragraph:
   • **Underline the verbs.** (There are 10.)
   • **Draw a circle around the subjects.** (There are 7.)
   • **If a subject is not stated but understood, write it underneath the verb.** (There are 3.)

   El señor Sólis es mi vecino. Vive en la casa amarilla. Su esposa trabaja mucho

   en su jardín. Ella siempre me saluda, y de vez en cuando hablamos por unos

   momentos. Pero a él nunca lo veo. Ella dice que su esposo trabaja siempre.

   Además, él viaja mucho por su trabajo. Su trabajo es muy importante para él.

C. In the following sentences:
   • **Underline the main clause.**   • **Put parentheses around any the dependent clause.**
   • **Circle the conjunction.**   • **Translate the sentence.**
   Example:

   <u>Me gusta la película</u>(que)(vimos).   *I like the movie that we saw.*

1. Espero que mis amigos vengan pronto.

   _____

2. Ellos admiran a las personas que son inteligentes y sinceras.

   _____

3. La oficina donde trabajamos está en el piso 20.

   _____

4. Mi compañero de casa nunca se acuerda de cerrar las ventanas cuando llueve.

   _____

5. ¿Te gustó la cena que ellos prepararon?

   _____

D. Complete the following sentences with a dependent clause. (Remember to use a connecting word.) **Translate each sentence.**

Examples:

¿Dónde está el libro *que acabo de sacar de la biblioteca?*

Where is the book *that I just checked out of the library?*

Por favor, invita a María a la fiesta *cuando la veas.*

Please invite María to the party *when you see her.*

1. Me gusta ir de compras _____

   I like to go shopping _____

2. Mis amigos quieren ir de vacaciones _____

   My friends want to go on vacation _____

3. Éste es el carro _____

   This is the car _____

4. Ella juega tenis con una amiga _____

   She plays tennis with a friend_____

The Answer Key begins on p.197.

Part I

The Present Subjunctive

A. How to Form the Present Subjunctive

How to Form the Present Subjunctive

Regular Verbs*:

1. Start with the "yo" form of the present indicative: hablo, tengo, como, conozco, etc.

2. Drop the -o.

3. Flip-flop the endings:
   -ar verbs take -er/-ir endings, and -er/-ir verbs take -ar endings:
   (habl**ar**) yo habl**e**, (ten**er**) tú teng**as**, (viv**ir**) ella viv**a**, etc.

   Note: the *yo* form of the subjunctive uses the same ending as the *él / ella / Ud.* form.

Verb Endings For the Present Subjunctive

	-ar verbs	**-er** / **-ir** verbs
yo	**-e**	**-a**
tú	**-e**s	**-a**s
él, ella, Ud.	**-e**	**-a**
nosotros, nosotras	-**e**mos	-**a**mos
ellos, ellas, Uds.	-**e**n	-**a**n

*****See p.12 for stem-change verbs.**

A. Indicative or subjunctive?
   Put a check next to the verbs in subjunctive.

_____1. viva   _____7. ayude

_____2. conozco   _____8. vengan

_____3. dormimos   _____9. durmamos

_____4. jugamos   _____10. compra

_____5. escribes   _____11. invita

_____6. preguntes   _____12. cante

B. Practice the "yo" form.

infinitive	yo, indicative	yo, subjunctive
1. hablar	*hablo*	*hable*
2. bailar		
3. pasar		
4. dejar		
5. tomar		
6. llamarse*		
7. quedarse*		
8. encontrar		
9. pensar		
10. comer		
11. creer		
12. querer		
13. perder		
14. vivir		
15. asistir		
16. seguir		
17. salir		
18. poner		
19. ver		
20. conocer		

*Reflexive pronouns (and object pronouns) go before the verb in subjunctive.
 Example: llamarse—me llame, te llames, se llame, nos llamemos, se llamen.

C. Practice the forms of the present subjunctive.

infinitive	yo	tú	él, ella, Ud.	nosotros, nosotras	ellos, ellas, Uds.
1. hablar	hable	hables	hable	hablemos	hablen
2. ayudar					
3. comprar					
4. estudiar					
5. quedarse					
6. escuchar					
7. usar					
8. cocinar					
9. comer					
10. comprender					
11. vender					
12. leer					
13. vivir					
14. dividir					
15. destruir					
16. caerse					
17. ver					
18. conocer					
19. tener					
20. hacer					

The Answer Key begins on p.197.

How to Form the Present Subjunctive

Stem-Change Verbs:

The subjunctive of stem-change verbs is formed the same way as regular verbs (see p.9), except for the "nosotros" form.

In the "nosotros" form:

- -ar. and -er stem-change verbs: use the same vowel as in the infinitive: ju gar, ju guemos.
- -ir stem-change verbs use **i** or **u**:
  If the vowel in the stem is **e**, it changes to **i**.: p e dir = p i damos,
  If the vowel in the stem is **o**, it changes to **u**: d o rmir = d u rmamos.

A. Practice stem-change verbs in the subjunctive.

infinitive	yo	tú	él, ella, Ud.	nosotros, nosotras	ellos, ellas, Uds.
1. encontrar					
2. cerrar					
3. querer					
4. poder					
5. perder					
6. volver					
7. morir					
8. seguir					

B. Practice stem-change and non-stem-change verbs in the subjunctive.

infinitive	yo	tú	él, ella, Ud.	nosotros, nosotras	ellos, ellas, Uds.
1. nadar					
2. construir					
3. mostrar					
4. preparar					
5. pedir					
6. servir					
7. pelear					
8. abrir					

C. Fill in the blanks with the correct form of subjunctive for the verbs in parentheses.

1. Ojalá* que mi amiga _____ (salir) sola.

2. Ojalá que el niño no _____ (caerse).

3. Ojalá que nosotros _____ (terminar) las tareas a tiempo.

4. Ojalá que tú _____ (poder) acompañarnos.

5. Ojalá que los jóvenes _____ (ayudar) al viejo.

6. Ojalá que Uds. _____ (dormir) bien.

7. Ojalá que yo _____ (tener) el tiempo.

8. Ojalá que tú _____ (ver) la película.

*"Ojalá" means "I hope," "let's hope," or "God grant." It is always followed by the subjunctive.

D. Ojalá.
   Change each of the following sentences into a clause following "Ojalá." (The verb will be in subjunctive.)
   Translate the new sentences.
   Example:

Se quedan en un buen hotel. *Ojalá que se queden en un buen hotel.*

I hope they stay in a good hotel.

1. Ellos no se pierden. _____

   _____

2. Nos vemos pronto. _____

   _____

3. No te pones nervioso. _____

   _____

4. Vendo mi carro. _____

   _____

5. Mi equipo gana. _____

   _____

6. Tu abuela no muere. _____

   _____

How to Form the Present Subjunctive

Irregular Verbs:

There are only six irregular verbs.
They are the verbs with a present tense "yo" form that doesn't end in a simple "-o."

```
dar............doy
estar.........estoy
ser............soy
ir...............voy
haber........he
saber........sé
```

Dar ....Use **d-** for the stem, and flip-flop the ending: **d**é*, **d**es, **d**é*, **d**emos, **d**en

Estar......Use **est-** for the stem: **est**é, **est**és, **est**é, **est**emos, **est**én**

Ser.........Use **se-** for the stem: **se**a, **se**as, **se**a, **se**amos, **se**an

Ir ....Use **vay-** for the stem: **vay**a, **vay**as, **vay**a, **vay**amos, **vay**an

Haber ....Use **hay-** for the stem: **hay**a, **hay**as, **hay**a, **hay**amos, **hay**an

Saber.....Use **sep-** for the stem: **sep**a, **sep**as, **sep**a, **sep**amos, **sep**an

Note: *Haber* is also the infinitive of *hay*. The subjunctive form is *haya*.

*The accent on *dé* distinguishes it from the preposition *de* as in *el libro de Juan.*
**The accent on the -a of the ending in the indicative forms of *estar* (example: *estás*),
is kept on the -e of the ending in subjunctive (example: *estés*).

A. Practice the subjunctive forms.

infinitive	yo	tú	él, ella, Ud.	nosotros, nosotras	ellos, ellas, Uds.
1. ser					
2. estar					
3. ir					
4. dar					
5. haber					
6. saber					

The Answer Key begins on p.197.

B. **Fill in the blanks with the correct form of subjunctive for the verbs in parentheses.**

1. Ojalá que mis tíos me _____ (dar) un regalo.

2. Ojalá que tú _____ (estar) bien.

3. Ojalá que nosotros siempre _____ (ser) amigos.

4. Ojalá que su esposo _____ (saber) la verdad.

5. Ojalá que _____ (haber) bastante comida.

6. Ojalá que ella _____ (ir) despacio.

C. Ojalá.
   **Change each of the following sentences into a clause following "Ojalá." (The verb will be in subjunctive.)
   Translate the new sentences.**

   Example:

   Se quedan en un buen hotel. *Ojalá que se queden en un buen hotel.*
   I hope they stay in a good hotel.

1. Ellos no están enfermos. _____

   _____

2. Nosotros sabemos las respuestas. _____

   _____

3. María les da las gracias por las flores. _____

   _____

4. Soy rico. _____ *algún día.*

   _____ *someday.*

5. Tú vas despacio. _____

   _____

6. Hay una fiesta. _____

   _____

Spelling Adjustments:

Sometimes a spelling change is needed to maintain the correct pronunciation of the final consonant of the stem.

- For verbs ending in -car, the "c" changes to "qu" before "e" (busca / bus**que**).
- For verbs ending in -gar, the "g" changes to "gu" before "e" (llega / lle**gue**).
- And because "ze" is generally not a combination found in Spanish, for verbs ending in -zar, the "z" changes to "c" before "e" (cazar / ca**ce**).

A. Spelling Changes
Fill in the subjunctive forms for the following verbs, making the necessary spelling changes.

infinitive	yo	tú	él, ella, Ud.	nosotros, nosotras	ellos, ellas, Uds.
1. buscar					
2. pagar					
3. sacar					
4. empezar*					
5. practicar					
6. regar*					

*Empezar and regar are stem-change verbs.

B. Fill in the blanks with the correct form of subjunctive for the verbs in parentheses.
Watch out for spelling changes.

1. Ojalá que yo_____ (llegar) a tiempo.

2. Ojalá que el comité _____ (organizar) bien el festival.

3. Ojalá que tú _____ (sacar) buenas notas.

4. Ojalá que nosotros _____ (jugar) bien.

5. Ojalá que la película _____ (empezar) pronto.

6. Ojalá que él _____ (tocar) la guitarra esta noche.

7. Ojalá que ellos_____ (buscar) un carro más seguro.

8. Ojalá que Uds. _____ (pagar) las cuentas.

C. Review Word Search
Write the subjunctive form of the verbs and find them in the puzzle below.

1. estar: tú _____

2. buscar: Ud. _____

3. jugar: tú y yo _____

4. abrir: él _____

5. cerrar: Ud._____

6. dar: ellos _____

7. ver: yo _____

8. saber: ella _____

9. escuchar: ellos _____

10. hacer: nosotras _____

11. oír: yo _____

12. servir: ella y él _____

13. divertirse: tú _____

14. ser: nosotros _____

15. mirar: tú _____

16. votar: él _____

```
V  B  N  S  M  A  U  X  B  K  I  V  O  T  E  Y  H  E
S  U  T  B  U  S  Q  U  E  Y  U  W  J  B  D  X  X  V
X  E  N  M  P  A  L  M  K  R  Q  B  Q  C  O  C  A  S
X  Q  A  C  V  C  P  A  Z  N  J  F  N  X  B  F  X  E
G  C  E  M  X  N  J  A  W  H  W  N  L  S  W  I  E  P
B  U  S  A  O  F  Z  P  A  I  M  T  B  N  K  R  B  A
H  W  T  T  B  S  F  U  S  B  K  K  E  O  O  S  R  R
J  F  É  Q  K  R  K  E  U  I  D  G  F  O  T  R  D  E
M  F  S  S  D  R  A  L  V  A  R  Q  F  Z  N  C  W  E
R  I  T  S  W  U  A  M  A  Y  H  V  O  M  Y  H  J  B
S  J  R  U  D  F  K  H  U  C  F  H  A  I  H  L  D  G
W  T  D  E  J  J  B  V  Z  B  F  X  H  N  G  C  E  X
F  X  R  P  S  J  U  G  U  E  M  O  S  V  E  A  N  I
U  J  V  Y  P  R  X  L  V  C  I  E  R  R  E  P  D  H
I  H  H  A  G  A  M  O  S  O  L  T  N  G  Z  S  P  O
E  J  F  T  C  M  P  F  T  N  J  A  U  M  X  K  K  Y
T  E  D  I  V  I  E  R  T  A  S  Y  E  J  D  Y  W  L
E  S  C  U  C  H  E  N  W  N  B  Z  V  C  W  C  J  X
```

Solution on p.36.

Part I

The Present Subjunctive

B. Step by Step

How to Use the Present Subjunctive

#1 Influence / Volition

When the subject of a sentence tries to influence or exert its will over another party, the indicative is used in the first part of the sentence and the subjunctive in the second part.

- The verb of influence / volition is information (indicative).
  The verb expressing what is willed is not information (subjunctive).

  Examples:

  Quiero que **limpies** tu cuarto.   *I **want** you to **clean** your room.*
  Ellos **insisten** en que **nos quedemos** con ellos.   *They **insist** we **stay** with them.*

  In the sentences above, *quiero* (I want) and *insisten* (they insist) are information (indicative). But *you cleaning your room* and *we staying with them* are not information—it's not known if the cleaning or staying will actually happen—so those verbs are in the subjunctive.

- The Influence / volition expressed can be strong and overt.

  Examples:

  Ellos exigen   They demand
  Yo mando   I order

  Or the influence / volition can be gentle and subtle.

  Examples:

  Sugerimos   We suggest
  ¿Prefieres?   Do you prefer?

- Because there are two conjugated verbs, "*que*" is needed to connect them.

- If only one subject is involved, then the second verb is not conjugated and there is no subjunctive.

  Examples:

  Quiero salir.   *I want to leave.*
  Esperamos llegar a tiempo.   *We hope to arrive on time.*

A. Circle the verbs that are in the subjunctive.

1. quiero	4. escribe	7. lees	10. decimos
2. salgan	5. hablamos	8. leas	11. salir
3. esté	6. ojalá	9. digamos	12. tenga

B. In the following Spanish sentences: • **underline the verb in indicative**
   • **circle the verb in subjunctive**   • **put a square around the connecting word (*que*).**

1. Queremos que haya paz en el mundo.   *We want there to be peace in the world.*

2. El general mandará que los soldados ataquen.   *The general will order the soldiers to attack.*

3. Sugiero que lo llames.   *I suggest you call him.*

4. Dicen que yo venga.   *They are telling me to come.*

5. ¿Aconsejas que estudiemos más ciencias?   *Do you advise us to study more science?*

C. Draw a line from the verbs of influence on the left to the correct translation on the right.

aconsejamos	we want
deseamos	he orders
dicen	they suggest
espera	I insist
exige	she hopes / expects
insisto	they tell
manda	we advise
necesito	do you forbid / prohibit?
obligan	we wish
permiten	do you all permit / allow?
pide	he demands
prefieren	they prefer
prohibe	I beg
propone	it proposes
queremos	they require
requieren	I need
ruego	is she asking?
sugieren	they force / oblige

D. Find each of the Spanish verbs of influence on p.22 in the word search below.

```
P O J S U G I E R E N Y P C O I
X R B S Z D I J R T P J J X B N
P D E L Q I Y R U Q R G D Z Z Q
N T F F I X L N J D O I E P Z O
G P J V I G J N W I P E S A W J
F D E V U E A R E C O V E C I V
E H P R E T R N S E N E A O N N
E C Q H M C G E R N E S M N S E
X N Q M P I D E N E U P O S I C
I L E P B G T A A G V E S E S E
G C R E Q U I E R E N R Y J T S
E G B G W X M A N D A A D A O I
E X H I Y I K C I J L D K M J T
I L A M M R Y Q U E R E M O S O
N B B U B X M R U E G O K S V V
P R O H I B E B O S I E X Q P O
```

The solution is on p.36.

E. Make a list of verbs of influence/volition (verbs that trigger the subjunctive).

1. *Querer*   5. _____   9. _____   13. _____

2. _____   6. _____   10. _____   14. _____

3. _____   7. _____   11. _____   15. _____

4. _____   8. _____   12. _____   16. _____

F. Use 5 of the verbs from exercise E in sentences that include a second verb in subjunctive.

1._____

2._____

3._____

4._____

5._____

G. Use 3 of the verbs from exercise E in sentences that do not use the subjunctive.

1._____

2._____

3._____

H. Translate the following sentences. (Note: Four of the sentences use no subjunctive.)

1. Do you *(tú)* want me to set the table *(poner la mesa)*?

_____

2. She will not permit her children to ski alone.*

_____

3. He wants to go to the party but he has to work.

_____

4. The school recommends that each student have their own computer.

_____

5. She needs to leave early.

_____

6. We will ask them to call tomorrow.*

_____

7. I hope to travel this summer.

_____

8. They suggest we make a reservation.

_____

9. *(Uds.)* Tell her to call me.

_____

10. The company requires its employees to take drug tests *(una prueba de detección de drogas)*.

_____

11. Do you *(Ud.)* prefer to do it, or do you prefer that I do it?

_____

12. The family wishes to see you *(tú)*.

_____

*Note: There is no separate form for future subjunctive.
The present subjunctive does double duty—present and future.

Decir

- *Decir* can introduce information (indicative).

  Example: Juan **dice** que su hermana **es** maestra.

  Juan says that his sister is a teacher.

  or

- *Decir* can be a verb of influence (meaning "to order") followed by the subjunctive.

  Example: Juan le **dice** a su hermana que **tenga** cuidado.

  Juan tells his sister to be careful.

I. **Put a check by the sentences in which "decir" expresses a command.
   Translate the sentences.**

_____1. Ella dice que su hijo va a llegar mañana.

_____

_____2. ¿Estás diciendo que ellos están mintiendo?

_____

_____3. La maestra les dice a los estudiantes que estudien para el examen.

_____

_____4. Te digo que bajes el volumen.

_____

_____5. No le digas a él que haga eso.

_____

_____6. Dicen que les gustó la película.

_____

The Answer Key begins on p.197.

J. Juan is about to graduate. His grandmothers are both concerned about his future.
Abuela Ana is very bossy. His other grandmother, Abuela Beatriz, prefers to be less direct.

Complete the following sentences.
Note: In their own way, both are trying to influence Juan, and so both will be using the subjunctive.

Abuela Ana	Abuela Beatriz

Examples: *Exijo que asistas a la universidad.*   *Ruego que no bebas la noche de su graduación*

      (I demand that you go to college.)   (I beg you not to drink graduation night.)

1. *Mando que tú*   *Sugiero que tú*

2. *Insisto en que*   *Recomiendo que*

3. *Prohibo que*   *Espero que*

K. María doesn't see her roommate much because of their work schedules, but she is not happy with her. María leaves notes for her in each room of their apartment.
Write the notes using the subjunctive.

Sala:

1. *No quiero que dejes ropa sucia en la sala.*

2. _____

3. _____

Cocina:

4. _____

5. _____

6. _____

Baño:

7. _____

8. _____

9. _____

#2 Emotion

- Verbs of emotion trigger the subjunctive.

- The verb expressing an emotion is information and so is in the indicative.

  Examples:

  Me alegro de que estés bien.   *I'm glad you're well.*
  Están tristes que ella esté enferma.   *They are sad that she's sick.*

- These verbs of emotion color the second verb, so that the second verb is in the subjunctive. (Also, when I say I'm happy that you're well, the focus of the sentence is on the information that I'm happy. The second part of the sentence, that you're well, isn't really information.)

  Examples:

  Me molesta que **no limpies** tu cuarto.   *It bugs me that you **don't clean** your room.*
  Están contentos que **nos quedemos** con ellos.   *They are happy that we're **staying** with them.*

- Because there are two conjugated verbs, "que" is needed to connect them.

- If only one subject is involved, then the second verb is not conjugated. And so there is no subjunctive.

  Examples:

  Odian **bailar**.   *They hate **to dance**.*
  Estamos contentos de **poder ayudar**.   *We are happy **to be able to help**.*

  Note: For information on the use of "*de*" in sentences of emotion, see p.205.

A. In the following Spanish sentences:
   • **underline the verb in indicative**
   • **put a square around the connecting word (*que*)**
   • **circle the verb in subjunctive.**

1. Nos enoja que siempre llegues tarde.   *It makes us mad that you always arrive late.*

2. La doctora se preocupa que su paciente no se mejore.   *The doctor is worried that her patient is not getting better / will not get better.**

3. Me inquieta que ellos fracasen.   *It worries me that they are failing / will fail.**

4. ¿Estás emocionada de que él se gradúe?   *Are you excited that he's graduating / will graduate?**

5. Los niños tienen miedo de que su perro esté perdido.   *The children are afraid their dog is lost.*

*Note: There is no separate form for future subjuctive.
      The present subjunctive does double duty—present and future.

B. Make a list of verbs and expressions of emotion (verbs that trigger the subjunctive).

1. _____   5._____   9. _____   13. _____

2. _____   6._____   10. _____   14. _____

3. _____   7._____   11. _____   15. _____

4. _____   8._____   12. _____   16. _____

C. Combine each set of 2 sentences to make one sentence.

Example:

El padre está enojado.   Su hija llega tarde.

   El padre está enojado que su hija llegue tarde.

1. El taxista se inquieta.   El precio de la gasolina sube.

   _____

2. Los niños están alegres.   Habrá* una fiesta de cumpleaños.

   _____

3. A María le encanta.   María sale a bailar.

   _____

4. Estamos contentos.   Puedes visitarnos.

   _____

5. Lamento.   Están enfermos.

   _____

6. ¿Tienes miedo?   No vienen.

   _____

*Note: The present subjunctive does double duty—present and future.
     There is no separate form for future subjunctive.

D. Translate the following sentences.

1. I don't like you *(tú)* traveling alone.

_____

2. She is proud that her children get good grades.

_____

3. The students are worried that the teacher will give* them a test tomorrow.

_____

4. We hate that you *(Uds.)* live like this *(así)*.

_____

5. He's embarrassed to admit it.

_____

6. Aren't you *(tú)* happy that it's not raining?

_____

7. They are afraid to tell you *(Ud.)* the truth.

_____

8. Don't be sad *(Uds.)* that it's ending *(acabarse)*.

_____

9. I'm sorry you *(tú)* have a headache.

_____

10. They're furious that it's turning out badly *(salir mal)*.

_____

*Note: The present subjunctive does double duty—present and future.
        There is no separate form for future subjunctive.

E. Present and Future
The subjunctive in the sentences below can be about the present or the future.
Translate each sentence below both ways.

Example:

Los padres se preocupan que sus hijos no saquen buenas notas.

present: *The parents are worried that their children aren't getting good grades.*

future: *The parents are worried that their children won't get good grades.*

1. El empleado está molesto que no le paguen más.

   present: _____

   future: _____

2. ¿Estás contenta que te ayuden?

   present: _____

   future: _____

3. Mi amigo se queja de que el viaje cueste mucho.

   present: _____

   future: _____

4. Nos alegramos de que tengan éxito.

   present: _____

   future: _____

5. Me encanta que haya música en vivo *(live)*.

   present: _____

   future: _____

The Answer Key begins on p.197.

F. You receive a message from a friend.
   Respond to each point, using a verb of emotion and the subjunctive.

> Hola,
>
> - Estoy de vacaciones en la Ciudad de México con unos amigos.
> - Nos divertimos mucho.
> - Hace buen tiempo.
> - Pero hay bastante contaminación y tengo los ojos irritados.
> - Vemos muchos lugares interesantes.
> - Mañana vamos a conocer el Museo Nacional de Antropología.
> - Te veo en algunos días.
>
>   Abrazos,
>   tu amigo

Hola,

1. *Me sorprende que estés de vacaciones en México.* _____

2. _____

3. _____

4. _____

5. _____

6. _____

7. _____

                                        Hasta pronto,

G. Use 3 verbs of influence/volition (p.24, ex. E) in sentences that include a second verb in subjunctive.

1. _____

2. _____

3. _____

H. Use 5 verbs of emotion (see p.30, ex. B) in sentences that include a second verb in subjunctive.

1. _____

2. _____

3. _____

4. _____

5. _____

I. Solve the puzzle.

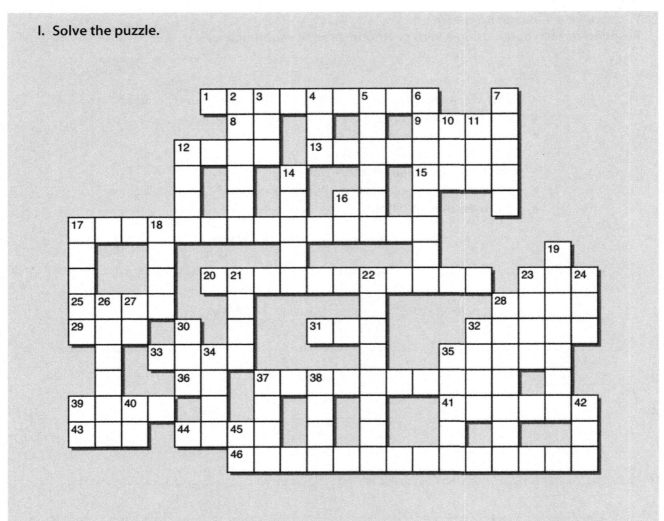

Solution on p.36.

Horizontal

1. it bugs me*

8. afirmativo

9. articulación del brazo

12. Juan dice que él _____ por correo.
    (votar)

13. they get mad*

15. animal simio de cola larga
    que vive en los árboles

16. ¿A tí _____ gusta?

17. she's embarrassed*

20. Are you *(tú)* afraid?*

23. cantina

25. Ojalá que el equipo _____.
    (ganar)

28. Te _____ mañana.
    (ver)

29. doce meses

31. Están orgullosos de que
    su hijo _____ médico.
    (ser)

32. no mojadas

33. Me alegro que _____ tiempo para hacerlo.
    (haber)

35. Cuando eran niños _____ muchas
    historietas. *(leer)*

36. —¿Tienes mi libro?
    —Sí, _____ tengo.

37. he worries*

39. enfermedad grave de inmunodeficiencia

41. camarones

43. Cuando me gradúe en dos años, _____
    a la Argentina *(ir)*

44. Me inquieto que él _____ tan mal.
    (comer)

46. we're sad*

*Translate into Spanish.

Vertical

2. Yo _____ triste cuando te vayas.
   (estar)

3. no la tuya

4. los niños y _____ niñas

5. Está impresionado que los niños_____
   con ser presidente. *(soñar)*

6. ¿Estás contento que ella te _____?
   (acompañar)

7. integridad

10. órgano de la vista

11. Juan dice que sus amigos _____ muchas
    fiestas. *(dar)*

12. Hoy vengo, ayer _____.

14. Quiero que ellos lo _____.
    (hacer)

16. ¿A ti _____ gusta?

17. Ojalá que ella _____ buena suerte.
    (tener)

18. viene al mundo

19. fruta cítrica

21. I would go*

22. I'm glad*

23. ayuda económica para los estudios

24. carne de vaca

26. poner más, agregar

27. negativo

28. Cuando éramos niños _____ mucha tele.
    (ver)

30. _____ y pimienta

32. Nos alegra que ella _____ la
    verdad. *(saber)*

34. un juguete

35. sitio

37. Espero que tú _____ feliz.
    (ser)

38. Este regalo es _____ ti.

39. if*

40. La organización está muy agradecida
    de que la gente le _____ dinero.
    (dar)

42. No son mis libros, son _____ libros.
    (their)

45. A mí _____ gusta.

Solution to the puzzle on p.34.

The crossword solution grid:

	M		E	M	O		L	E		S	T		A				H	
			S	Í		A		U				C	O	D	O			
	V	O	T	A		S	E	E	N	O	J	A	N					
	I			R		A		H				Ñ		M	O	N	O	
	N			R		A		E	P			P					R	
I	E	N	E	V	E	R	G	Ü	E	N	Z	A						
E		A						A			Ñ				N			
N		C		T	I	E	N	E	S	M	I	E	D	O	B	A	R	
G	A	N	E	R					M			V	E	R	E			
A	Ñ	O		S			S	E	A		S	E	C	A	S			
D		H	A	Y	A				L		L	E	Í	A	N			
		L	O		S	E	P	R	E	O	C	U	P	A		J		
S	I	D	A	Y		E	A	G	G	A	M	B	A	S			
I	R	É		C	O	M	A	R	R	A		O			U		
				E	S	T	A	M	O	S	T	R	I	S	T	E	S	

Solution to the puzzle on p.17.

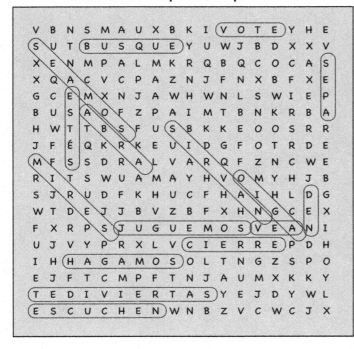

Solution to the puzzle on p.23.

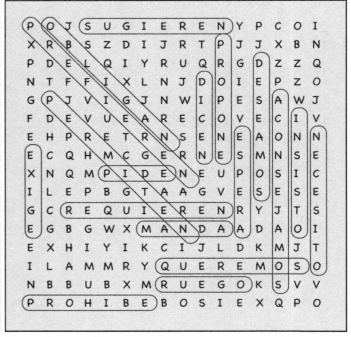

#3 Impersonal Expressions

- An impersonal expression consists of a form of the verb *ser* + an adjective.

  It's "impersonal" because it is not tied to a person. It translates as "it."

Es importante	*It's important*
Es triste	*It's sad*
Será fantástico	*It will be fantastic*

- The impersonal expression is information, and so is in the indicative.
  If another conjugated verb follows, it is in the subjunctive.*

  Examples:

  Es sorprendente que **se casen** tan rápido.   *It's surprising that they're **getting married** so quickly.*
  Es bueno que **nos llevemos** bien.   *It's good that we **get along** well.*

  *Because there are two conjugated verbs, "*que*" is needed to connect them.

- Exception:

  If an impersonal expression asserts a truth, then the second verb is information
  and so is in the indicative.

  Examples:

  Es verdad que **somos** amigas.   *It's true that **we're** friends.*
  Es evidente que él te **admira.**   *It's evident that he **admires** you.*
  No es mentira que le **tienen** miedo.   *It's not a lie that they **are afraid** of him.*

- Impersonal expressions can be followed by an infinitive if the second verb refers to no one
  in particular.

  Examples:

  Es importante estudiar.   *It's important to study.*
                vs.
  Es importante que tú **estudies**.   *It's important that **you** study.*

A. In the following Spanish sentences:
- **underline the impersonal expression**
- **put a square around any connecting word** *(que)*
- **circle the second verb <u>if</u> it is in subjunctive.**

1. Es horrible que me digas eso.   *It's horrible that you say that to me.*

2. Es fantástico que nos visiten.**   *It's fantastic that you're going to visit us.*

3. Es verdad que un carro como ése cuesta un dineral.   *It's true that a car like that costs a fortune.*

4. ¿Es necesario que salgamos ahora?   *Is it necessary for us to leave now?*

5. Es increíble que existan los OVNIs.   *It's incredible that UFOs exist.*

6. Es preciso pagar por adelantado.   *It's necessary to pay in advance.*

** **The present subjunctive is used to express both the present and the future.**

B. List some impersonal expressions that trigger the subjunctive.

1. _____   5. _____   9. _____

2. _____   6. _____   10. _____

3. _____   7. _____   11. _____

4. _____   8. _____   12. _____

C. List some impersonal expressions that require the second verb to be in indicative.

1. _____   3. _____

2. _____   4. _____

D. Put an impersonal expression before each of the following statements.
If the impersonal expression asserts a truth, leave the verb in the indicative.
If it does not, change the verb to the subjunctive.
Example:
Llueve mucho aquí.   *Es verdad que llueve mucho aquí.*
                      Es molestoso que llueva mucho aquí.

1. Su hijo está enfermo. _____

2. No hay mucho tráfico ahora. _____

3. María estudiará para ser abogada. _____

4. Caracas es la capital de Venezuela. _____

5. Venden carros eléctricos. _____

6. La guerra terminará. _____

7. Ellos beben mucho. _____

8. Hacemos ejercicio todos los días. _____

9. Tú ves fantasmas. _____

10. Tengo miedo a las serpientes. _____

E. Translate the following sentences.

1. It's fun to ski.

_____

2. It's dangerous for the children to play in the street.

_____

3. It's not right *(correcto)* for them to leave him alone / on his own.

_____

4. It's true that he knows how to drive. But it's not true that he drives well.

_____

5. It's wonderful that you *(tú)* are getting married.

_____

6. It's incredible that it costs so much.

_____

F. Review ways to use the subjunctive.
   Use 3 verbs of influence/volition (p.24, ex. E) in sentences that include a second verb in subjunctive.

1. _____

2. _____

3. _____

   Use 3 verbs of emotion (see p.30, ex. B) in sentences that include a second verb in subjunctive.

4. _____

5. _____

6. _____

G. Use 5 impersonal expressions in sentences that include a second verb in subjunctive.

1._____

2._____

3._____

4._____

5._____

H. Choose a book or movie and make comments about the plot using impersonal expressions.
   Example:

Título: *"El Mago de Oz" ("The Wizard of Oz")*_____

   *Es horrible que la mujer le quite Toto a Dorotea.*_____

   *Es fantástico que un tornado se lleve la casa de Dorotea.*_____

   *Es bueno que la bruja buena le dé las zapatillas rojas a Dorotea.*_____

   Es necesario que Dorotea y sus amigos vayan a Oz para hablar con el Mago de Oz.

Título: _____

_____

_____

_____

_____

_____

_____

_____

The Answer Key begins on p.197.

#4 Doubt and Negation

- Some verbs of doubt and negation:

Dudar	*To doubt*
Negar	*To deny*
No creer	*To not believe*
No estar seguro de	*To not be sure*
No es	*It's not*
No es cierto	*It's not true*
No parece	*It doesn't seem*

- The first verb in a sentence of doubt or negation is information, and so is in the indicative. If a conjugated verb follows, it is in the subjunctive (because you cannot give information about something that is not true or that is not believed to be true).

Examples:

Dudamos que **tengan** suficiente dinero.　　*We **doubt** that they **have** enough money.*
No es que yo **quiera** salir.　　*It's not that I **want** to leave.*
No creo que **llegues** a tiempo.　　*I **don't believe** that you'll **arrive** on time.*
Ella **niega** que tal documento **exista**.　　*She **denies** that such a document **exists.***

- **Note:**

Dudar expresses doubt, but **no dudar** does not.
No creer negates the existence of what follows, but **creer** generally asserts a truth.
No parece introduces something not believed to be true; **parece** introduces a perceived truth.

Therefore, a verb following "no dudar" "creer" or "parece" or a similar expression is usually information, and so is in the indicative.

Examples:

No dudo que ella **es** muy inteligente.　　*I **don't doubt** that she **is** very intelligent.*
Creen que los **comprendemos**.　　*They **think** that we **understand** them.*
No negamos que **tienes** razón.　　*We **don't deny** that you're right.*

See p.46 for more further information on "creer" and "no creer."

A. In the following Spanish sentences:
- **put an X in front of the sentences that are an expression of doubt or that negate something**
- **put a check in front of the sentences that assert a truth.**

_____1. Es verdad que mañana es jueves.　　　*It's true that tomorrow is Thursday.*

_____2. No niego que él es guapo.　　　*I don't deny he's good-looking.*

_____3. No creen que existan los extraterrestres.　　*They don't believe that extraterrestrials exist.*

_____4. Dudamos que él sea de confianza.　　　*We doubt that he's trustworthy.*

_____5. Es que la tierra sí es plana.　　　*The thing is that the earth really is flat.*

_____6. Creo que salimos a las 9:00.　　　*I think we'll leave at 9:00.*

B. Make a list of expressions of doubt or negation that may trigger the subjunctive.

1. _____   4. _____   7. _____

2. _____   5. _____   8. _____

3. _____   6. _____   9. _____

C. List expressions that assert a truth.

1. _____   3. _____   5. _____

2. _____   4. _____   6. _____

D. Translate the following sentences.

1. He doesn't believe it's true.

_____

2. They doubt that she knows how to cook paella.

_____

3. I don't think he drives well.

_____

4. We're not sure that they will come to the party.

_____

5. She doesn't think that we should work there.

_____

E. Use 3 verbs of doubt/negation in sentences that include a second verb in subjunctive.

1. _____

2. _____

3. _____

F. Use 3 verbs that express certainty or that assert a truth in sentences that include a second verb in indicative.

1. _____

2. _____

3. _____

G. Change these sentences from exercise A as indicated.

1. Es verdad que mañana es jueves.

   _____

   It's true that tomorrow is Thursday.

   It's not true that tomorrow is Thursday.

2. No niego que él es guapo.

   _____

   I don't deny he's good-looking.

   I deny he's good-looking.

3. No creen que existan los extraterrestres.

   _____

   _____

   They don't believe that extraterrestrials exist.

   They believe that extraterrestrials exist.

   They believe that extraterrestrials do not exist.

4. Dudamos que él sea de confianza.

   _____

   We doubt that he's trustworthy.

   We don't doubt that he's trustworthy.

5. Es que la tierra sí es plana.

   _____

   The thing is that the earth really is flat.

   It's not that the earth is flat.

6. Creo que salimos a las 9:00.

   _____

   I think we'll leave at 9:00.

   I don't think we'll leave at 9:00.

Bizarro: © 2013 Dan Piraro
Distributed by King
Features Syndicate, Inc.

H. Two criminals, Jorge and David, are planning a bank robbery in collusion with a bank employee, Sara.
Jorge is unrealistically optimistic.
Read what Jorge plans, then write Sara's opinions and observations on the plan.
Use several expressions of doubt and negation.

Jorge: Vamos a robar el banco.
- El primero del mes es el mejor día porque ese día hay más dinero.
- Podemos robar $50.000.000.
- Pondremos el dinero en nuestros bolsillos *(pockets)*.
- Necesitamos armas. No quiero que usemos pistolas. Recomiendo granadas.
- El guarda no es problema.
- Porque hay cámaras de seguridad, llevaremos barbas falsas.
- Sara, tú nos abrirás la caja de seguridad *(safe)*.
- Podemos escaparnos en bicicleta.
- El siguiente día, yo voy a comprar un Porsche rojo.
- ¿Qué vas a comprar tú, Sara?

Sara:

_____

_____

_____

_____

_____

_____

_____

_____

_____

_____

_____

I. Review ways to use the subjunctive.

Use 3 verbs of influence/volition (p.24, ex. E) in sentences that include a second verb in subjunctive.

1._____

2._____

3._____

Use 3 verbs of emotion (see p.30, ex. B) in sentences that include a second verb in subjunctive.

4._____

5._____

6._____

Use 3 impersonal expressions in sentences (see p.38, ex. B & C).

7._____

8._____

9._____

J. Write about some things you believe and don´t believe. Use expressions of doubt and negation.

_____

_____

_____

_____

_____

_____

NOTE: *The Fact That* **&** *It's Hard to Believe*

- **el que**
  el hecho de que
  que

  These expressions all mean "the fact that."

  Although it seems that these expressions should introduce the indicative, they do not. They require the subjunctive.

  (This may be because you're talking about something known and don't want to insult the listener by presuming to inform.)

  Example:

  El hecho de que Washington **sea** la sede de gobierno afecta la economía de esa ciudad.
  The fact that Washington is the seat of government affects the economy of that city.

- **Parece mentira que**

  Parece mentira que means: "it seems a lie that," or "it's hard to believe that."
  Even though this seems to introduce a truth, *parece mentira* requires the use of subjunctive.
  (Think of it as a synonym of *es increíble que*.)

  Example:

  Parece mentira que llevemos 20 años en el mismo trabajo.
  It's hard to believe that we've been in the same job for 20 years.

NOTE: *Creer & No Creer*

The speaker's doubt or certainty determines the use of subjunctive or indicative.

Although a verb or expression of doubt usually calls for the use of subjunctive,
and a verb or expression of certainty usually calls for the use of indicative,
with the verb "creer" it is actually the speaker's doubt or belief that determines the
choice of subjunctive or indicative.

Consider the following examples:

CREER — In questions

• Although the indicative generally follows "creer":
   Creo que va a llover.
   I think it's going to rain.

And the subjunctive generally follows "no creer":
   No creen que **haya** fantasmas.
   They don't believe that there are ghosts.

when asking a question about what someone believes, it is your opinion that determines
whether the second verb is in indicative (you believe it) or subjunctive (you do not believe it).
Your bias will be evident.

Examples: ¿No crees que ellos **son** intelligentes?
                   Don't you think they are intelligent?   (I certainly do.)

                   ¿Crees que ellos **sean** intelligentes?
                   Do you think they are intelligent?   (I don't or I haven't made up my mind.)

CREER — in statements

• Although the indicative generally follows "creer," there is some wriggle room when
   expressing your own opinion—using the subjunctive can express a lack of conviction.

Examples: Creo que ellos **vienen**.
                   I think they're coming.   (I'm convinced that this is true—information.)
                   Creo que ellos **vengan.**
                   I think they are (probably) coming.   (I have a doubt in my mind—subjunctive.)

• You may also use indicative after "no creer" when someone else's opinion runs counter
   to your information.

Examples: Él no cree que yo **estoy** enferma.
                   He doesn't believe that I'm sick.   (I know I am—information.)
                   Ella no cree que la quiero.
                   She doesn't believe I love her.   (I know I do—information.)

#5 Compound Verbs*

- A compound verb consists of a helping verb and a participle.
  To make a compound verb subjunctive, put the helping verb in the subjunctive.

  Examples:

  Indicative: Lo **estás** pasando bien.   *You **are** having a good time.*
  Subjunctive: Se alegran de que lo **estés** pasando bien.
                   *They are glad **you're** having **a** good time.*

  Indicative: El **sigue** comportándose bien.   *He **keeps** behaving himself.*
  Subjunctive: Ojalá que él **siga** comportándose bien.
                   *I hope he **keeps** behaving himself.*

  Indicative: **Ha** tenido tanto éxito.   *She **has** been so successful.*
  Subjunctive: Es impresionante que **haya** tenido tanto éxito.
                   *It's impressive that **she's** been so successful.*

  Indicative: Ellos **han** estado trabajando.   *They **have** been working.*
  Subjunctive: Dudamos que ellos **hayan** estado trabajando.
                   *We doubt that they **have** been working.*

* To brush up on compound verbs, see pp.47-52.
For exercises on the subjunctive, skip ahead to p.53.

What is a compound Verb?

- A compound verb has several parts: a helping verb and one or two participles.

  "Escribo" (*I write*) is a simple verb.
  "He escrito" (*I have written*) is a compound verb.
  "Estoy escribiendo" (*I am writing*) is also a compound verb.

Participles and Helping Verbs

- A participle is a verb particle, a piece of a verb.
  It has no tense or person, and it does not function as a verb on its own.

  Examples: *comido* = eaten, *pintando* = painting

- A compound verb gets its tense and person from its helping verb.
  The helping verb can be in any tense: present, future, past, etc.

  Examples:

  He comido. = ***I have*** *eaten.* **Habíamos** comido. = ***We had*** *eaten.* **¿Habrás** comido? = *Will you have eaten?*
    (*yo*, present tense)   (*nosotros*, imperfect tense)   (*tú*, future tense)

- There are present participles and past participles.

  Present participles express "in progress."   **Example:** *está pintando* = he is painting (right now).
  (Tenses with a present participle are called progressive tenses.)

  Past participles express completion.   **Example:** *ha pintado* = he has painted (completed action).
  (Tenses with a past participle are called perfect tenses, the action is perfected, completed.)

Present Participles
&
Progressive Tenses

- A progressive tense is made up of a helping verb and a present participle.
  The helping verb is conjugated in any tense, indicative or subjunctive.

  (Progressive tenses are named for the tense of their helping verb: present progressive, future progressive, etc.)

- The helping verbs used with present participles are:
  estar, seguir, and verbs of motion (**ir, venir, andar**, etc.)

- Present participles indicate "in progress."
  The progressive tenses are similar to English tenses with -ing.
  But they are only used to emphasize that the action is in progress, and so are used much less frequently in Spanish than in English.

  (The present tense in Spanish is often enough to express that the action is in progress. *Estudio español* can be translated as *I study* or *I am studying Spanish*.)

How To Form Present Participles

- Drop the -ar, -er or -ir ending from the infinitive and add the following participle endings:

  -ar ....-ando   (examples: habl**ando**, estudi**ando**, jug**ando**)
  -er/-ir ....-iendo   (examples: com**iendo**, viv**iendo**, hac**iendo**)

  Examples: Estoy viaj**ando**.   *I am traveling.*
  Estaba estudi**ando**.   *He was studying.*
  Siguen com**iendo**.   *They keep eating.*
  Vendremos cant**ando**.   *We will come singing.*

- There are no irregular present participles.

Notes

- Spelling Adujstments
  The only spelling adjustment is to avoid three vowels in a row.
  This calls for the "i" in the "-iendo" ending to change to "y."
  leer ....le**ye**ndo   oír ....o**ye**ndo

  And in Spanish a word cannot begin with a dipthong (*ie* or *ue*), so the *iendo* of *ir* becomes:

  ir ....**ye**ndo

- Stem Changes
  -ar and -er stem-change verbs have no stem change in the present participle.
  -ir stem-change verbs have the following stem changes:

  "-e" becomes "-i":   p**e**dir ....p**i**diendo   div**e**rtir ....div**i**rtiendo
  "-o" becomes "-u":   d**o**rmir.......d**u**rmiendo   m**o**rir............m**u**riendo

- Pronoun Placement
  Reflexive, direct and indirect object pronouns are attached to the end of the participle or placed before the conjugated helping verb.
  Example: Estamos divirti**é**ndo**nos**.   (Add an accent mark to maintain the pronunciation.)

  Nos estamos divirtiendo.

- No word may be placed between a helping verb and its participle.
  Example: Siempre **vienes quejándo**te.   *or*   **Vienes quejándo**te siempre.

Past Participles
&
Perfect Tenses

- A perfect tense is made up of a helping verb and a past participle.
  The helping verb is conjugated in any tense, indicative or subjunctive.

  (Tenses with past participles are called perfect tenses, because the action is completed or perfected.)
  (Perfect tenses are named for the tense of their helping verb: "present perfect," "future perfect," etc.
  The "imperfect perfect" would be a clumsy name; Instead it is called the "pluperfect.")

- The helping verb used with past participles is: **haber**.

Present Tense (indicative):		**Imperfect Tense*** (indicative):	
he	(yo)	**había**	(yo)
has	(tú)	**habías**	(tú)
ha	(él, ella, Ud.)	**había**	(él, ella, Ud.)
hemos	(nosotros, nosotras)	**habíamos**	(nosotros, nosotras)
han	(ellos, ellas, Uds.)	**habían**	(ellos, ellas, Uds.)

* The imperfect tense of haber is used to form the past perfect. (The preterite forms—hube, hubiste, hubo, hubimos, hubieron—have a very specific function, and are seldom used in conversation as helping verbs.)

- Past participles indicate completion.
  The perfect tenses are equivalent to the English perfect tenses: to have done something.

How To Form Past Participles

- Drop the -ar, -er or -ir ending from the infinitive and add the following participle endings:

  -ar ....-ado   (examples: habl**ado**, estudi**ado**, jug**ado**)
  -er/-ir ....-ido   (examples: com**ido**, viv**ido**, ped**ido**)

  Examples: He viaj**ado**.   *I have traveled.*
  Había estudi**ado**.   *He had studied.*
  Habrán com**ido**.   *They will have eaten.*

- Common irregular past participles:

abrir	abierto	morir	muerto
decir	dicho	poner	puesto
escribir	escrito	romper	roto
freír	frito	ver	visto
hacer	hecho	volver	vuelto

Notes

- Spelling Adjustments
  The only spelling adjustment is to add an accent mark to the "i" in the "-ido" ending
  when it follows a vowel: leer ....le**í**do   oír.........o**í**do   caer ....ca**í**do

- Stem Changes: There are no stem changes in past participles.

- Pronoun Placement
  Reflexive, direct and indirect object pronouns are placed before the conjugated helping verb.
  Example: **Nos** hemos divertido.

- No word can be placed between a helping verb and its participle.
  Example: Él siempre se **ha quejado**. *or* Él se **ha quejado** siempre.

A. Practice Participles
Identify the infinitives of the following past and present participles.

1. hablado *hablar* _____

2. comiendo _____

3. viviendo _____

4. hecho _____

5. leyendo* _____

6. dando _____

7. durmiendo** _____

8. visto _____

9. viniendo** _____

10. perdido _____

* This participle includes a spelling adjustment
** This participle includes a stem change.

B. Practice Participles
Write the present and past participles of the following verbs.

1. hablar *hablando / hablado* _____

2. correr _____

3. salir _____

4. leer* _____

5. dormir** _____

6. hacer*** _____

7. practicar _____

8. ver*** _____

9. morir**/*** _____

10. escribir*** _____

11. tomar _____

12. llegar _____

13. continuar _____

14. ser _____

15. escuchar _____

16. jugar _____

*   This present participle includes a spelling adjustment.
**   This present participle includes a stem change.
*** This past participle is irregular.

C. Practice the forms of helping verbs.

Estar:

	yo	tú	él, ella, Ud.	nosotros, nosotras	ellos, ellas, Uds.
present indicative					
present subjunctive					

Seguir:

	yo	tú	él, ella, Ud.	nosotros, nosotras	ellos, ellas, Uds.
present indicative					
present subjunctive					

Haber:

	yo	tú	él, ella, Ud.	nosotros, nosotras	ellos, ellas, Uds.
present indicative					
present subjunctive					

D. Rewrite the following sentences changing the subject.

No lo he hecho. *(I haven't done it.)*

1. Mi hermano _____
2. Mis hermanos _____
3. Tú y yo_____
4. Uds. _____
5. Yo _____
6. Tú _____
7. Ellos_____
8. Ud. y su familia _____

Estoy escuchándola. *(I'm listening to her.)*

9. Tú _____
10. Nosotros _____
11. Sus amigos _____
12. Uds._____
13. Yo _____
14. El comité _____
15. Mi profesor _____
16. Tú y yo _____

E. Practice Participles
   Choose the correct helping verbs for the following participles.
   Translate the phrases.

1. _____esperando   _____
      (sigo / he)

2. _____mirado   _____
      (estamos / hemos)

3. _____tocado   _____
      (él estaba / él había)

4. _____roto   _____
      (se seguirá / se habrá)

5. _____diciendo   _____
      (andan / han)

6. _____dicho   _____
      (estás / has)

7. _____vivido   _____
      (Ud. viene / Ud. ha)

8. _____divirtiéndome   _____
      (estaba / he)

F. Translate the following phrases in indicative:

present participle	past participle
1. I am listening _____	I have listened _____
2. he keeps yelling _____	he has yelled _____
3. they were coming _____	they had come _____
4. she will be giving _____	she will have given _____
5. we are writing _____	we have written _____
6. it is making _____	it has made _____
7. they keep meeting *(reunirse).* _____	they have met _____
_____	_____
8. we are enjoying ourselves _____	we have enjoyed ourselves _____
_____	_____

Note:

FYI—Other Uses of Participles

- Present participles in English are frequently used as nouns, as in: ***Swimming*** *is good exercise.*
  Present participles in Spanish are <u>never</u> used this way.
  (But infinitives can be used as nouns: **Nadar** es buen ejercicio.   ***Swimming*** *is good exercise.*

  Present participles (with no helping verb) are sometimes used as adverbs:
  Practicando se aprende más rápido.   ***By practicing***, *one learns more quickly.*

- Past participles (with no helping verb) are often used as adjectives.
  When used as an adjective, the ending shows number and gender:
  La serpiente se escapó por una ventana **abierta**.   *The snake escaped through an **open** window.*
  Los niños están **aburridos** y **cansados**.   *The children are **bored** and **tired**.*

G. Practice the Subjunctive
 • **Circle the helping verbs in subjunctive in the following sentences.**
 • **Translate the sentences.**

1. Dudo que nuestro hijo haya terminado.

   _____

2. Ojalá que no se nos haya acabado la leche.

   _____

3. Es feo que siga lloviendo.

   _____

4. Estamos impresionados que hayas pasado la tarde limpiando tu cuarto.

   _____

5. María espera que Juan esté escuchando.

   _____

6. El maestro no está convencido de que los alumnos hayan estado estudiando.

   _____

H. Put each of the following phrases in the subjunctive (in the person of your choice).
Then build a sentence around it and translate the sentence.
Examples:

estar cocinando _____esté cocinando_____

_____Estoy sorprendida que él esté cocinando._____   _I'm surprised that he is cooking._

haber llegado tarde _hayamos llegado tarde_____

_____Es una lástima que hayamos llegado tarde._____   _It's a pity that we've arrived late._

1. estar jugando al béisbol _____

   _____

2. seguir esperando _____

   _____

3. haber salido para México _____

   _____

4. haber pedido un café _____

   _____

5. haber comprado un carro nuevo _____

   _____

I. Translate the following sentences.

1. It bugs me that they keep calling.

   _____

2. We are afraid that they've gotten lost.

   _____

3. She thinks he's talking on the telephone.

   _____

4. They don't think that you've _(tú)_ done it.

   _____

J. Complete the puzzle.

Horizontal

3. _____ una lástima que salgan.
5. ** Le encanta que se hayan _____.
(quedar)
10. Única
11. *Ella está contenta que (nosotros)
la _____ comprendido.
13. El otro lado
15. *Nos alegra de que (tú) te
_____ graduado.
17. *Es bueno que los niños
_____ durmiendo.
19. *Es triste que (ellos) _____
peleándose.
21. No venir
23. Es el libro _____ profesor.
25. **Creo que estén _____.
(enamorarse)
27. _____ quiero, mi amor.
28. **Me fascina que eso siga_____.
(ocurrir)
32. ** Es impresionante que él haya
_____ este cuadro.
(pintar)

Vertical

1. **No me importa que hayan
_____ la película. (ver)
2. Parte de la mano
4. _____ y pimienta
6. ** Creo que le han _____. (escribir)
7. Yo le _____ el regalo mañana.
8. *Me molesta que los precios _____ subido.
9. *Esperan que yo _____ pagado la cuenta.
12. No vienen
14. **Es increíble que hayan _____ su casa. (vender)
16. *Dudo que ella _____ jugando al golf.
18. **No es verdad que estén_____ la televisión. (ver)
20. No allá
22. Demás
24. Ella _____ el periódico.
26. No reciben
29. Lo que se viste
30. *No creo que (tú) _____ haciendo eso.
31. **Es improbable que hayan _____ una ⬜esta. (dar)

* Supply an appropriate helping verb.
** Change the verb in parentheses to
the correct participle.

Solution on p.58.

K. Comment on the following statements using a compound tense in the subjunctive.

Example:

María ganó la lotería.   *Me alegro que haya ganado la lotería.*
María won the lottery.

Juan anda mintiendo sobre ella.   *Dudo que él ande mintiendo sobre ella*
Juan's going around lying about her.

1. María dio a luz a gemelos. _____
   María gave birth to twins.

2. Juan está buscando un nuevo empleo._____
   Juan is looking for a new job.

3. María recibió un aumento._____
   María got a raise.

4. A Juan se le ha roto la pierna. _____
   Juan has broken his leg.

5. María sigue ofreciéndose como voluntaria. _____
   María keeps volunteering.

6. Juan ha estado ayudando a sus padres. _____
   Juan has been helping his parents.

7. María se negó a pagar sus impuestos. _____
   María refused to pay her taxes.

8. Juan y María se divorciaron. _____
   Juan and María got divorced.

The Answer Key begins on p.197.

L. Review ways to use the subjunctive.

Use 3 verbs of influence/volition (see p.24, ex. E).

1. _____

2. _____

3. _____

Use 3 verbs of emotion (see p.30, ex. B).

4. _____

5. _____

6. _____

Use 3 impersonal expressions in sentences (see p.38, ex. B & C).

7. _____

8. _____

9. _____

Use 3 expressions of doubt/negation in sentences (see p.42, ex. B).

10. _____

11. _____

12. _____

Use 2 expressions that assert a truth (see p.42, ex. C).

13. _____

14. _____

Solution to the puzzle on p. 55.

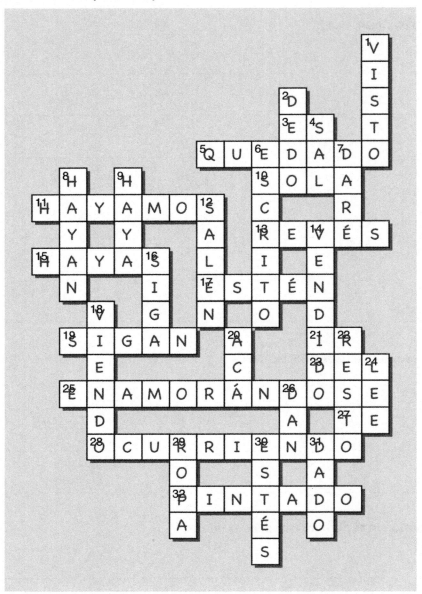

#6 Intended Purpose

- Expressions of intended purpose trigger the subjunctive.
  (This is because the sentence is about intention. It does not tell us whether the purpose or goal becomes fact.)

- PARA QUE is the most common expression of intended purpose.
  It means "so that" or "in order that" and always requires the subjunctive.

  Example:

  Ellos van a llevar a sus hijos a Colombia **para que conozcan** a sus tíos.
  *They are going to take their children to Colombia **so that they can meet** their aunts and uncles.*

- If there is only one subject, *"para"* + an infinitive is used.

  Example:

  Voy a Colombia **para conocer** a mis tíos.   *I'm going to Colombia to meet my aunts and uncles.*

  Note: If "in order that" can be inserted in a sentence in English, the Spanish equivalent must use *"para."*
  Although the "in order that" is often left out in English (as in, "I'm going to Colombia to meet my
  aunts and uncles.") in Spanish, the *"para"* is never omitted.

- Any phrase that means "so that" or "in order that" requires the subjunctive.
  For example: de manera que   de modo que   a fin de que

  All of the expressions above are interchangeable with *"para que."*
  They all mean the same thing: "so that" / "in order that."

  Examples:

  Mira como preparo este plato **de manera que** luego lo hagas correctamente.
  Watch how I make this dish so that later you can make it correctly.

  Voy a tomar unas aspirinas **de modo que** no duela tanto.
  I'm going to take some aspirin so that it doesn't hurt so much.

  Tomamos unos cursos de capacitación **a fin de que** nos den un aumento de sueldo.
  We're taking some training courses so that they'll give us a pay raise.

A. In the following Spanish sentences, circle the expressions of intended purpose.

1. Juan trabaja mucho para mantener a su familia.   *Juan works hard to support his family.*

2. Mi tía me manda dinero a fin de que yo les compre   *My aunt sends me money to buy the*
   regalos a los niños.   *children presents.*

3. Les escribimos de modo que sepan la buena noticia.   *We're writing to them so that they'll*
                                                            know the good news.

4. Nos encanta esta canción. Voy a subir el volumen   *We love this song. I'm going to turn up*
   para que la oigamos mejor.   *the volume so that we can hear it better.*

5. ¿Quieres que yo te lleve al aeropuerto de manera que   *Do you want me to take you to the airport*
   no tengas que pagar el estacionamiento?   *so you don't have to pay for parking?*

6. Van a plantar los rosales aquí para que reciban   *They're going to plant the rose bushes*
   suficiente sol.   *here so that they get enough sun.*

B. Translate the following sentences:

1. They're going to Sara's so that she can help them with their homework.

    _____

2. I'm picking my neighbors up *(recoger)* at the airport tonight so they don't have to take a taxi.

    _____

3. They don't go out much in order to save money.

    _____

4. He's explaining it to you *(Uds.)* so that you understand.

    _____

5. His parents insist he study every day so that he gets good grades.

    _____

6. Are you *(tú)* going to Mexico to study or to visit friends?

    _____

C. Choose the best phrase from the list on the right to complete each sentence.
   Translate the completed sentence.
   (Remember, if there is only one subject, use "*para*" + infinitive.
   But if there are two, use "*para que*" + a verb in subjunctive.)

1. Hacen ejercicio _____   para confirmar la cita.

    _____   para que ella compre un carro.

2. Sus padres le van a prestar dinero _____   para que su equipo gane.

    _____   para bajar su fiebre.

3. Ella toma aspirina _____   para que dure mucho tiempo.

    _____   para alcanzar el autobús a tiempo.

4. Llamamos _____   para recibir una beca.

    _____   para ser sanos y fuertes.

5. El mantiene bien su carro_____

    _____

6. Corremos _____

    _____

7. Él practica fútbol mucho _____

    _____

8. Él practica fútbol mucho _____

    _____

D. Write sentences using the expression indicated.

1. para que _____

2. para _____

3. de modo que _____

4. a fin de que _____

5. de manera que _____

E. Review ways to use the subjunctive.

    Use 2 verbs of influence/volition (see p.24, ex. E).

1. _____

2. _____

    Use 2 verbs of emotion (see p.30, ex. B).

3. _____

4. _____

    Use 2 impersonal expressions in sentences (see p.38, ex. B & C).

5. _____

6. _____

    Use 2 expressions of doubt/negation in sentences (see p.42, ex. B).

7. _____

8. _____

    Use 1 expression that asserts a truth (see p.42, ex. C).

9. _____

    Use 1 compound tense (see p.47).

10. _____

F. **Write about what's going to happen during the next week or two.**
   Include at least 4 intended purposes for those actions.
   Example: Mañana voy al dentista a fin de que me repare un diente roto.
   (I'm going to the dentist tomorrow to get a broken tooth fixed.)

   Luego voy a casa para descansar un rato.
   (Then I'm going home to rest awhile.)

_____

_____

_____

_____

_____

_____

_____

_____

_____

_____

_____

_____

#7 Contingencies

- Conjunctions like the ones listed below trigger the subjunctive when they introduce a contingency or a condition that must be in place for the action to happen.

  Example: Te llamo **en cuanto** Juan llegue.   *I will call you **as soon as** Juan arrives.*

  The main clause—"Te llamo" / "*I will call you*"—is information (indicative).
  But my calling is dependent on Juan's arrival (subjunctive). "Juan llegue" is a future contingency.

a menos que..............	*unless*
con tal (de) que	*provided that*
siempre que...............	*provided that, as long as*
antes (de) que	*before*
después (de) que	*after*
en caso de que..........	*in case that*
sin que	*without*
mientras que.............	*while, as long as*
hasta que..................	*until*
luego que..................	*as soon as, after*
así que	*as soon as*
tan pronto como	*as soon as*
en cuanto..................	*as soon as*

- **Note:** A sentence may start with either the main clause or with the contingency.

  Example: Te llamo **en cuanto Juan llegue.**   *I will call you **as soon as Juan arrives**.*
   En cuanto Juan llegue, te llamo.   ***As soon as Juan arrives,** I'll call you.*

A. In the following sentences, circle and translate the contingency statement including the conjunction.

  Example: Te llamo (en cuanto Juan llegue.) _____ *as soon as Juan arrives.* _____

1. Van a jugar al béisbol a menos que llueva. _____

2. Hasta que ella se gradúe, va a vivir con sus padres. _____

3. Nadie puede entrar en la casa sin que yo lo sepa. _____

4. Antes de que salgas, quiero que limpies tu cuarto. _____

5. Su hijo puede usar el carro siempre que pida permiso. _____

6. En caso de que la jefa no esté, haga el favor de dejar el informe con la recepcionista.

_____

B. Translate the list of conjunctions below into English, and find them in Spanish in the word search.

a menos que _____

antes de que _____

así que _____

con tal de que_____

después de que _____

en caso de que _____

en cuanto _____

hasta que _____

luego que _____

mientras que _____

siempre que _____

sin que _____

tan pronto como _____

Solution on p.74.

```
V  A  O  C  X  H  U  G  V  W  X  C  R  D  G
A  A  M  M  V  L  D  Q  T  S  N  C  G  P  R
N  F  N  E  I  R  S  G  B  N  U  O  F  X  X
A  V  L  T  N  E  U  D  G  R  V  N  P  A  E
B  P  U  G  E  O  N  L  T  B  B  T  I  S  N
F  M  E  B  V  S  S  T  P  H  I  A  B  Í  C
D  R  G  O  S  K  D  Q  R  B  U  L  K  Q  A
C  K  O  R  Q  I  F  E  U  A  F  D  R  U  S
L  L  Q  Z  M  F  N  B  Q  E  S  E  O  E  O
M  Z  U  O  O  I  U  Q  W  U  C  Q  U  K  D
S  I  E  M  P  R  E  Q  U  E  E  U  A  E
E  N  C  U  A  N  T  O  G  E  K  E  X  E  Q
H  A  S  T  A  Q  U  E  L  N  E  P  X  B  U
Q  T  A  N  P  R  O  N  T  O  C  O  M  O  E
H  D  E  S  P  U  É  S  D  E  Q  U  E  I  G
```

C. Underline the conjunction and translate the following sentences.

1. No me iré a menos que quieras que me vaya.

   _____

2. No me iré mientras que no quieras que me vaya.

   _____

3. No me iré sin que quieras que me vaya.

   _____

4. Me iré tan pronto como quieras.

   _____

5. No me iré siempre que no quieras que me vaya.

   _____

6. No me iré hasta que quieras que me vaya.

   _____

7. No me iré antes de que quieras que me vaya.

   _____

8. Me iré con tal de que quieras que me vaya.

   _____

9. Me iré después de que me digas que me vaya.

   _____

10. Me iré en cuanto me digas que me vaya.

    _____

11. Me iré así que me digas que me vaya.

    _____

12. No me iré en caso de que me necesites.

    _____

13. Me iré luego que nos despidamos.

    _____

D. Translate the following sentences.

1. I will tell him as soon as I see him.

_____

2. He will go with us to the movies providing we pay.

_____

3. Before you all get mad, listen to us.

_____

4. Unless they study, they are not going to do well *(salir bien)* on the test.

_____

5. Take *(tú)* your umbrella in case it rains.

_____

E. Answer the following questions with a contingency or condition.

1. ¿Cuándo vas al parque?

_____

2. ¿Van de vacaciones a Europa sus amigos?

_____

3. ¿Quieren Uds. comprarlo?

_____

4. ¿En dónde van Uds. a quedarse?

_____

5. ¿Dónde quieren vivir Uds.?

_____

6. ¿Hasta cuándo debemos quedarnos?

_____

7. ¿Vas a llamarme?

_____

8. ¿Quién trabaja mañana?

_____

F. Review ways to use the subjunctive.

Use 2 verbs of influence/volition (see p.24, ex. E).

1._____

2._____

Use 2 verbs of emotion (see p.30, ex. B).

3._____

4._____

Use 2 impersonal expressions in sentences (see p.38, ex. B & C).

5._____

6._____

Use 2 expressions of doubt/negation in sentences (see p.42, ex. B).

7._____

8._____

Use 1 expression that asserts a truth (see p.42, ex. C).

9._____

Use 1 compound tense (see p.47).

10._____

Use "para," "para que" or other expressions of intended purpose (see p.59).

11._____

12._____

G. It's a telenovela: Jorge is leaving Ana (who is pregnant) for another woman—Ana is not taking it well. In the following dialogue, write who says each line, Jorge or Ana.

_____: Oye, estoy enamorado de otra. Me voy.

_____: No. Nadie se va a menos que lo mande. Y yo no lo mando.

_____: No somos felices. Es mejor que me vaya antes de que nos odiemos.

_____: No quiero que te vayas hasta que nos odiemos. No me dejes.

_____: Además, no debes abandonarme hasta que nazca la criatura.

_____: Llámame después de que des a luz para que yo pueda conocer a mi hijo.

_____: Te prometo mandar dinero para mantener a mi hijo siempre que nos dejes en paz a mí y a mi nueva mujer.

_____: Nunca los dejaré en paz ni a ti ni a la fulana esa hasta que yo esté muerta.

_____: En serio. Y antes de que yo permita que veas a tu hijo, te mato.

_____: No seas así. Tan pronto como seas razonable, cumpliré con mis responsabilidades.

_____: Seré razonable así que renuncies a esa mujer.

_____: Podemos ser felices de nuevo con tal de que abandones a la fulana esa.

_____: Nunca, jamás. Pero no quiero irme sin que me prometas ser razonable.

_____: Quédate entonces.

_____: No, Ana. Adiós.

H. Write a dialogue in which two people negotiate something.
   For example: an employer and employee / a parent and child / spouses / housemates, etc.
   Write three or four lines for each speaker and use the subjunctive at least five times.

_____

_____

_____

_____

_____

_____

_____

_____

_____

_____

_____

_____

The Answer Key begins on p.197.

#8 Cuando

- **Cuando** (*when*) is a conjunction that can introduce a verb in subjunctive or in indicative.

Example:

La visito **cuando voy** a Miami.   *I visit her when / whenever I go to Miami.*

> **Note:** The verb in the main clause (*visito*) is in the present tense.
> The verb following "cuando" is **indicative**, because it gives information about a customary action.

La visitaré **cuando yo vaya** a Miami.   *I will visit her when I go to Miami.*
Cuando vayas a Miami, visita a tu abuela.   *When you go to Miami, visit your grandmother.*

> **Note:** The verbs in the main clauses above are a future tense (*visitaré*) and a command (*visita*).
> The verb following "cuando" is **subjunctive**—it introduces a future contingency or anticipated action.

- If the verb in the main clause is a present tense, use the **indicative** after "cuando."
  If the verb in the main clause is about the future or is a command, use the **subjunctive**.

- **Note:** A sentence may start with either the main clause or with the clause beginning with "cuando."

Example:

Pagarán la cuenta **cuando la reciban**.   *They will pay the bill **when they receive it.***
Cuando reciban la cuenta, la pagarán.   ***When they receive the bill**, they will pay it.*

See pp.178-179 for information on the future tense.

A. In the following sentences:
- indicate if they are about customary actions (C) or about future contingencies (F)
- translate the sentences.

Example:

_C_   Cierro la puerta con llave cuando salgo de casa.

I lock the door when I leave the house.

1. _____ Cuando mis amigos oyen música, bailan.

2. _____ Llevo mi computadora portátil *(laptop)* cuando viajo.

3. _____ Cuando vayas a la universidad, cómprame una camiseta.

4. _____ Lo invitamos a cenar cuando preparamos paella.

5. _____ Mi amiga me recogerá en el aeropuerto cuando yo la llame.

6. _____ Cuando su hija cumpla 15, le darán una gran fiesta.

B. Connect the phrases in the first column to phrases in the second column to make correct and logical sentences. Write the sentences and their translation on the lines provided.

Keep in mind: If the main clause is in the present tense, "cuando" is followed by a verb in indicative.
If the main clause is about the future or is a command, "cuando" is followed by a verb in subjunctive.

1. Cuando él habla,

2. Les escribiré

3. Vamos de compras

4. Cuando veas a Mercedes,

5. Cuando terminen el curso sobre la Guerra Civil,

6. José se pone de mal humor

7. Llámame

8. Cuando vamos al cine,

a. cuando me den su dirección.

b. nos gusta salir a comer antes.

c. salúdala de mi parte.

d. cuando llegues a casa.

e. debes escuchar.

f. cuando tenemos dinero y tiempo libre.

g. Uds. comprenderán mejor esa época.

h. cuando llueve mucho.

1. _____

_____

2. _____

_____

3. _____

_____

4. _____

_____

5. _____

_____

6. _____

_____

7. _____

_____

8. _____

_____

C. Translate the following sentences that are about customary actions (no subjunctive).

1. Do you *(Ud.)* use butter when you make cookies?

_____

2. He always pays when we go to the movies.

_____

3. She always takes off her shoes when she gets home.

_____

4. When he studies, he does well *(salir bien)* on tests.

_____

5. They don't always answer the phone when it rings.

_____

D. Translate the following sentences that are about future contingencies (subjunctive).

1. When you *(Ud.)* make the cookies for the party, don't use butter.

_____

2. He will pay when we go to the movies tomorrow.

_____

3. When she arrives at the airport, she'll call us.

_____

4. When you *(Uds.)* study for the test, do it in the library.

_____

5. When the phone rings, I'll answer it.

_____

6. When you *(tú)* go to Spain, visit the art museums.

_____

The Answer Key begins on p.197.

E. Translate the following sentences, deciding whether or not to use the subjunctive.

1. When we travel, the neighbor takes care of our dog.

   _____

2. He hopes to buy a car when he gets a job.

   _____

3. They'll get angry when he tells them the news.

   _____

4. They worry when I don't call.

   _____

5. She always brings flowers when she visits us.

   _____

6. When you *(Ud.)* arrive at the corner, turn left.

   _____

F. Review ways to use the subjunctive.

   Use a verb of influence/volition in a sentence (see p.24, ex. E).

1. _____

   Use a verb of emotion in a sentence (see p.30, ex. B).

2. _____

   Use an impersonal expression in a sentence (see p.38, ex. B & C).

3. _____

   Use an expression of doubt/negation in a sentence (see p.42, ex. B).

4. _____

   Use an expression that asserts a truth in a sentence (see p.42, ex. C).

5. _____

   Use a compound tense in a sentence (see p.47).

6. _____

   Use *para*, *para que* or another expression of intended purpose (see p.59).

7. _____

   Use 3 conjunctions that introduce contingencies in sentences (see p.63).

8. _____

9. _____

10. _____

G. Answer the following questions with a complete sentence containing two verbs and "cuando."

1. ¿Cuándo verás a tus amigos?

_____

2. ¿Cuándo corren ellos en el parque?

_____

3. ¿Por lo general, cuándo va Ud. de compras?

_____

4. ¿Cuándo irá Ud. de compras?

_____

5. ¿Cuándo alquilan Uds. un carro?

_____

6. ¿Cuándo viajará ella al Perú?

_____

7. ¿Cuándo quieres salir mañana?

_____

8. ¿Va Ud. a llamarme?

_____

**H. Give directions from a location of your choice to your house.
Use four to six steps, and use "cuando" at least 3 times.**

_____

_____

_____

_____

_____

_____

_____

_____

Solution to the word search on p.64:

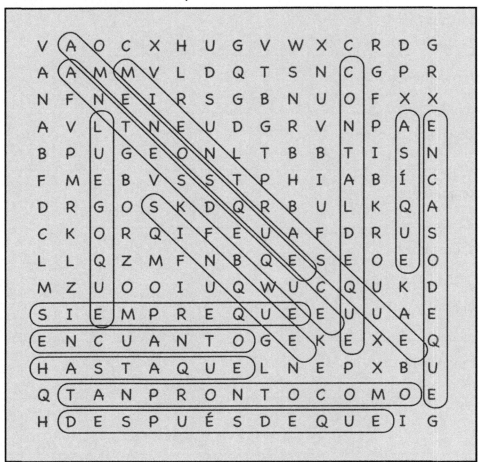

Solution to the word search on p.79:

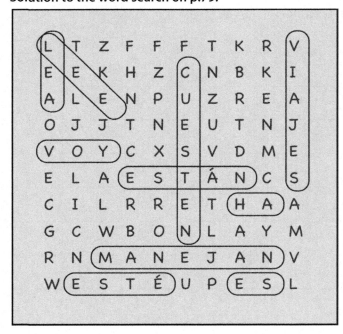

#9 Aunque

- **AUNQUE** *("although" or "even though")* is a conjunction that can introduce a verb in subjunctive or indicative. The decision to use subjunctive or indicative depends on whether you want to give information or you wish to be noncommittal.

Example:

Aunque Juan **es** inteligente, en este caso está equivocado.
Although Juan is intelligent, in this case he's wrong.

In the example above, Juan is indeed intelligent, and so the verb following *aunque* is indicative.

Aunque Juan sea inteligente, está equivocado.
Although Juan **may be** intelligent, he's wrong.

In this example, the verb is in subjunctive because it is not necessarily true that Juan is intelligent, or the speaker does not know and so cannot give information about his intelligence.

- **Note:** Whether a sentence with "aunque" contains the subjunctive or not, it may start with either the main clause or with the clause beginning with "aunque."

Example:

Aunque nos gusta la comida china, casi nunca la comemos.
Although we like Chinese food, we almost never eat it.

or

Casi nunca comemos la comida china, **aunque nos gusta.**
We almost never eat Chinese food, although we like it.

A. Translate the following sentences that affirm a truth (no subjunctive).

1. Even though it rains a lot, I like the climate here.

_____

2. We go to the movies every weekend, although it's expensive.

_____

3. Although she gets good grades, it's hard for her.

_____

4. They seldom visit us, even though they don't live far.

_____

B. Translate the following sentences that are noncommittal (subjunctive).

1. Although / even though they leave early tomorrow, they won't arrive until evening.

_____

2. Even though it may be beautiful there, they prefer to stay home this weekend.

_____

3. Although mysteries may be interesting, we only read science fiction.

_____

4. He never responds even though he may know the answer.

_____

C. Translate the following sentences, deciding whether to use indicative or subjunctive.

1. He wants to have a dog even though he travels a lot.

_____

2. She has a cat even though she has allergies.

_____

3. Although they may get angry, you *(tú)* have to tell them the truth.

_____

4. Although you *(Uds.)* may be busy, please call us.

_____

5. He will want to drive even though there may be a lot of traffic.

_____

6. Although I haven't been to your *(Uds.)* house before, I will find it.

_____

D. Review ways to use the subjunctive.

Use a verb of influence/volition in a sentence (see p.24, ex. E).

1. _____

Use a verb of emotion in a sentence (see p.30, ex. B).

2. _____

Use an impersonal expression in a sentence (see p.38, ex. B & C).

3. _____

Use an expression of doubt/negation in a sentence (see p.42, ex. B).

4. _____

Use an expression that asserts a truth in a sentence (see p.42, ex. C).

5. _____

Use a compound verb in a sentence (see p.47).

6. _____

Use "para," "para que" or another expression of intended purpose (see p.59).

7. _____

Use 2 conjunctions that introduce contingencies in sentences (see p.63).

8. _____

9. _____

Write a sentence with "cuando" (see p.69).

10. _____

E. In the following sentences with "cuando" and "aunque":
  • **fill in the correct form of the verb and also write its conjugated form in the list on the right in Exercise F.**
  • **translate the sentence.**

1. Cuando _____ (ir) al centro, me gusta almorzar en un restaurante.

   _____

2. Vamos a trabajar en el jardín mañana, aunque _____ (estar) lloviendo.

   _____

3. Aunque ellos siempre _____ (manejar) demasiado rápido, no han tenido ningún accidente.

   _____

4. Aunque él _____ (haber) buscado mucho, no ha encontrado un empleo.

   _____

5. Cuando tú _____ (viajar) a Colombia, cómprame un CD de cumbias.

   _____

6. Cuando ellos _____ (estar) nerviosos, no comen.

   _____

7. No sé cuánto costarán los boletos para el concierto, pero los compraré aunque

   _____ (costar) $100.

   _____

8. Aunque él _____ (ser) mi amigo, a veces me vuelve loco.

   _____

9. Cuando ella _____ (leer) novelas, siempre empieza leyendo el final.

   _____

10. Pero voy a recomendar que ella no haga eso cuando _____ (leer) este misterio.

   _____

F. Write your answers from p. 78 below. Then find the words in the word search.

1._____

2. _____

3._____

4._____

5._____

6._____

7._____

8._____

9._____

10._____

```
L T Z F F F T K R V
E E K H Z C N B K I
A L E N P U Z R E A
O J J T N E U T N J
V O Y C X S V D M E
E L A E S T Á N C S
C I L R R E T H A A
G C W B O N L A Y M
R N M A N E J A N V
W E S T É U P E S L
```

Solution on p.74.

G. Answer the following questions with a complete sentence containing "aunque."

1. Vas a acompañarme al cine, ¿verdad?

_____

2. ¿Crees lo que él dice?

_____

3. ¿Crees que podamos superar esta situación?

_____

H. The president is visiting your community next week.

    1. Explain the situation and your and/or your community's plans.

or

    2. Write about what you and/or your community want to talk to the president about.
       Use "aunque" at least 5 times, and use a mix of subjunctive and indicative.

_____

_____

_____

_____

_____

_____

_____

_____

_____

_____

_____

_____

_____

The Answer Key begins on p.197.

#10 Non-existent People & Objects

- We use the indicative to state that people and things exist or not because it's giving information. But (in a dependent clause) any description of something or someone unreal cannot be information—they do not exist—so the subjunctive is used.

   Example:

   No hay estudiante que **encuentre** fácil esto.   *There is no student who **finds** this easy.*

   (That the student does not exist is information, and so is in the indicative; but since such a person is non-existent, any description of them is in the subjunctive.)

   Hay dos estudiantes que **encuentran** fácil esto.   *There are two students who **find** this easy.*

   (That there are two students is information, and so is in the indicative, and these are actual, specific people, so any description of them is also information: indicative.)

- See pp.85-86 for a review of negatives.

A. The following sentences contain a description of a person or object:
   - **Circle the person or object.**
   - **Underline the verb of the description.**
   - **If the sentence is about a non-existent person or object, put an X before the sentence.**
   - **Translate the sentence.**

   <u> X </u>   Ya no vive ninguna (persona) que <u>sepa hablar</u> el egipcio de los faraones.

   No person is now alive who knows how to speak the Egyptian of the pharaohs.

_____1. No hay nadie aquí que conozca Bolivia.

_____

_____2. Sólo hay dos de mis vecinos que no tienen perros.

_____

_____3. No existe ninguna universidad en este estado que dé cursos de maya.

_____

_____4. No tenemos computadora que funcione.

_____

B. Translate the following sentences that describe someone or something that doesn't exist (subjunctive).

1. There is no one in the office who speaks Russian.

_____

2. I don't have any books that explain Mexican history.

_____

3. I don't know anyone who works there.

_____

4. They want to buy a house in this neighborhood, but they can't find one that has four bedrooms.

_____

C. Translate the following sentences that may or may not be describing a non-existent person or object (decide between subjunctive and indicative).

1. The team does not exist that has better players.

_____

2. I'm buying the car that does not use a lot of gas.

_____

3. There is nobody in his family who has graduated from college.

_____

4. She's never written a book that's boring.

_____

5. We bought pants, but not shoes.

_____

D. **Review ways to use the subjunctive.**

Use a verb of influence / volition in a sentence (see p.24, ex. E).

1._____

Use a verb of emotion in a sentence (see p.30, ex. B).

2._____

Use an impersonal expression in a sentence (see p.38, ex. B & C).

3._____

Use an expression of doubt / negation in a sentence (see p.42, ex. B).

4._____

Use an expression that asserts a truth in a sentence (see p.42, ex. C).

5._____

Use a compound tense in a sentence (see p.47).

6._____

Use "para," "para que" or another expression of intended purpose (see p.59).

7._____

Use 2 conjunctions that introduce contingencies in sentences (see p.63).

8._____

9._____

Write a sentence with "cuando" (see p.69).

10._____

Write a sentence with "aunque" (see p.75).

11._____

E. A Rant
   Translate the following example of what an unhappy teenager might say about school:

Odio la escuela.
No tengo ningún profesor que no sea aburrido.
No hay ninguna clase que valga la pena.
No hay plato en la cafetería que no me dé asco.   (dar asco = *to make sick, to be disgusting*)
No conozco a nadie que me comprenda.

_____

_____

_____

_____

_____

Now assume an identity, and write a rant about something or someone who does not exist.

_____

_____

_____

_____

_____

_____

_____

_____

The Answer Key begins on p.197.

Negatives

no...	*no, not*
nadie...	*nobody, not anybody*
nada	*nothing, not anything*
ningún, ninguno, ninguna...........	*none, not one, not any*
ninguna parte	*nowhere, not anywhere*
nunca..	*never, not ever*
jamás..	*never, not ever*

(often used with nunca, as in nunca jamás = never ever)

de ninguna manera	*in no way, not (in) any way*
de ningún modo	*in no way, not (in) any way*
tampoco	*neither*
ni...	*nor, not even*

(when used as ni....ni = neither....nor)

• In a negative sentence or clause, "no" or another negative word must precede the verb.

   Example: Ojalá que **no** lleguen tarde.   *I hope they don't arrive late.*

   Ojalá que **nadie** llegue tarde.   *I hope no one arrives late.*

• Use as many negatives as required in the sentence—unlike English, two negatives do not cancel each other out.

   Example: Es importante que **no** compres **nunca ninguna** cosa de ese sitio web.

   It's important that you never buy anything from that website.

A. Write the negative counterpart in Spanish for the following words and phrases.

1. siempre *(always)* _____

2. algo *(something)* _____

3. algún *(some, any)* _____

4. alguien *(someone, anyone)* _____

5. de alguna manera *(someway / anyway)* _____

6. sí *(yes)* _____

7. o....o *(either...or)* _____

8. también *(also)* _____

9. alguna parte *(somewhere)* _____

B. Translate the following sentences.
   Note: If a sentence or clause is negative, everything in that sentence or clause must be negative.

1. I don't want to see any movie with that actor.

   _____

2. I have no reason to call him.

   _____

3. We hope that you *(tú)* never say anything to him either.

   _____

4. He never went anywhere with anybody.

   _____

5. No way did she ever say that.

   _____

6. They don't want to visit either you *(Ud.)* or me.

   _____

7. I'm glad that you *(tú)* haven't lost anything.

   _____

C. Answer the following questions as negatively as possible.

1. ¿Alguna vez ha conocido Ud. a alguien famoso?

   _____

2. ¿Qué dejaron en la mesa?

   _____

3. ¿Es importante que todo el mundo sepa todo sobre esto?

   _____

4. ¿Cuándo me lo dirás?

   _____

5. ¿Quieren Uds. estos libros o ésos?

   _____

6. ¿Adónde los has llevado?

   _____

#11 Hypothetical People & Objects

- Because you can't give information about something or someone who is hypothetical, the subjunctive is used in the clause that describes that person or thing.

Example:

Desean emplear un recepcionista **que sea** bilingüe.
They want to hire a receptionist who is bilingual.

(In the example above, that they want to hire a receptionist is information[indicative], but the description of this hypothetical / unspecified person is in subjunctive.)

Acaban de emplear a una recepcionista **que es** bilingüe. Se llama Marisol.
They just hired a receptionist who is bilingual. Her name is Marisol.

(In the example above, that they just hired a receptionist is information [indicative], and because Marisol is a specific person, the description is also in indicative.)

- The verbs "querer," "desear," "buscar," and "necesitar" are verbs that commonly introduce hypothetical objects.

Example:

Él quisiera casarse con una mujer **que sea** rica y guapa.
He would like to marry a woman who's rich and good-looking.

Buscamos una aplicación **que pueda** ayudarnos a aprender vocabulario.
We are looking for an app that can help us learn vocabulary.

- **Note:** The personal "a" is omitted before a hypothetical / unspecified person.

Example:

Conozco **a** ese actor.
I know that actor. (specific person)
But:
¿Conoces un actor que sea famoso?
Do you know an actor who's famous? (hypothetical / unspecified person—no "a.")

A. The following sentences contain a description of a person or object.
- Circle the person or object.
- Underline the verb of the description.
- If the sentence is about a hypothetical person or object, put an X before the sentence.
- Translate the sentence.

    X   Necesitamos (un carro) que <u>use</u> menos gasolina.

We need a car that uses less gas.

_____1. Él desea asistir a una universidad que no esté muy lejos de su casa.

_____

_____2. Quiero esos plátanos que están maduros.

_____

_____3. Ella necesita un empleo que pague mejor.

_____

_____4. Ellos no quieren zapatos que no les queden *(fit)* bien.

_____

_____5. Estoy buscando el libro que me prestaste.

_____

_____6. Estoy buscando un libro que me interese.

_____

The Answer Key begins on p.197.

B. Translate the following sentences that describe a hypothetical person or thing (subjunctive).

1. They need an interpreter who speaks English, Spanish and Mayan.

_____

2. Do they sell toys that are safe?

_____

3. I want to see a movie that you *(tú)* will like too.

_____

4. She's looking for an adult dog that needs a home and that isn't too big.

_____

**C. Translate the following sentences that may or may not be describing a hypothetical object .
Decide between subjunctive and indicative.**

1. The team wants players who know how to play well.

_____

2. I'm buying a car that does not use a lot of gas. I'm picking it up tomorrow.

_____

3. Let's go to a movie that makes us laugh.

_____

4. They're looking for a babysitter who drives and who can work nights.

_____

5. I want to talk to the person who wrote this.

_____

D. In the following crossword, decide if the verbs in parentheses should be in indicative or subjunctive.

Horizontal

1. Voy a darte el libro que yo (acabar) de leer.

5. Voy a presentarte a unas personas que (conocer) bien Chile.

6. Buscan una casa que (tener) cinco habitaciones.

8. No conozco a nadie que (hablar) ruso.

9. Voy a darles un regalo que (costar) menos de $20.

Vertical

2. El preᬨere ir a un médico que (comprender) español.

3. Queremos vivir en una casa que (contar) con dos baños.

4. Quieren emplear un jardinero que (saber) mucho sobre los frutales.

6. Pásame ese libro que (tener) el cubierto azul.

7. No hay ninguna casa en este barrio que me (gustar).

Solution on p.94.

E. Review ways to use the subjunctive.

Use a verb of volition or emotion in a sentence (see p.24, ex. E and p.30, ex. B).

1. _____

Use an impersonal expression in a sentence (see p.38, ex. B & C).

2. _____

Use an expression of doubt / negation in a sentence (see p.42, ex. B).

3. _____

Use a compound tense in a sentence (see p.47).

4. _____

Use "para," "para que" or another expression of intended purpose (see p.59).

5. _____

Use a conjunction that introduces a contingency in a sentence (see p.63).

6. _____

Write a sentence with "cuando" (see p.69).

7. _____

Write a sentence with "aunque" (see p.75).

8. _____

Write 2 sentences about people and/or objects that doesn't exist (see p.81).

9. _____

10. _____

F. **Assume an identity and write a personal ad.**
   Your description of yourself will be information (indicative).
   In the description of the person you're looking for, use at least four verbs in subjunctive.

Soy _____

_____

_____

_____

_____

Busco un hombre / una mujer que _____

_____

_____

_____

_____

_____

G. Describe your dream vacation house. Use at least four verbs in subjunctive.

Sueño con una casa / un condominio que

_____

_____

_____

_____

_____

H. José and Sonia, two successful professionals, adore their three-year-old daughter.
Describe the child (indicative) and use subjunctive to explain what they are looking for in a nanny (*niñera*).
Use at least four verbs in subjunctive.
Note: They have very high standards.

La hija de José y Sonia: _____

_____

_____

_____

_____

Buscan una niñera que: _____

_____

_____

_____

_____

Solution to the crossword on p.90.

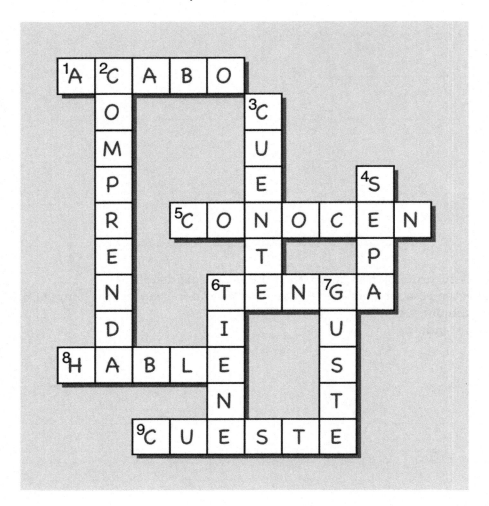

#12 "Si" Clauses

- "Si" is inherently different from other conjunctions.
  It is in a class by itself with its own rules.

- "Si" can **never** be followed by the present subjunctive.

- If "si" is followed by the present indicative, the verb in the main clause will:
  1.) be in the present indicative, 2.) refer to the future, or 3.) be a command.

Examples:

1. Vamos a montar en bicicleta **si hace** sol.   *We're going to ride our bikes **if it's** sunny.*
2. Pero **si llueve**, tomaremos el autobús.   *But **if it rains**, we'll take the bus.*
3. **Si ves** un libro bueno sobre verbos,   ***If you see** a good book on verbs,*
   cómpramelo.   *buy it for me.*

Note: See Part II, p.177 for more uses of "si."
See p.179 for information on the future tense.

A. Translate the following sentences.

1. No hagas ejercicio fuerte si hace mucho calor.

_____

2. Si hay mucho tráfico, vamos a tomar otra ruta.

_____

3. Si Uds. llegan tarde esta noche, por favor, no me llamen hasta la mañana.

_____

4. Iremos por tren si tenemos el tiempo.

_____

B. Translate the following sentences.

1. If *(tú)* you're hungry, order a pizza.

_____

2. I'm going to stay here, if you *(a Uds.)* don't mind *(importar)*.

_____

3. If you *(Ud.)* don't like the hotel, tell me.

_____

4. If we see them before the party, we will invite them.

_____

C. Complete the following sentences.

1. Si hace mucho calor _____

2. Dámelo si _____

3. Si hay tiempo mañana _____

4. Irán de vacaciones a España si _____

D. María has invited friends for dinner.
Her motto is "Always be prepared." She even tends to make backup plans for her backup plans.
Write about her plans using "si" at least 5 times.
(Remember: Do not use the present subjunctive with "si.")

_____

_____

_____

_____

_____

_____

_____

_____

_____

#13 Verbs of Influence: A Shortcut

- In *#1 Influence/Volition*, we saw that the subjunctive can be used to express one person's attempt to influence another's actions (see p.21).

  Examples:

  Pido que cierren la puerta con llave.   *I ask them to lock the door.*
  Prohibo que mi hijo fume.   *I forbid my son to smoke.*

- A number of verbs of influence/volition commonly bypass the subjunctive and instead use an indirect object pronoun and an infinitive.   (The indirect object pronouns are: me, te, le, nos, les.)

  Examples:

  Les hago **cerrar** la puerta con llave.   *I have **them lock** the door.*
  A mi hijo* **le** prohibo **fumar**.   *I forbid (him) my son **to smoke**.*
         or
  Le prohibo **fumar** a mi hijo*.   *I forbid (him) my son **to smoke**.*

  *"A + noun" is used to clarify or emphasize the indirect object pronoun.

- Common verbs used in this way:

aconsejar...*to advise*	mandar ......*to order*	prohibir ....*to forbid, prohibit*
dejar**........*to let, allow*	pedir ....*to request, ask*	recomendar ...*to recommend*
hacer ....*to have (done)*	permitir ......*to permit*	sugerir ....*to suggest*

  **Dejar takes a direct object pronoun: No la/lo/las/los dejo fumar....*I don't let her/him/them smoke.*

  Some other verbs used this way:

animar a (*to encourage*)	impedir (*to prevent*)	proponer (*to propose*)
convencer (*to convince*)	obligar a (*to make, to force*)	rogar (*to beg, plead*)
disuadir de (*to talk out of*)	ordenar (*to order*)	suplicar (*to ask, pray, plead*)
exigir (*to demand*)	persuadir a (*to persuade*)	urgir (*to urge*)

A. Write the indirect object pronoun (*me, te, le, nos, les*) that corresponds to the following words.

1. yo _____

2. tú y yo _____

3. Juan _____

4. María_____

5. Juan y María _____

6. nosotras _____

7. los niños _____

8. la compañía_____

B. Translate the following sentences.

1. Mi profesor me aconseja practicar más. _____

_____

2. ¿No lo dejas manejar tu carro? _____

3. A mi hermana no le permito usar mis cosas. _____

_____

4. Les haré pintar la casa. _____

5. ¿Nos sugieres tomar un taxi? _____

C. Change the shortcut sentences from Exercise B into sentences that use the subjunctive.

Example: Les mando quitarse los zapatos lodosos.

Mando que se quiten los zapatos lodosos.

1. Mi profesor me aconseja practicar más.

_____

2. ¿No lo dejas manejar tu carro?

_____

3. A mi hermana no le permito usar mis cosas.

_____

4. Les haré pintar la casa.

_____

5 ¿Nos sugieres tomar un taxi?

_____

D. Translate the following sentences in 2 ways: with the subjunctive and with an infinitive.

Example:

I always have them check the oil.

Subjunctive *Siempre hago que revisen el aceite.*

Infinitive *Siempre les hago revisar el aceite.*

1. They don't let us travel alone.

Subjunctive _____

Infinitive_____

2. They prohibit their employees from making personal calls.

Subjunctive _____

Infinitive_____

3. Do you *(Ud.)* recommend that I call her?

Subjunctive _____

Infinitive_____

#14 Indirect Commands

- In *#1 Volition*, we saw that the subjunctive can be used to express one person's attempt to influence another's actions (see p.21).

    Examples:

    Quiero que llegues temprano.   *I want you to arrive early.*
    Prohibo que mis hijos fumen.   *I forbid my children to smoke.*

- An indirect command is similar to those above, but the main clause has been dropped.

    Examples:

    1. Que lo pasen bien.   *Have a good time.*
    2. Que le vaya bien.   *May all go well for you.*
    3. Que lo haga ella.   *Let her do it / have her do it.*
    4. Que laven los platos ellos. *Let them wash the dishes / have them wash the dishes.*

    An indirect command is sometimes translated into English as a direct command as in #1 above.
    Sometimes it is translated by using "may" as in #2.
    And sometimes with "let"* or "have" as in #3 and #4.

    *"Let" in these sentences does not mean "to permit," but is an expression of the speaker's will.

- In a few common expressions, the "que" is dropped:
    Dios le bendiga   *May God bless you.*
    ¡Viva México!   *Long live Mexico!*

A. Translate the following indirect commands.

1. ¡Que se diviertan *(Uds.)*!

_____

2. ¡Que no te caigas!

_____

3. ¡Que salgamos juntos!

_____

4. ¡Que nos llamen tus padres!

_____

5. ¡Que limpie ella su propio cuarto!

_____

6. ¡Que fumen afuera los empleados

_____

B. Some indirect commands can be rewritten as direct commands.
The first 3 sentences in Exercise A can be changed into direct commands.
Change these indirect commands into direct commands and translate them.

1. ¡Que se diviertan (Uds.)! _____   _____

2. ¡Que no te caigas! _____   _____

3. ¡Que salgamos juntos! _____   _____

C. In the following conversations:
   • Translate the first sentence.
   • Change the 2nd sentence (the part in italics) into an indirect command.
   • Translate the indirect command.

   Example:
   — Hay muchos platos sucios. _There are lots of dirty dishes._
   — ¿Por qué no pides que los niños los laven? _¡Que los niños los laven!_
   Have the children wash them.

1. —No hay autobús a esa hora. _____

   —Entonces, deben caminar. _____

   _____

2. —Nos vamos. _____

   —Bueno. Espero que Uds. lo pasen bien. _____

   _____

3. —Sacaron muy malas notas. _____

   —Por eso insistimos en que ellos estudien más. _____

   _____

4. —No puedo terminar a tiempo. _____

   —Pues, pide que él te ayude. _____

   _____

D. Add a thought—framed as an indirect command—to the following statements. Translate both sentences.

Example:

Te voy a extrañar.   *¡Que me llames!*

I'm going to miss you. Call me!

1. No es mi turno para poner la mesa *(set the table).*_____

_____

2. No es bueno que ella haga tanto. _____

_____

3. ¿Estás diciéndome mentiras?_____

_____

4. ¿Por qué tienes tanta prisa?_____

_____

E. Respond to the following statements with an indirect command. Translate both sentences.

Example:

—Juan tiene una pregunta sobre esto.   *"Juan has a question about this."*

—Pues, que me llame, y se lo explico.   *"Well, have him call me, and I'll explain it to him"*

1. —¡Ay! Casi me caí.   1._____

— _____   _____

2. — La boda va a ser afuera.   2._____

— _____   _____

3. —No tengo bastante dinero.   3._____

— _____   _____

4. —Ya me voy.   4._____

— _____   _____

The Answer Key begins on p.197.

F. Review ways to use the subjunctive.

Use a verb of influence/volition or emotion in a sentence (see p.24, ex. E and p.30, ex. B).

1. _____

Use an impersonal expression in a sentence (see p.38, ex. B & C).

2. _____

Use an expression of doubt/negation in a sentence (see p.42, ex. B).

3. _____

Use a compound tense in a sentence (see p.47).

4. _____

Use "para," "para que" or another expression of intended purpose (see p.59).

5. _____

Use a conjunction that introduces a contingency in a sentence (see p.63).

6. _____

Write a sentence with "cuando" (see p.69).

7. _____

Write a sentence with "aunque" (see p.75).

8. _____

Write a sentence about a person or object that doesn't exist (see p.81).

9. _____

Write a sentence about a hypothetical / nonspecific person or object (see p.87).

10._____

Write a sentence in the present tense with "si" (see p.95).

11._____

Write an indirect command (see p.99).

12._____

#15 The "-Ever"s

- In dependent clauses, "que" + the subjunctive is normally used after these expressions:
  1. cualquier (+ noun) ....*whatever, whichever (noun)*
  2. cualquiera...*whatever, whichever*
  3. quienquiera..*whoever, whomever*
  4. (a)dondequiera....................................*(to) wherever*
  5. cuandoquiera.......................................*whenever*
  6. por + (adjective or adverb) + que ....*however (adjective or adverb)*

  Note: *Cualesquiera* and *quienesquiera* are the plural forms of *cualquiera* and *quienquiera*.

  The subjunctive is used because what is referred to is not specific, not information.

  Examples:
  1. Leeré **cualquier** biografía o   *I'll read whatever biography*
     cualquier misterio que **tengas**.   *or whatever mystery you have.*
  2. Dame **cualquiera** que **recomienden**.   *Give me whichever one they recommend.*
  3. Hablaré con **quienquiera** que **conteste**.   *I'll talk with whomever answers.*
  4. Vivirá **dondequiera** que **encuentre** empleo.   *He will live wherever he finds work.*
  5. Irán a los conciertos de ese conjunto   *They will go to that group's concerts*
     cuandoquiera y adondequiera que **sean**.   *whenever and wherever they may be.*
  6. **Por difícil que sea**, lo haremos.   *However difficult it may be, we will do it.*
     Por rápido que corran, no van a   *However fast they run, they're not going*
     alcanzarla.   *to catch up with her.*

- Expressions 1 through 5 can be used without a dependent clause.
  Examples: Cualquiera funciona.   *Whichever one works.*
                 Iremos adondequiera.   *We'll go wherever.*

- Subjunctive + *lo que* + subjunctive
  Examples:
     digan lo que digan   *whatever they say, no matter what they say*
     hagas lo que hagas   *whatever you do, no matter what you do*
     coma lo que coma (él)   *whatever he eats, no matter what he eats*

- "Lo que + verb" can be in indicative (if it's information) or subjunctive (if it's not specific).
  Examples:
     Esto es **lo que quiero**.   *This is what I want.*   *(information—indicative)*
     Haz l**o que quieras**   *Do whatever you want.* *(not specific—subjunctive)*
     Lo que me importa es tener buenos amigos.   *What's important to me is having good friends.*
                                                (information—indicative)

     —¿Qué quieres hacer?   *What do you want to do?*
     —**Lo que sea**.   *Whatever.*   *(not specific—subjunctive)*

- el / la / los / las (noun) + verb*
  Use the subjunctive if the meaning is "whichever "or "whatever."
  Examples: Veremos **la** película **que** Uds. **quieran**.   *We'll see whatever movie you want.*
                 Veremos **la que** Uds. **quieran**.   *We'll see whichever one you want.*
                                   vs.
                 Veamos "Casablanca." Es la que Uds. **quieren**.
                 Let's see "Casablanca." It's the one that you want.   *(specific—indicative)*

  * Often the verb is *querer*.

A. Translate the following sentences.

1. Cueste lo que cueste, vale la pena.

   _____

2. Por barato que sea, no lo compres.

   _____

3. Cualquier madre diría lo mismo.

   _____

4. Adondequiera que él lleve su carro, no podrán repararlo.

   _____

5. Veremos cualquier película que les interese a Uds.

   _____

6. ¡Lo que sea!

   _____

7. Quienquiera que pague, decide.

   _____

'8. —Cuál de estas camisas prefieres?

   _____

   —Cualquiera. Me da igual. *(It's all the same to me.)*

   _____

9. Juan hará lo que le dé la gana. *(dar la gana = to feel like)*

   _____

10. Por despacio y claro que yo hable, ellos nunca me comprenden.

   _____

The Answer Key begins on p.197.

B. Translate the following sentences.

1. The police will find him wherever he may go.

   _____

2. Whoever knows her, admires her.

   _____

3. However much they may work, their money isn't enough *(no alcanzar para)* to pay their bills.

   _____

4. Whatever house they buy, they will make it attractive and comfortable.

   _____

C. Write a dialogue for María and Juan.
   María asks Juan several questions about his preferences for their upcoming vacation.
   Juan's answers are nonspecific and noncommittal.
   Use at least 4 "-ever" expressions.

   _____

   _____

   _____

   _____

   _____

   _____

   _____

   _____

   _____

D. Translate the following phrases and find the Spanish phrases in the word search below.

cualquier niño _____

diga lo que diga _____

cualquiera _____

lo que sea _____

cualesquiera _____

lo que quieras _____

dondequiera _____

cuandoquiera _____

por feo que canten _____

por fácil que sea _____

quienquiera _____

```
A  A  W  Q  U  I  E  N  Q  U  I  E  R  A  P  D  Ú  Ú
L  P  Ú  J  O  Y  Ó  R  S  G  H  W  T  R  Ü  I  C  H
Ó  O  J  L  O  Q  U  E  Q  U  I  E  R  A  S  G  Ó  E
Í  R  N  Ü  J  U  Í  Ñ  Ü  P  B  K  O  B  Q  A  L  B
B  F  Í  B  Í  K  D  Q  O  Í  S  S  H  A  Z  L  O  M
F  E  D  L  V  Ñ  D  O  V  U  G  K  Í  E  Q  O  Q  O
C  O  E  V  X  Ú  Ü  N  Ñ  Q  V  A  S  E  Q  U  Ñ
W  Q  K  Á  Y  Ü  Ó  C  K  D  Ñ  N  R  E  Z  U  E  I
H  U  F  O  Í  S  C  J  R  A  E  Ó  E  U  Y  E  S  N
M  E  R  U  E  G  L  Í  R  Q  E  Q  I  Q  Ü  D  E  R
É  C  K  J  Ú  Ó  I  E  Ñ  W  M  P  U  L  O  I  A  E
J  A  A  J  Í  Ñ  I  T  N  G  F  Q  Q  I  D  G  Y  I
L  N  N  J  B  U  B  É  Í  L  S  Z  S  C  E  A  Q  U
X  T  Ó  É  Q  D  J  Ú  C  X  E  I  E  Á  D  R  R  Q
Z  E  F  L  X  M  B  D  F  N  F  V  L  F  E  Q  A  L
O  N  A  G  Á  E  H  Y  Á  S  D  I  A  R  U  Ü  S  A
K  U  M  O  É  E  A  F  N  L  E  P  U  O  Y  A  R  U
C  U  A  N  D  O  Q  U  I  E  R  A  C  P  Y  U  Y  C
```

Solution on p.108.

#16 Expressions of Possibility (Single Clause)

- **Indicative**—the following expressions of possibility are used only with the indicative:

a lo mejor	*perhaps, probably*
mejor que	*it's better that, it's best that*
menos mal que	*at least, it's not so bad that*
o sea que	*in other words, that is to say*
qué + (adjective / adverb / noun) + que......	*how interesting (adj.), how quickly (adv.), what a problem (noun), etc.*

Examples:

A lo mejor nos **gustará**.	*We'll probably like it.*
O sea que nos gustó.	*In other words, we liked it.*
Menos mal que nos **gusta**.	*At least we like it.*
Qué suerte que nos **gusta**.	*How lucky that we like it.*

Note: if the above expressions are restructured as impersonal expressions (see p.37), they are followed by the subjunctive.

Examples:

Mejor que lo **saben.**	*It's best that they know.*	*(indicative)*
Es mejor que lo **sepan.**	*It's best that they know.*	*(subjunctive)*
Qué afortunado que **han ganado**.	*How fortunate that they've won.*	*(indicative)*
Es afortunado que **hayan ganado**.	*It's fortunate that they've won.*	*(subjunctive)*

- **Subjunctive**—the following expressions of possibility are used only with the subjunctive, even if there is only one clause in the sentence:

posiblemente	*possibly*
puede ser que	*it could be, possibly*

Examples:

Posiblemente no se **conozcan**.	*Possibly they don't know each other.*
Puede ser que ella se lo **diga** a él.	*It could be that she'll tell him.*

- **Subjunctive** or **indicative**—the following expressions of possibility may be used with either:

tal vez	*perhaps, maybe*
quizá....................................	*perhaps, maybe*
quizás	*perhaps, maybe*

The use of indicative with these expressions shows more certainty. Subjunctive shows more doubt.

Examples:

Tal vez no se **dan** cuenta.	*Maybe they don't realize.* *(I think that's the case—indicative.)*
Tal vez no se **den** cuenta.	*Maybe they don't realize.* *(But I doubt that's so—subjunctive.)*

A. For the following expressions, write the letters of the phrases that can complete the sentences. There will be more than one answer.

Tal vez _____

Quizás _____

Puede ser que _____

A lo mejor _____

Qué sorpresa que_____

Es sorprendente que _____

Posiblemente _____

Quizá _____

a. pueden ayudar.

b. puedan ayudar.

c. Juan se muda pronto.

d. Juan se mude pronto.

e. se casan en septiembre.

f. se casen en septiembre.

Solution to the word search on p.106.

Part II

The Past Subjunctive

A. How to Form the Past Subjunctive

How to Form the Past Subjunctive

1. Start with the "ellos" form of the preterite: *hablaron, comieron, tuvieron, pidieron,* etc.
2. Drop the final "-on."
3. Add the following endings:

Verb Endings For the Past Subjunctive

-ar / **-er** / **-ir** verbs

yo	**-a**
tú	**-a**s
él, ella, Ud.	**-a**
nosotros, nosotras	**-a**mos
ellos, ellas, Uds.	**-a**n

Notes:

- There are no irregular verbs, stem-change verbs or spelling adjustments that are not already found in the "ellos" form of the preterite.

  Examples of conjugations for the past subjunctive:

infinitive	yo	tú	él, ella, Ud.	nosotros, nosotras	ellos, ellas, Uds.
hablar	hablara	hablaras	hablara	habláramos	hablaran
correr	corriera	corrieras	corriera	corriéramos	corrieran
vivir	viviera	vivieras	viviera	viviéramos	vivieran
jugar	jugara	jugaras	jugara	jugáramos	jugaran
pedir	pidiera	pidieras	pidiera	pidiéramos	pidieran
ir, ser	fuera	fueras	fuera	fuéramos	fueran
querer	quisiera	quisieras	quisiera	quisiéramos	quisieran
leer	leyera	leyeras	leyera	leyéramos	leyeran

- In the "nosotros" form, an accent is added to the "a" or the "e" in the syllable before the "-amos" ending. This keeps the stress on the same syllable as in the other forms.

Examples: yo habl**a**ra   yo com**ie**ra   yo tuv**ie**ra
nosotros habl**á**ramos   nosotros com**ié**ramos   nosotros tuv**ié**ramos

Review: The "Ellos" Form of the Preterite (Indicative)

	-ar	-er / -ir	irregular
Verb Endings for "ellos, ellas, Uds.":	-aron	-ieron	-ieron (-eron if it follows a "j")
examples:	habl**aron** estudi**aron**	com**ieron** viv**ieron**	hic**ieron** dij**eron**

Irregular Verb Stems

andar	anduv-	anduvieron
caber	cup-	cupieron
decir	dij-	dijeron
estar	estuv-	estuvieron
haber	hub-	hubieron
hacer	hic-	hicieron
poder	pud-	pudieron
poner	pus-	pusieron
producir	produj-	produjeron
querer	quis-	quisieron
saber	sup-	supieron
tener	tuv-	tuvieron
traducir	traduj-	tradujeron
traer	traj-	trajeron
venir	vin-	vinieron

Totally Irregular Verbs:

ir, ser	fueron
dar	dieron

Stem-Change Verbs:

- "-ar" and "-er" stem-change verbs have no stem change in the preterite.
- "-ir" stem-change verbs use "i" or "u":

    If the vowel in the stem is **e**, it changes to **i**: p**e**dir = p**i**dieron,
    If the vowel in the stem is **o**, it changes to **u**: d**o**rmir = d**u**rmieron.

Spelling Changes:

- "-er" and "-ir" verb stems ending in "e": the "i" of the ending changes to "y."
    - examples: **cre**er .....cre**y**eron   **le**er ....le**y**eron

- verb stems ending in "ñ": the "i" in the ending is dropped.
    - examples: **gruñ**ir .....gruñeron   **reñ**ir ....riñeron

- verb stems with a stem change ending in "i": the "i" of the ending is dropped.
    - examples: **re**ír ....**ri**eron   **fre**ír ....**fri**eron

A. Practice the "ellos" form of preterite (indicative).

infinitive	ellos, preterite	yo, past subjunctive
1. hablar	*hablaron*	*hablara*
2. bailar		
3. pasar		
4. dejar		
5. tomar		
6. llevarse*		
7. perderse*		
8. encontrar		
9. pensar		
10. comer		
11. creer		
12. querer		
13. ir, ser		
14. vivir		
15. asistir		
16. seguir		
17. salir		
18. poner		
19. ver		
20. conocer		

* Reflexive pronouns (and other object pronouns) go before the verb in subjunctive.
Example: quedarse—me quedara, te quedaras, se quedara, nos quedáramos, se quedaran.

B. Practice the forms of the past subjunctive.

infinitive	yo	tú	él, ella, Ud.	nosotros, nosotras	ellos, ellas, Uds.
1. hablar	hablara	hablaras	hablara	habláramos	hablaran
2. invitar					
3. pensar					
4. comprender					
5. comer					
6. poder					
7. vivir					
8. ser, ir					
9. estar					
10. tener					
11. vender					
12. leer					
13. hacer					
14. decir					
15. dar					
16. caerse					
17. ver					
18. conocer					
19. saber					
20. querer					
21. volver					
22. seguir					
23. haber					
24. servir					
25. morir					

The Other Past Subjunctive

There is another set of endings for the past subjunctive.

The final -ron is dropped from the "ellos" form of the preterite, and the following endings used:
-se, -ses, -se, -semos, -sen.   (An accent is added to the "nosotros" form as it is to the forms on p.111.)

Examples: hablar: hablase, hablases, hablase, hablásemos, hablasen
comer: comiese, comieses, comiese, comiésemos, comiesen
ir / ser: fuese, fueses, fuese, fuésemos, fuesen
hacer: hiciese, hicieses, hiciese, hiciésemos, hiciesen

For the most part, the two forms are interchangeable.

In conversation, the forms above are used more in Spain than in Latin America.
They are also seen frequently in writing.

But for conversation in Latin America, the endings on p.111 are more commonly used. These -ara /-iera endings will be the ones used in the Answer Key.

C. Indicative or subjunctive?
Put a check next to the verbs in subjunctive (past or present).

_____1. viva

_____2. conocíamos

_____3. dormimos

_____4. jugaré

_____5. escribieras

_____6. preguntases

_____7. ayudáramos

_____8. vengan

_____9. ayudamos

_____10. compra

_____11. invitaste

_____12. cantaras

D. Fill in the blanks with the correct form of past subjunctive for the verbs in parentheses.

1. Ojalá* que mi amiga me (dar) _____un regalo.

2. Ojalá que el niño (estar) _____bien.

3. Ojalá que nosotros (ser) _____amigos.

4. Ojalá que tú (poder)_____acompañarnos.

5. Ojalá que mi familia no (vivir) _____tan lejos.

6. Ojalá que Uds. (dormir) _____bien.

7. Ojalá que yo (tener)_____el tiempo.

8. Ojalá que (haber) _____bastante comida.

* Ojalá with past subjunctive means "if only" or "I wish" as in:
Ojalá que él estuviera............. *If only he were here / I wish he were here.*
Ojalá que fuera así................. *If only it were so / I wish it were so.*

E. Word Search
Write the past subjunctive form of the verbs and find them in the puzzle below.

1. estar: tú _____

2. buscar: Ud. _____

3. jugar: tú y yo _____

4. abrir: él _____

5. cerrar: Ud. _____

6. dar: ellos _____

7. ver: yo _____

8. saber: ella _____

9. escuchar: ellos _____

10. hacer: nosotras _____

11. oír: yo _____

12. servir: ella y él _____

13. divertirse: tú _____

14. ser: nosotros _____

15. mirar: tú _____

16. llover: (*it*) _____

```
Z E Q J P F S E S C U C H A R A N I
A B R I E R A T G M T I R U S R K Y
N L N D L H J F S X E Z P J K G Q Z
E C A I L I Y D W H D K R U P O F E
E S T U V I E R A S I Y T G I H P N
M F Y T N P V F D N V R Á D I L U
Q D U V S I I D J H I W Y R S C B D
X P X É Z U Q I Z T R P U A K I U W
I B J U R G P J X K T Y U M H É S U
E F E P E A D I L G I J J O Q R C M
P V K T Q U M O E T E C D S P A A D
J C O R J M R O M R R O E J N M R I
C E R R A R A W S M A Y P I S O A E
Z L L O V I E R A Z S A J I R S W R
A F J B X S H O O Y E R A R C P Q A
V A M B Y I K R S I R V I E R A N N
M I R A R A S T U Y I S I P Q G H S
J I L L G L W Y J K V I E R A A T M
```

Solution on p.118.

F. Ojalá

In the following sentences:
• change the sentence into a clause following "Ojalá"
• put the verb in past subjunctive
• translate the new sentences.

Example:

Se quedan en un buen hotel.   *Ojalá que se quedaran en un buen hotel.*

If only they were staying in a good hotel.

1. Yo comprendo esto. _____

_____

2. Nosotros llegamos a tiempo. _____

_____

3. No te pones tan nervioso. _____

_____

4. Sé las respuestas. _____

_____

5. Mis hijos estudian más. _____

_____

6. El bebé duerme toda la noche. _____

_____

7. Hay una fiesta. _____

_____

8. Ellos ganan la lotería. _____

_____

9. Sacas buenas notas en tus clases. _____

_____

10. Él baila mejor. _____

_____

The Answer Key for the past subjunctive begins on p.233.

Courtesy Expressions

The following past subjunctive verbs, when used alone or in main clauses, function as polite forms:

Quisiera.............*would want, would like*
Debiera ....*should*
Pudiera..............*could*

Examples:

Quisiéramos una habitación, por favor. ....*We would like a room, please.*
¿Quisieras un café? ....*Would you like some coffee?*
Debiera hacerlo. ....*You should do it.*
¿Pudiera ayudarme?..*Could you help me?*

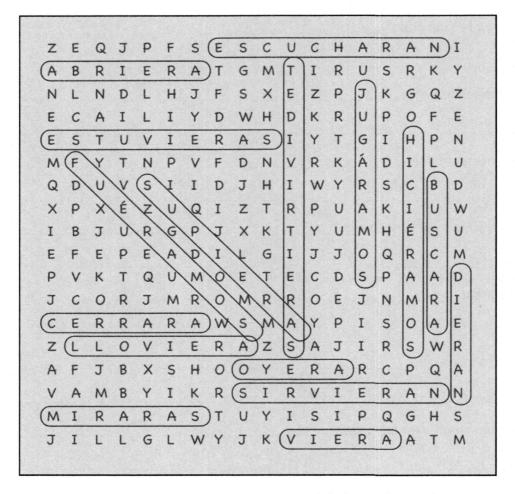

Solution to the puzzle on p.116.

Part II

The Past Subjunctive

B. Step by Step

How to Use the Past Subjunctive

Coordinating Tenses

- The first part of this book dealt with sentences with a main clause and a dependent clause. They combined verbs from the choices in the box below.

Indicative
present
future
   (and their compound forms)

Subjunctive
present
   (and its compound forms)

Commands

Examples:

Quiero   que   me **ayudes**.
(present indicative) +   (present subjunctive)
I want   *you to help me.*

Nos **ha sorprendido** que no se **hayan esforzado**.
(present perfect indicative) + (present perfect subjunctive)
It has surprised us   *that*   *they haven't made an effort.*

Lo **leeré**   cuando   **esté** de vacaciones.
(future)   +   (present subjunctive)
I will read it   *when*   *I'm on vacation.*

Llámame   tan pronto como   **puedas.**
(command)   +   (present subjunctive).
Call me   *as soon as*   *you can.*

- The second part of this book will also deal with sentences with a main clause and a dependent clause, but the verbs used will come from the choices in the box below. For the most part, it's important to stay either within the box above or the one below.

Indicative
preterite*
imperfect*
conditional
   (and their compound forms)

Subjunctive
past
   (and its compound forms)

Examples:

Insistí   en que   lo ayudaran.
(preterite)   +   (past subjunctive).
I insisted   *that*   *they help him.*

Me alegraba de que se hubiera graduado.
(imperfect)   +   (past perfect subjunctive)
I was glad   *that*   *he had graduated.*

Lo habría leído si hubiera tenido tiempo.
(conditional perfect) + (past perfect subjunctive)
I would have read it *if*   *I'd had time.*

- **Exception**

If the main clause is about the present and the dependent clause is about the past, many speakers will simply jump between the boxes above and put the dependent clause in a past tense.

Example: Me alegro   que   vinieran.   *I'm glad they came.*
       present indicative + *past subjunctive*

Although it's possible to stay within one box:
      Me alegro   que   hayan venido.   *I'm glad they've come.*
      present + *present perfect*

*See pp.122-124 for a review of preterite and imperfect.

Verb Endings for Preterite

	-ar	**-er / -ir**	**irregular**
yo	-é	-í	-e
tú	-aste	-iste	-iste
él, ella, Ud.	-ó	-ió	-o
nosotros, nosotras	-amos	-imos	-imos
ellos, ellas, Uds.	-aron	-ieron	-ieron*

*-eron if it follows a "j"

Examples:

hablar:	hablé	hablaste	habló	hablamos	hablaron
comer:	comí	comiste	comió	comimos	comieron
vivir:	viví	viviste	vivió	vivimos	vivieron
tener:	tuve	tuviste	tuvo	tuvimos	tuvieron

(See p.112 for information on irregulars, stem changes and spelling changes.)

Verb Endings for Imperfect

	-ar	**-er / -ir**
yo	-aba	-ía
tú	-abas	-ías
él, ella, Ud.	-aba	-ía
nosotros, nosotras	-ábamos	-íamos
ellos, ellas, Uds.	-aban	-ían

Examples:

hablar:	hablaba	hablabas	hablaba	hablábamos	hablaban
comer:	comía	comías	comía	comíamos	comían
vivir:	vivía	vivías	vivía	vivíamos	vivían

There are no stem changes in the imperfect.

There are 3 irregulars:

ir:	iba	ibas	iba	íbamos	iban
ser:	era	eras	era	éramos	eran
ver:	veía	veías	veía	veíamos	veían

A Summary of Preterite vs. Imperfect

Preterite is used for:	**Imperfect** is used for:
Beginnings La clase empezó a las dos. Se echó a correr. **Ends** La clase terminó a las tres. Llegamos tarde. Murió ayer.	**When the beginning or end is not the focus** —¿Qué hacían Uds. en ese momento? —Practicábamos los verbos.
Specified number of times Visité a mi amiga en México dos veces. Fuimos a ese restaurante algunas veces. **For a specified period of time** Estudiamos por dos horas. El imperio duró por siglos.	**Customary or habitual action** Cada verano íbamos de camping. Cuando era niña, estudiaba mucho.
Discrete action* (viewed as complete, over and done) Lincoln fue un presidente importante. Escribió esos libros.	**Ongoing action** Leíamos el periódico. A las cuatro ella tomaba café.
Sequence of events Salimos a comer y luego fuimos al cine. Juan insultó a Pepe, y Pepe le pegó.	**Simultaneous actions** Miraba la tele mientras los niños dormían. Escuchaba música mientras pagaba las cuentas. **Interrupted actions** (not a sequence) Yo estaba limpiando la cocina cuando llamaste.
*Consider how the characteristics of the preterite tense can affect the meaning of these verbs: tener: ....had, got saber: ....knew, found out conocer: ....knew, met poder: ....could, managed to, succeeded in no poder: ......could not, failed to querer:...........wanted, tried to no querer:......didn't want, refused to	**Description, background info, circumstances** Era mecánico. Era listo. Era moreno. Estaba cansado. Trabajaba con mi hermano. Vivía lejos de aquí. Llevaba una chaqueta azul marino.

A. Write the preterite and imperfect forms of the following verbs:

Example: estudio _____ *estudié* _____ *estudiaba* _____

Verbs of Influence / Volition	preterite	imperfect
1. quiero		
2. ¿mandas?		
3. sugiere		
4. decimos		
5. insisten		

Verbs of Emotion	preterite	imperfect
6. me alegro		
7. ¿estás triste?		
8. le molesta		
9. tenemos miedo		
10. se preocupan		

Verbs of Impersonal Expressions	preterite	imperfect
11. es bueno		
12. es increíble		

Verbs of Doubt and Negation	preterite	imperfect
13. dudo		
14. ¿no crees?		
15. no quiere decir		
16. negamos		
17. no creo		
18. no están seguras		

The Answer Key for the past subjunctive begins on p.233.

How to Use the Past Subjunctive

#1. Influence / Volition (see p. 21)

#2. Emotion (see p.29)

#3. Impersonal Expressions (see p.37)

#4. Doubt and Negation (see p.41)

- Verbs of influence/volition, verbs of emotion, most impersonal expressions,*
  and expressions of doubt and negation** trigger the subjunctive.

  The tense of these verbs in the main clause determines the tense of the subjunctive
  in the dependent clause. (See p.121.)

  If the main clause is in a present or future tense, the dependent clause will be in the **present subjunctive**.
  If the main clause is in a past or conditional tense, the dependent clause will be in the **past subjunctive.**

  Examples:

Ellos **piden** que **llegues** a tiempo.	*They ask that you arrive on time.*
Ellos **pidieron** que **llegaras** a tiempo.	*They asked that you arrive on time.*
Están tristes que ella **esté** enferma.	*They are sad that she's sick.*
Estaban tristes que ella **estuviera** enferma.	*They were sad that she was sick.*
Es sorprendente que **se casen** tan rápido.	*It's surprising that they're getting married so quickly.*
Fue sorprendente que **se casaran** tan rápido.	*It was surprising that they got married so quickly.*
No creo que **sea** buena idea.	*I don't think it's a good idea.*
No creía que **fuera** buena idea.	*I didn't think it was a good idea.*

- Because there are two conjugated verbs, "que" is needed to connect them.

- If only one subject is involved, then the second verb is not conjugated.

Examples:		
	Quería **salir**.	*I wanted to leave.*
	Estuvimos contentos de **poder ayudar**.	*We were happy to be able to help.*
	Fue difícil **estudiar**.	*It was difficult to study.*

  * Impersonal expressions that assert a truth are followed by the indicative.
  Example: **Era verdad** que él te **admiraba.**   *It was true that he admired you.*

  ** Expressions denying doubt or negation assert a truth and are followed by the indicative.
  Example: **No dudé** que habían dicho la verdad.   *I did not doubt that they had told the truth.*

A. Change the following sentences to the past tense. (Use the preterite or imperfect in the main clause.)

1. Queremos que haya paz en el mundo.

    _____

2. El general mandará que los soldados ataquen.

    _____

3. Sugiero que lo llames.

    _____

4. Dicen que yo venga.

    _____

5. ¿Aconsejas que estudien más ciencias?

    _____

6. Nos enoja que siempre llegues tarde.

    _____

7. La doctora se preocupa de que su paciente no se mejore.

    _____

8. El empleado está molesto que no le paguen más.

    _____

9. ¿Estás emocionada de que ellos se casen?

    _____

10. Los niños tienen miedo de que su perro esté perdido.

    _____

11. Es horrible que me digas eso.

    _____

12. Es fantástico que nos visiten.

    _____

B. **Combine each set of two sentences to make one sentence.**
   (Use a verb in the past subjunctive, if possible.)

Example:

El padre estaba enojado.   Su hija llegaba tarde.

El padre estaba enojado que su hija llegara tarde.

1. El taxista se inquietó.   El precio de la gasolina subiría.

_____

2. Los niños estaban alegres.   Habría una fiesta de cumpleaños.

_____

3. A Luz María le encantaba.   Ella salía a bailar.

_____

4. Estábamos contentos.   Pudiste visitarnos.

_____

5. Lamenté.   Estaban enfermos.

_____

6. ¿Tuviste miedo?   No vinieron.

_____

7. Mi amigo se quejó. El viaje costó mucho.

_____

8. Me encantó. Había música en vivo *(live)*.

_____

The Answer Key for this chapter begins on p.237.

C.   Translate the following sentences. (Not all the sentences require the subjunctive.)

1. Did you *(tú)* want me to set the table *(poner la mesa)*?

_____

2. She did not permit her children to ski alone.

_____

3. He wanted to go to the party, but he had to work.

_____

4. The school recommended that students have their own computer.

_____

5. She needed to leave early.

_____

6. We asked them to call us on Tuesday.

_____

7. They suggested we make a reservation.

_____

8. The company required its employees to take drug tests *(una prueba de detección de drogas)*.

_____

9. The family wished to see him.

_____

10. I didn't like you *(tú)* traveling alone.

_____

11. She was proud that her children got good grades.

_____

12. The class was worried that the teacher would give them a test.

_____

13. He was embarrassed to admit it.

_____

14. Weren't you *(tú)* happy that it wasn't raining?

_____

15. They were afraid to tell you *(Ud.)* the truth.

_____

16. I was sorry that you *(tú)* had a headache.

_____

17. They were furious that it was turning out badly *(salir mal)*.

_____

18. It was dangerous for the children to play in the street.

_____

19. It was not right *(correcto)* for them to leave him alone / on his own.

_____

20. It was true that he knew how to drive. But it was not true that he drove well.

_____

21. It was incredible that it cost so much.

_____

22. He didn't believe it was true.

_____

23. They doubted that she knew how to cook paella.

_____

24. We were not sure that they would come to the party.

_____

25. She didn't think that we should work there.

_____

26. It was sad that it was over *(acabarse)*.

_____

D. Use 3 verbs of influence/volition in sentences that include a second verb in the past subjunctive.

1. _____

2. _____

3. _____

E. Use 3 verbs of emotion in sentences that include a second verb in the past subjunctive.

1. _____

2. _____

3. _____

F. Use 3 impersonal expressions in sentences that include a second verb in the past subjunctive.

1. _____

2. _____

3. _____

G. Use 3 expressions of doubt or negation in sentences that include a second verb in the past subjunctive.

1. _____

2. _____

3. _____

H. Write a dialogue in the *present tense* between two people who are arguing about something. Write at least 3 lines for each person and include at least 4 verbs in the present subjunctive.

Example: *Juan:*   *Yo quiero que laves los platos.*
　　　　　María: *No creo que sea mi turno para lavarlos.*

_____

_____

_____

_____

_____

_____

_____

I. One of the people above tells a friend about the argument.
(The verbs above in present subjunctive should appear below in the past subjunctive.)

Example: *Yo dije que quería que ella lavara los platos.*
　　　　　Ella dijo que no creía que fuera su turno para lavarlos.

_____

_____

_____

_____

_____

J. Write a dialogue between two people who are talking about something that happened in the past. Give their reactions to the event. Write at least 3 lines for each person, and include at least 4 verbs in the past subjunctive.

Persona 1: ¿Recuerdas

Ojalá

- *Ojalá* can only be used with the subjunctive.

- *Ojalá* with the present subjunctive asserts volition over a current or future action.
  Examples:
  Ojalá que estén bien.   *I hope they are well.*
  Ojalá que lleguen mañana.   *I hope they arrive tomorrow.*

- *Ojalá* with the past subjunctive expresses the wish that something were different than it is, and often translates as "If only" or "I wish."
  Example:
  Ojalá que estuvieran bien.   *If only they were well. (But they're sick.)*

A. Translate the following sentences into English.

1. Ojalá que ella los ayude con sus tareas.

   _____

2. Ojalá que ya hayan llegado sin problema y que ahora estén en su hotel.

   _____

3. Ojalá que él no dijera tales cosas.

   _____

4. Ojalá que yo no le hubiera dicho eso a mi cuñada *(sister-in-law)*.

   _____

5. Ojalá que él saque buenas notas.

   _____

6. Ojalá que no fuera cierto.

   _____

B. Translate the following sentences into Spanish.

1. I wish I had finished. _____

2. I hope it begins soon. _____

3. If only we had left earlier. _____

4. I hope it doesn't rain tomorrow. _____

5. If only it weren't so hot out. _____

6. I hope they have voted. _____

C. Think of a novel you've read, or a movie you've seen.
What might someone who's in the middle of it say with *Ojalá*.

Examples for *The Wizard of Oz* :

<u>Hopes about how it will turn out (present subjunctive):</u>

Ojalá que la bruja no **mate** a Dorotea.
I hope the witch doesn't kill Dorothy.

<u>MIsgivings about what is happening or has happened (past subjunctive):</u>

Ojalá que a la bruja no le **importaran** las zapatillas rojas de Dorotea.
If only the witch didn't care about Dorothy's ruby slippers. (But she does.)

Ojalá que Dorotea no **hubiera salido** durante la tormenta.
If only Dorothy hadn't gone out during the storm. (But she did.)

Write 5 sentences about how the person hopes the book or movie will turn out (present subjunctive).

1. _____

2. _____

3. _____

4. _____

5. _____

Write 5 sentences expressing what the person wishes were different (past subjunctive).

6. _____

7. _____

8. _____

9. _____

10. _____

#5 Compound Verbs—The Past Tense
(See pp.47-49.)

- To make a compound verb subjunctive, the helping verb is put in the subjunctive.

- The tense of the main clause determines whether to use the present or past subjunctive in the dependent clause. (See p.121.)

If the main clause is in a present or future tense, the dependent clause will be in the **present subjunctive**.
If the main clause is in a past or conditional tense, the dependent clause will be in the **past subjunctive**.

Examples:

Se alegran de que lo **estés** pasando bien.
*They are glad **you're** having a good time.*

Se alegraban de que lo **estuvieras** pasando bien.
*They were glad **you were** having a good time.*

Esperamos que él **siga** comportándose bien.
*We hope he **keeps** behaving himself.*

Esperábamos que él **siguiera** comportándose bien.
*We hoped that he **would keep** behaving himself.*

Es impresionante que **haya** tenido tanto éxito.
*It's impressive that she **has** been so successful.*

Fue impresionante que **hubiera** tenido tanto éxito.
*It was impressive that she **had** been so successful.*

Dudo que ellos **hayan** estado trabajando.
*I doubt that they **have** been working.*

Dudé que ellos **hubieran** estado trabajando.
*I doubted that they **had** been working.*

A. Write the forms of the past subjunctive for the following helping verbs.

	haber	estar	seguir
yo			
tú			
él, ella, Ud.			
nosotros, nosotras			
ellos, ellas, Uds.			

B. Change the following sentences to the past tense and translate the new sentences.

1. Dudan que su hijo haya terminado.

_____

_____

2. Me sorprende que se nos haya acabado la leche.

_____

_____

3. Es feo que siga lloviendo.

_____

_____

4. Estamos impresionados que hayas pasado la tarde limpiando tu cuarto.

_____

_____

5. María espera que Juan esté escuchando.

_____

_____

6. El maestro no está convencido de que los alumnos hayan estado estudiando.

_____

_____

The Answer Key for this chapter begins on p.240.

C. Put the following phrases in the past subjunctive (in the person of your choice).
Then build a sentence around it and translate the sentence.
Example:

estar cocinando   *estuviera cocinando*

   Estaba sorprendida de que él estuviera cocinando.

   I was surprised that he was cooking.

haber llamado antes   *hubiéramos llamado antes*

   Fue una lástima que no hubiéramos llamado antes.

   It was a pity that we hadn't called first.

1. estar jugando al béisbol _____

_____

_____

2. seguir esperando _____

_____

_____

3. haber salido para México _____

_____

_____

4. haber pedido un café _____

_____

_____

5. haber comprado un carro nuevo _____

_____

_____

D. Translate the following sentences.

1. It bugged me that they kept calling.

   _____

2. We were afraid that they had gotten lost.

   _____

3. She thought that he was talking on the telephone.

   _____

4. They didn't think that you *(tú)* had done it.

   _____

**E. Comment on the following statements using a compound tense in the past subjunctive.
Example:**

María ganó la lotería.   *Me alegré de que María hubiera ganado la lotería.*
María won the lottery.

Juan andaba mintiendo sobre ella.   *Dudo que él anduviera mintiendo sobre ella,*
Juan was going around lying about her.

1. María dio a luz a gemelos. _____
   María gave birth to twins.

2. Juan estába buscando un nuevo empleo. _____
   Juan was looking for a new job.

3. María recibió un aumento. _____
   María got a raise.

4. A Juan se le rompió la pierna. _____
   Juan broke his leg.

5. María seguía ofreciéndose como voluntaria. _____
   María kept volunteering.

6. Juan había estado ayudando a sus padres._____
   Juan had been helping his parents.

7. María se negó a pagar sus impuestos. _____
   María refused to pay her taxes.

8. Juan y María se divorciaron. _____
   Juan and María got divorced.

Frank and Ernest

F.   Review ways to use the subjunctive.

Use 3 verbs of influence/volition in sentences that include a second verb in the past subjunctive.

1. _____

2. _____

3. _____

Use 3 verbs of emotion in sentences that include a second verb in the past subjunctive.

4. _____

5. _____

6. _____

Use 3 impersonal expressions in sentences that include a second verb in the past subjunctive.

7. _____

8. _____

9. _____

Use 3 expressions of doubt or negation in sentences that include a second verb in the past subjunctive.

10. _____

11. _____

12. _____

#6 Intended Purpose—The Past Tense
(See p.59.)

- Expressions of intended purpose always trigger the subjunctive, no matter the tense.
(This is because the sentence does not tell us whether the purpose or goal becomes or became fact.)

- PARA QUE is the most common expression of intended purpose. It means "so that" or "in order that." It always requires the subjunctive.

  Examples:

  Ellos van a llevar a sus hijos a Colombia **para que conozcan** a sus tíos.
  *They are going to take their children to Colombia **so that they can meet** their aunts and uncles.*

  Ellos iban a llevar a sus hijos a Colombia **para que conocieran** a sus parientes.

  *They were going to take their children to Colombia **so that they could meet** their relatives.*

  Any phrase that means "so that" requires the subjunctive.
  For example: de manera que   de forma que
                de modo que   a fin de que

- If there is only one subject, use *para* + an infinitive instead of the subjunctive.
  Example:

  Fui a Colombia **para conocer** a mis tíos.   *I went to Colombia to meet my aunts and uncles.*

A. Change the following sentences to past tenses and translate the new sentences.

1. Juan trabaja mucho para mantener a su familia.

   _____

   _____

2. Mi tía me manda dinero a fin de que yo les compre regalos a los niños.

   _____

   _____

3. Les escribimos de modo que sepan la buena noticia.

   _____

   _____

4. Porque nos encanta esta canción, siempre subo el volumen para que la oigamos mejor.

   _____

   _____

5. Quieren que yo los lleve al aeropuerto de manera que no tengan que pagar el estacionamiento.

   _____

   _____

6. Van a plantar los rosales allí de forma que reciban suficiente sol.

   _____

   _____

B. Translate the following sentences.

1. They were going to Sara's so that she could help them with their homework.

   _____

2. I picked my kids up *(recoger)* at school yesterday so that they didn't have to walk home in the rain.

   _____

3. They didn't go out much in order to save money.

   _____

4. He explained it to you *(Uds.)* so that you would understand it.

   _____

5. His parents insisted that he study every day so that he would get good grades.

   _____

6. Did you *(tú)* go to Mexico to study or to visit friends?

   _____

C. Write sentences using the expression indicated. Use at least 3 past subjunctives.

1. para que: _____

2. para:_____

3. de modo que:_____

4. de forma que:_____

5. a fin de que:_____

6. de manera que: _____

D. Review ways to use the subjunctive.

Use 3 verbs of influence/volition in sentences that include a second verb in the past subjunctive.

1. _____

2. _____

3. _____

Use 3 verbs of emotion in sentences that include a second verb in the past subjunctive.

4. _____

5. _____

6. _____

Use 3 impersonal expressions in sentences that include a second verb in the past subjunctive.

7. _____

8. _____

9. _____

Use 3 expressions of doubt or negation in sentences that include a second verb in the past subjunctive.

10. _____

11. _____

12. _____

Use compound verbs in 2 sentences that include verbs in the past subjunctive.

13. _____

14. _____

The Answer Key for this chapter begins on p.242.

E. **Write about what you and your friends and family did last month.**
Include at least 4 intended purposes for those actions.
Example: Fui al dentista la semana pasada a fin de que me reparara un diente roto.
   (I went to the dentist last week to get a broken tooth fixed.)

   Luego volví a casa para descansar un rato.
   (Then I returned home to rest awhile.)

_____

_____

_____

_____

_____

_____

_____

_____

_____

_____

_____

_____

#7 Contingencies / Anticipated Actions (see p.63)
#8 Cuando (see p.69)

A conjunction that introduces a contingency or an anticipated action requires the subjunctive. A conjunction that reports a completed action will use the indicative.

- **The following conjunctions always require the subjunctive:**
  (This is because they always express a contingency.)

a menos que	*unless*
con tal (de) que	*provided that*
antes (de) que	*before*
en caso de que	*in case that*
sin que*	*without*

- **The following conjunctions may use either the subjunctive or indicative:**

cuando	*when*
siempre que	*provided that, as long as, every time*
después (de) que	*after*
mientras / mientras que	*while (indicative) / as long as (subj.)*
hasta que	*until*
luego que	*as soon as, after*
tan pronto como	*as soon as*
en cuanto	*as soon as*
así que	*as soon as*

- **If the conjunction simply reports an action that has taken place, it will use the indicative.**
  Examples — Indicative:

  Te llamé **en cuanto** Juan llegó.   *I called you **as soon as** Juan arrived.*

  (Both "I called" and "Juan arrived" are information about completed actions — no contingency, so no subjunctive.)

  No salí **hasta que** Juan llegó.   *I didn't leave **until** Juan arrived.*

  (Juan's arrival is not a contingency, but information about a completed action —so indicative.)

- **If the conjunction introduces a contingency or anticipated action from the point of view of the past, it requires the subjunctive.**
  Examples — Subjunctive:

  No quería salir **hasta que** Juan llegara.   *I didn't want to leave **until** Juan arrived.*
  (Juan's arrival is a contingency, an anticipated event—so in the subjunctive.)

  Juan iba a salir **cuando** dejara de llover.   *Juan was going to leave **when** it stopped raining.*
  (It's a contingency, an anticipated event in the past—so subjunctive.)

- **Note:** A sentence may start with either the main clause or with the dependent clause.
  Example: Te llamé **en cuanto** Juan llegó.   *I called you **as soon as** Juan arrived.*
  En cuanto Juan llegó, te llamé.   ***As soon as** Juan arrived, I called you.*

* *Sin que may not express a contingency in the past, but it requires subjunctive because it introduces something that did not in fact occur.*

Some Notes on the Indicative and Tense

Future & Conditional

- The future and conditional tenses are closely related.
  (See pp.178-180 for a review.)

  When a verb in the future tense is changed to the past, the conditional is used.
  Example:

future	conditional
Me dicen que **vendrán** el lunes.	Me dijeron que **vendrían** el lunes.
*They said they **will come** on Monday.*	*They say they **would come** on Monday.*

Ir a + Infinitive

- When a form of "va a + infinitive" is changed to the past, a form of "iba a + infinitive" is used.
  Example:

present	past
Vamos a comprar una impresora.	**Íbamos* a** comprar una impresora.
We're going to buy a printer.	*We were going to buy a printer.*

  *This verb is in the imperfect tense. In the preterite, the sentence is: ***Fuimos*** *a comprar = we **went** to buy.*

Preterite & Imperfect

- When a verb in the present tense is changed to the past, a choice must be made between preterite and imperfect.
  (See pp.122-124 for a review of preterite and imperfect.)

  The preterite is used to describe an action that is viewed as done and over, or that happened a specific number of times.

  The imperfect is used when the focus is on the action in progress (rather than on its beginning or end), or to describe an action that was habitual.

  Example:

preterite	imperfect:
Plantaron los rosales**.**	**Plantaban** rosales.
They planted the rose bushes.	*They planted rose bushes.*
	They used to plant rose bushes.
	They would plant rose bushes.
	They were planting rose bushes.

A. Practice changing present and future verbs to a past tense.

Future to Conditional   (Translate both verbs)

ex.: hablarán _____*hablarían*_____   _____*they will talk*_____ / _____*they would talk*_____

1. estudiaré _____   _____ / _____

2. haremos _____   _____ / _____

3. ¿irás? _____   _____ / _____

4. ella comprenderá _____   _____ / _____

Ir a + Infinitive   (Translate both verb phrases)

ex.: voy a hablar _____*iba a hablar*_____   _____*I'm going to talk*_____ / _____*I was going to talk*_____

5. vamos a dar _____   _____ / _____

6. ellas van a llegar _____   _____ / _____

7. ¿vas a organizar? _____   _____ / _____

8. él va a morir _____   _____ / _____

Present to Preterite and Imperfect   (Translate the two past-tense verbs)

ex.: hablo _____*hablé* / *hablaba*_____   _____*I talked* / *I used to talk, I was talking*_____

9. él pide _____   _____ / _____

10. hacemos _____   _____ / _____

11. ellos van _____   _____ / _____

12. comes _____   _____ / _____

Present Subjunctive to Past Subjunctive. (No translation)

ex.: yo hable _____*hablara*_____

13. pregunten _____   15. sepas _____

14. salgamos _____   16. Ud. lea _____

Review: The following verbs are in the present or future tense.
Change them to a past tense as in the exercises above. (No translation.)

17. llueve _____

18. haga sol _____

19. vamos a volar _____

20. viajaré _____

21. él tiene _____

22. compras _____

23. venderemos _____

24. voy a dormir _____

Note: These conjunctions are always followed by the subjunctive:

> a menos que ....*unless*
> con tal (de) que ....*provided that*
> antes (de) que ....*before*
> en caso de que............*in case that*
> sin que ....*without*

B. Change the following sentences to the past (see p.146) and translate the new sentences.

1. No iré a la fiesta a menos que me inviten.

_____

_____

2. Damos un paseo en el parque todos los domingos con tal de que no llueva.

_____

_____

3. Monto mi bicicleta antes de que haya mucho tráfico.

_____

_____

4. En caso de que mi equipo gane el campeonato, tengo lista una buena botella de champán.

_____

_____

5. Nunca puedo visitarla sin que ella me repita esa misma historia.

_____

_____

6. Vamos a comprar una casa antes de que suban los precios de nuevo.

_____

_____

7. Me imagino que están trabajando en la computadora, a menos que tengan que cuidar a los niños.

_____

_____

C. Translate the following sentences.

1. She knew what I was thinking without me saying a word.

   _____

2. We ate before they arrived. _____

3. Were you *(tú)* going to let me know *(avisarme)* before I left?

   _____

4. They used to leave a plate of cookies on the table in case the children got hungry.

   _____

5. Unless they gave him a raise, he wasn't going to be able to buy a car.

   _____

6. I would have invested *(invertir)* in that company provided that you *(Ud.)* had invested in it too.

   _____

> **Note: The following conjunctions may use either the subjunctive or the indicative.**
>
> cuando ....*when*
> siempre que ....*as long as, every time that*
> después (de) que.......*after*
> mientras ....*while (indicative)*
> mientras que ....*as long as (subjunctive)*
> hasta que ....*until*
> luego que ....*as soon as, after*
> tan pronto como.........*as soon as*
> en cuanto ....*as soon as*
> así que ....*as soon as*
>
> **Note: This is not a complete list of conjunctions.**

D. In the following English sentences, the conjunction is underlined. (Its translation follows.)
Write an F (for Fact) in the blank if the conjunction introduces a completed action.
Write A/C (for Anticipated Action/Contingency) if it introduces an anticipated action or contingency.

Example: ___*F*___ I waited <u>until</u> the rain stopped. *(hasta que)*
[The rain stopping is a fact.]

___*A/C*___ I told him to wait <u>until</u> the rain stopped. *(hasta que)*
[The rain hadn't yet stopped when I told him to wait.]

_____1. I came <u>as soon as</u> I could. *(luego que / tan pronto como / en cuanto / así que)*

_____2. I was going to pay you <u>as soon as</u> I had the money. *(luego que / tan pronto como / en cuanto / así que)*

_____3. All year I looked forward to visiting Honduras <u>after</u> my classes ended. *(después de que)*

_____4. I went to Honduras in June <u>after</u> my classes ended. *(después de que)*

_____5. He watched the game <u>as long as</u> it lasted. *(mientras que / siempre que)*

_____6. He said he would lend it to me <u>as long as</u> I returned it. *(mientras que / siempre que)*

Some Notes on the Present Tense Indicative

- The name of a tense can be misleading.
  For example, in English, the present tense is not really the present tense—it expresses customary actions. As in: "I speak Spanish." (Which doesn't mean I'm speaking Spanish now, in the present.)

- In Spanish, the "present" tense is used in a number of ways:

customary action

Llaman a sus padres todos los días. ....*They call their parents every day.*
No limpio ventanas...*I don't wash windows.*

asking for instructions

¿Dónde pongo esto?..*Where shall I put this?*
¿Te ayudo?..*Shall I help you?*

present action

Un momento. Hablo con mis padres. ....*One moment. I'm talking with my parents.*
¿Qué haces? ....*What are you doing?*

immediate future

Te llamo mañana...*I'll call you tomorrow.*
Nos acompañas a la playa, ¿verdad? ....*You're going to the beach with us, right?*

narrative past

Les hablo, y de repente... ....*I'm talking to them and suddenly...*
Un pingüino entra en un bar... ....*A penguin goes into a bar...*

- What happens to a present-tense verb when changed to the past depends not on the name of the tense, but on the meaning and usage of the verb.

Examples:

customary action

Desayuno antes de que llegue el autobús.............*I eat breakfast before the bus arrives.*

Desayunaba antes de que llegara el autobús. ....*I would eat breakfast before the bus arrived.*
I used to eat breakfast before the bus arrived.

present action

Desayuno antes de que llegue el autobús. ....*I'm eating breakfast before the bus arrives.*

Desayuné antes de que llegara el autobús............*I ate breakfast before the bus arrived.*

immediate future

Desayuno antes de que llegues. ....*I'll eat breakfast before you arrive.*

Iba a desayunar antes de que llegaras.................*I was going to eat breakfast before you arrived.*

Dije que desayunaría antes de que llegaras.........*I said I would eat breakfast before you arrived.*

E. Translate the following sentences. Use the following conjunctions.

cuando ....*when*
siempre que ....*as long as, every time that, whenever*
después (de) que.......*after*
mientras ....*while (indicative)*
mientras que ....*as long as (subjunctive)*
hasta que ....*until*
luego que ....*as soon as, after*
tan pronto como ....*as soon as*
en cuanto ....*as soon as*
así que ....*as soon as*

Note: all of the conjunctions below introduce verbs that express completed actions (indicative).

1. I told him *(it)* as soon as I saw him.

   _____

2. Did you *(Ud.)* use butter when you made these cookies?

   _____

3. He would go with us to the movies whenever we invited him.

   _____

4. We danced until the orchestra stopped playing.

   _____

5. He would always pay when we went out to eat.

   _____

6. His parents let him use the car after he turned *(cumplir)* 16 and got his license.

   _____

   _____

7. She used to always take off her shoes when she got home.

   _____

8. As soon as she got the tattoo *(el tatuaje)*, she showed it to us.

   _____

F. Translate the following sentences—do not translate the phrases in brackets.

Note: the conjunctions below all introduce verbs that introduce contingencies or anticipated actions (subjunctive).

1. I planned to tell him (it) as soon as I saw him.

   _____

2. I wanted to see that movie when it came out. [It hadn't come out yet.]

   _____

3. He promised that they would take us to the movies whenever *(siempre que)* we visited.
   [We hadn't visited yet.]

   _____

4. She told us that she would call when she arrived at the airport. [She hadn't arrived yet.]

   _____

5. We were going to dance until the sun came up.

   _____

6. His parents said he could use the car after he turned *(cumplir)* 16 and got a license. [He's still 15.]

   _____

   _____

7. They gave us their address in case we wanted to visit them.

   _____

8. She recommended that you *(tú)* visit the art museums when you went to Spain. [You hadn't gone yet.]

   _____

   _____

9. We crossed the mountains before it snowed.

   _____

10. I was going to open the package as soon as it arrived.

   _____

G. Answer the following questions with a contingency or anticipated action (subjunctive). Use one of the suggested conjunctions.

1. ¿Cuándo fue el niño al parque?   (antes de que)

_____

2. ¿Iban a hacer un viaje a Europa sus amigos? (tan pronto como / mientras que / a menos que / cuando)

_____

3. ¿Pensaban Uds. comprarle a ella una bicicleta?   (con tal que / tan pronto como)

_____

4. ¿En dónde se quedó Ud.?   (en caso de que / sin que)

_____

5. ¿Dónde querían vivir Uds.?   (antes de que / hasta que / a menos que / con tal de que)

_____

6. ¿Cuándo querías salir?   (antes de que / así que / cuando / tan pronto como)

_____

7. ¿Cuándo ibas a decírmelo?   (antes de que / luego que / cuando)

_____

8. ¿Les daban ellos regalitos a sus nietos cuando los visitaban? (con tal de que / a menos que / sin que)

_____

H. Answer the following questions with information about completed actions (indicative). Use the following conjunctions: cuando / siempre que / después (de) que / mientras / hasta que / luego que / tan pronto como / en cuanto / así que.

1. ¿Cuándo fue el niño al parque?

_____

2. ¿HIcieron sus amigos un viaje a Cuba?

_____

3. ¿Le compraron Uds.una bicicleta a ella?

_____

4. ¿En dónde se quedó Ud.?

_____

5. ¿Dónde vivieron Uds.?

_____

6. ¿La llamaste?

_____

I. Translate the following sentences, deciding whether or not to use the subjunctive.
   Note: There are 8 verbs in subjunctive.

1. Before you *(Uds.)* took your trip, did you make reservations?

   _____

2. We made reservations as soon as he confirmed the dates of his vacation.

   _____

3. He hoped to buy a car when he got a job.

   _____

4. As soon as the garage fixed their tire, they continued with their trip.

   _____

5. More innocent people would die unless the war ended.

   _____

6. They worried when I didn't call.

   _____

7. He was afraid they would get angry when he told them the news.

   _____

8. I cooked the turkey until it was brown *(dorarse)* .

   _____

9. He was going to call as soon as we arrived, but there was no coverage *(cobertura)*.

   _____

10. She wanted to work in the garden until the sun set.

   _____

11. She worked in the garden until the sun set.

   _____

12. I used to take care of their dog when they traveled, as long as it was for less than a week.

   _____

   _____

Extra Practice with "Cuando"

J. Change the following sentences to the past tense (see p.146) and translate the new sentences.
Note: In the past tense these sentences are all about completed actions (indicative).

1. Siempre cierro la puerta con llave cuando salgo de casa._____

_____

2. Cuando mis amigos oyen música, bailan._____

_____

3. Cuando viajo, llevo mi computadora portátil *(laptop)*. *La semana pasada*_____

_____

4. ¿Cuando vayas a la universidad, me compras una camiseta?_____

_____

5. Lo invitamos a cenar cuando preparamos paella. *Siempre*_____

_____

6. Mi amiga me recoge en el aeropuerto cuando yo la llamo. *Anoche*_____

_____

7. Cuando su hija cumpla 15, le darán una gran fiesta. *El año pasado*_____

_____

8. Lavo el carro cuando está sucio._____

_____

K. Answer the following questions with a complete sentence containing two verbs and "cuando."
Note: 4 are about facts (indicative) and 4 are about anticipated events/contingencies (subjunctive).

1. ¿Cuándo vio a tus amigos?_____

2. ¿Cuándo corrían ellos en el parque?

_____

3. ¿Cuándo iba Ud. a ir de compras?

_____

4. ¿Cuándo fue Ud. de compras? _____

5. ¿Cuándo alquilaban Uds. un carro?

_____

6. ¿Cuándo pensaba ella viajar a Chile?

_____

7. ¿Cuándo querías salir? _____

8. ¿Ibas a llamarme?_____

L. Solve the following puzzle by translating the clues.

Solution on p.161.

Horizontal

3. I send
6. your
8. as soon as
9. when
12. *[he built the ark]*
14. she is
15. dates
16. we remember
    (present subj.)
18. case
20. unless
21. I would eat
23. he was lying
24. he laughs
    (present subj.)
25. I take out
    (present subj.)
26. from

28. ear of corn
    (South America)
31. they use
    (present subj.)
32. *[a kind of big snake]*
33. I put
34. while
35. it went
37. garlic
38. feet
39. they would go
40. as long as
43. alone
44. he sees
45. as soon as
46. they loved
    (the other past subj.)

Vertical

1. without
2. you are
   (present subj.)
4. they see
5. bears
6. as soon as
7. one
10. before
11. after
13. she called
    (past subj.)
15. provided that
17. in case that
18. I fell
19. himself
22. I took off
23. snot

27. in, on
29. there is
    (present subj.)
30. dough
33. could you?
    (polite form)
35. the
36. this
38. you pass
    (present subj.)
40. sun
41. peep
42. that
44. she goes

M. Review ways to use the subjunctive.

Use 2 verbs of influence/volition in sentences that include a second verb in the past subjunctive.

1. _____

2. _____

Use 2 verbs of emotion in sentences that include a second verb in the past subjunctive.

3. _____

4. _____

Use 2 impersonal expressions in sentences that include a second verb in the past subjunctive.

5. _____

6. _____

Use 2 expressions of doubt or negation in sentences that include a second verb in the past subjunctive.

7. _____

8. _____

Use a compound verb in the past subjunctive.

9. _____

Use "para que" with the past subjunctive.

10. _____

The Answer Key for this chapter begins on p.244.

N. It's a telenovela: Jorge is leaving Ana (who's pregnant) for another woman—she's not taking it well. Report on what was said.

Example:

Jorge: Oye, estoy enamorado de otra. Me voy.

Jorge dijo que estaba enamorado de otra y que se iba.

Ana: Nadie va a irse a menos que lo mande.

Ana dijo que nadie

Y yo no mando que te vayas.

Ana dijo que ella

Jorge: No somos felices.

Jorge dijo que ellos

Es mejor que me vaya antes de que nos odiemos.

Jorge dijo que

Ana: No quiero que te vayas hasta que nos odiemos.

Ana dijo que ella

No me dejes.

Ana le dijo que

Además, no debes abandonarme hasta que nazca la criatura.

Ana dijo que

Jorge: Llámame después de que des a luz para que yo pueda conocer a mi hijo.

Jorge le dijo que

Jorge: Te prometo mandar dinero para mantener a mi hijo siempre que dejes en paz a mí y a mi nueva mujer.

Jorge dijo que

Ana: Nunca los dejaré en paz ni a ti ni a la fulana esa hasta que yo esté muerta.

         Ana dijo que nunca _____

_____

         Te mataré antes de que yo permita que veas a tu hijo.

         Ana dijo que _____

Jorge: No seas así.

         Jorge le dijo que _____

         Tan pronto como seas razonable, cumpliré con mis responsabilidades.

         Jorge dijo que _____

_____

Ana: Seré razonable así que renuncies a esa mujer.

         Ana dijo que _____

         Podemos ser felices de nuevo con tal de que abandones a la fulana esa.

         Ana dijo que _____

_____

Jorge: No quiero irme sin que me prometas ser razonable.

         Jorge dijo que _____

Ana: Quédate entonces.

         Ana le dijo que _____

Jorge: Adiós, Ana.

         Jorge dijo— Adiós, Ana. _____

O. Report a dialogue between two people who negotiated something.
Write what each person said (*El padre dijo que...*, etc.).
For example: an employer and employee / a parent and child / spouses / housemates / etc.
Write three or four lines for each speaker and use the subjunctive at least five times.
(You may want to report on the dialogue you wrote for Exercise H, p.68.)

_____

_____

_____

_____

_____

_____

_____

_____

_____

_____

_____

_____

_____

_____

_____

_____

_____

_____

Solution to the puzzle on p. 156.

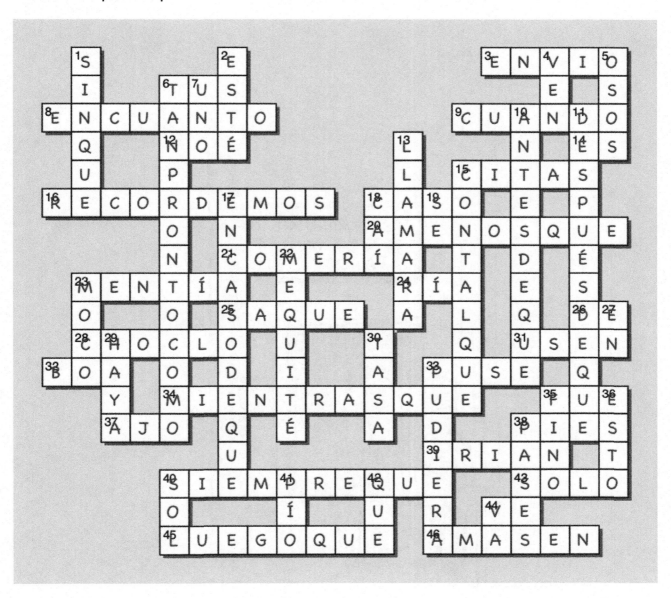

"And remember—no more subjunctive where the correct mood is indicative."

#9 Aunque—The Past Tense (see p.75)

- **AUNQUE** *(although, even though, or even if)* is a conjunction that in both the present and past tenses can introduce a verb in subjunctive or indicative.

  Examples—Indicative:

  Aunque Juan **es** inteligente, en este caso está equivocado.
  Although Juan is intelligent, in this case he's wrong.

  Aunque Juan **era** inteligente, en ese caso estuvo equivocado.
  Although Juan was intelligent, in that case he was wrong.

  In the examples above, Juan is indeed intelligent, and so the verb following *aunque* is indicative.

  Examples—Subjunctive:

  Aunque Juan sea guapo, María no está interesada en él.
  Although *Juan **may be** attractive, María's not interested in him.*

  Aunque Juan fuera guapo, María no estaría interesada en él.
  Even if *Juan **were** attractive, María would not be interested in him.*

  In the examples above:
  In the present tense, the verb is in subjunctive because it is not necessarily true that Juan is attractive, or the speaker does not know and so cannot give information about his appearance. And in the past tense, it expresses something contrary to fact. In other words, Juan is not attractive.

- **AUNQUE,** when followed by the past subjunctive, translates as "even if," and the verb in the main clause will be in the conditional.   **(See pp.178-179 for information on the conditional.)**

  Even when the conditional refers to the present or the future, the clause with *aunque* will be in the past subjunctive.   **(See p.121 about coordinating tenses.)**

  Examples:

  Juan **seguiría** jugando videojuegos aunque se le **cayera** el techo.
  Juan would keep playing video games even if the roof fell in on him.

  María **lograría** llegar mañana aunque se **descompusiera** su carro.
  María would manage to arrive tomorrow even if her car broke down.

- **Note:** A sentence may start with either the main clause or with the clause beginning with *aunque*.

  Example:

  Aunque trabajaran día y noche, sería muy difícil terminar a tiempo.
  Even if they were to work day and night, it would be difficult to finish on time.

  or

  Sería muy difícil terminar a tiempo **aunque trabajaran día y noche.**
  It would be difficult to finish on time, even if they were to work day and night.

A. Translate the following sentences that affirm a truth (indicative).

1. Although it rained a lot, we had a good time *(pasarlo bien)*.

_____

2. We went to the movies every weekend, even though it was expensive.

_____

3. Although she passed *(aprobar)* the class, it was hard for her.

_____

4. They only visited us a couple *(un par)* of times, even though they didn't live far.

_____

B. Translate the following sentences that talk about something contrary to reality (subjunctive).

1. Even if you *(Uds.)* left at 5:00 in the morning, you would not arrive until evening.

_____

2. Even if I didn't have work to do, I would prefer to stay home this weekend.

_____

3. Even if they had offered me the job, I would not have accepted it.

_____

4. We wouldn't plant a vegetable garden (una huerta) even if we had the space.

_____

The Answer Key for this chapter begins on p.250.

C. Translate the following sentences with *aunque*, deciding whether or not to use the subjunctive, and whether to use the present or past subjunctive.

1. They wanted to have a dog even though they traveled a lot.

   _____

2. She has a cat even though she has allergies.

   _____

3. Although they may get angry, you *(tú)* have to tell them the truth.

   _____

4. She would call us even if she were busy.

   _____

5. He wanted to drive even though there was a lot of traffic.

   _____

6. He would want to drive even if there were a lot of traffic.

   _____

7. Even if I knew (it), I would not tell you *(Ud.)* (it).

   _____

8. We bought it even though it cost a lot.

   _____

9. We will buy it even though it may cost a lot.

   _____

10. We would buy it even if it cost a lot.

    _____

D.   Review ways to use the subjunctive.

Use 2 verbs of influence/volition in sentences, one with present subjunctive, one with past subjunctive.

1. _____

2. _____

Use 2 verbs of emotion in sentences, one with present subjunctive, one with past subjunctive.

3. _____

4. _____

Use 2 impersonal expressions in sentences, one with present subjunctive, one with past subjunctive.

5. _____

6. _____

Use 2 expressions of doubt or negation in sentences, one with present subjunctive, one with past subjunctive.

7. _____

8. _____

Use a compound verb in the past subjunctive.

9. _____

Use "para que" in 2 sentences, one with present subjunctive, one with past subjunctive.

10. _____

11. _____

Use 3 conjunctions from p.145 in a past tense.

12. _____

13. _____

14. _____

E. In the following sentences with *cuando* and *aunque*:
   • **fill in the correct form of the verb**
   • **translate the sentence.**

1. Cuando_____(ir) al centro, me gustaba almorzar en un restaurante.

   _____

2. Vamos a trabajar en el jardín mañana, aunque_____ (estar) lloviendo.

   _____

3. Aunque ellos siempre _____ (haber) manejado demasiado rápido, nunca han tenido ningún accidente.

   _____

4. Aunque él _____(haber) buscado mucho, no habría encontrado un empleo.

   _____

5. Cuando tú _____(viajar) a Colombia, cómprame algo.

   _____

6. Cuando ellos _____ (estar) nerviosos, no comían.

   _____

7. Él habría comprado los boletos para el concierto, aunque _____ (haber) costado $500.

   _____

8. Aunque él _____ (ser) mi amigo, a veces me volvía loco.

   _____

9. Cuando ella _____ (leer) novelas, siempre empieza leyendo el final.

   _____

10. Al darle ese misterio a ella, le hice prometer que no haría eso cuando lo

   _____ (leer).

   _____

F. Answer the following questions with a complete sentence containing *aunque*.

1. Lo acompañaste al cine. ¿Verdad?

   _____

2. ¿Creíste lo que él dijo?

   _____

3. ¿Creerías a ellos?

   _____

4. ¿Crees que podamos superar esta situación?   (superar = *to overcome / to get through / to get over*)

   _____

5. ¿Pudieron Uds. superar esa situación?

   _____

6. ¿Fuiste de compras ayer?

   _____

7. ¿Van Uds. a la playa mañana?

   _____

8. ¿Te gustó la película?

   _____

**G. You took a trip, but there were various hitches.
Use *aunque* at least 5 times, and use a mix of subjunctive and indicative.**

_____

_____

_____

_____

_____

_____

_____

_____

_____

#10 Non-existent People & Objects —The Past Tense
(See p.81.)

#11 Hypothetical People & Objects —The Past Tense
(See p.87.)

- Because you can't give information about something or someone who does not exist, or about something or someone who is hypothetical, the subjunctive is used in the dependent clause, both in the present and past tenses.

  Examples:

  No hay estudiante que **encuentre** fácil esto.   *There is no student who **finds** this easy.*
  No había estudiante que **encontrara** fácil esto.   *There was no student who **found** this easy.*

  Desean emplear alguien **que sea** bilingüe.   *They want to hire someone who **is** bilingual.*
  Desearon emplear alguien **que fuera** bilingüe.   *They wanted to hire someone who **was** bilingual.*

- The verbs *querer*, *desear*, *buscar*, and *necesitar* are verbs that commonly introduce hypothetical/non-specific people and things.

  Examples:

  Él quería casarse con una mujer **que fuera** rica y guapa.
  He wanted to marry a woman who was rich and good-looking.

  Buscamos una aplicación **que pudiera** ayudarnos a aprender vocabulario.
  We looked for an app that could help us learn vocabulary.

- **Note:** The personal *a* is omitted before a hypothetical person,
  but it is not omitted before non-existent person.

  Examples:

  ¿Conociste actores que fueran famosos?   *Did you meet actors who were famous?*
  (hypothetical person)

  No conocí **a** nadie que fuera famoso.   *I didn't meet anyone who was famous.*
  (non-existent person)

A. Change the following sentences to the past tense and translate the new sentence.
   (Note: Sentences about specific, real people and things use the indicative.)

1. No hay nadie allí que conozca Bolivia. _____

   _____

2. Sólo hay dos de mis vecinos que no tienen perros. _____

   _____

   _____

3. No existe ninguna universidad en este estado que dé cursos de maya. _____

   _____

   _____

4. No tenemos impresora que funcione. _____

   _____

5. Él desea asistir a una universidad que no esté muy lejos de su pueblo. _____

   _____

   _____

6. Quiero esos plátanos que están más maduros. _____

   _____

   _____

7. Ella necesita un empleo que pague mejor. _____

   _____

8. Ellos nunca compran zapatos que no les queden bien. _____

   _____

   _____

9. Estoy buscando el libro que me prestaste. _____

   _____

10. Estoy buscando un libro que me interese. _____

   _____

B. Translate the following sentences that describe someone or something that doesn't exist (subjunctive).

1. There was no one in the office who could speak Russian.

   _____

2. I didn't have any books that explained Mexican history clearly.

   _____

3. I didn't know anyone who worked there.

   _____

4. They tried to buy a house in this neighborhood, but they couldn't find one that had four bedrooms.

   _____

   _____

C. Translate the following sentences that may or may not be describing a non-existent person or object (subjunctive or indicative).

1. A team did not exist that had better players.

   _____

2. I bought a car that did not use a lot of gas.

   _____

3. There was nobody in his family who had graduated from college.

   _____

4. She had never written a book that was boring.

   _____

5. We bought pants, but not shoes.

   _____

D. Translate the following sentences that describe a hypothetical/nonspecific person or thing (subjunctive).

1. They needed an interpreter who could speak English and French.

_____

2. Were they selling toys that were dangerous?

_____

3. I wanted to see a movie that you *(tú)* might like too.

_____

4. She was looking for an adult dog that needed a home and that wasn't too big.

_____

E. Translate the following sentences that may or may not be describing a hypothetical person or thing (subjunctive or indicative).

1. The team wanted players who knew how to play well.

_____

2. We saw a movie that made us laugh.

_____

3. They were looking for a babysitter who could drive and work nights.

_____

4. I wanted to talk to the person who wrote this.

_____

The Answer Key for this chapter begins on p.253.

F. Review ways to use the subjunctive.

Use 2 verbs of influence/volition in sentences, one with present subjunctive, one with past subjunctive.

1. _____

2. _____

Use 2 verbs of emotion in sentences, one with present subjunctive, one with past subjunctive.

3. _____

4. _____

Use 2 impersonal expressions in sentences, one with present subjunctive, one with past subjunctive.

5. _____

6. _____

Use 2 expressions of doubt or negation in sentences, one with present subjunctive, one with past subjunctive.

7. _____

8. _____

Use a compound verb in the past subjunctive.

9. _____

Use "para que" in 2 sentences, one with present subjunctive, one with past subjunctive.

10. _____

11. _____

Use 2 conjunctions from p.145 in a past tense.

12. _____

13. _____

Use "aunque" in 2 sentences, one with a present/future tense, one with a past/conditional tense.

14. _____

15. _____

G. A Rant

This is what an unhappy teenager says about school.

Change it to the past tense (his or her memories of that time).

Odio la escuela.

No tengo ningún profesor que no sea aburrido.

No hay ninguna clase que valga la pena.

No hay plato en la cafetería que no me dé asco.

No conozco a nadie que me comprenda.

Cuando yo era estudiante

_____

_____

_____

_____

Write a rant about something in the past, or take the rant you wrote for exercise E, p.84, and change it to the past tense.

_____

_____

_____

_____

_____

_____

_____

_____

_____

H. When you were a child or teenager, what did you think the perfect mate would be like?
   List what you would have said were the 10 most important characteristics for the perfect mate.
   Use verbs in the past subjunctive.

La Pareja Perfecta
(The Perfect Mate)

1. *Quería una pareja que* _____

2. _____

3. _____

4. _____

5. _____

6. _____

7. _____

8. _____

9. _____

10. _____

I. When you were a child or teenager, what did you think the perfect job would be like?
   Use verbs in the past subjunctive.

Cuando era niño/niña soñaba con ser _____

_____

_____

_____

_____

_____

_____

J. The first time you looked for a house, apartment or car to buy or rent, describe what you were looking for. Use at least four verbs in the past subjunctive.

_____

_____

_____

_____

_____

_____

_____

_____

_____

_____

_____

#12 "Si" Clauses — The Past Tense
(See p.95.)

- "Si" is inherently different from other conjunctions. (It's not like "cuando," "a menos que," etc.) "Si" is in a class by itself, with its own rules.

- "Si" can never be followed by the present subjunctive. But it can be followed by the past subjunctive.

- In other words, "si" can be followed by:

1. present indicative*

or

2. past subjunctive

Here's the formula:

—If the verb in the main clause is in the **present** or **future** tense (indicative), then "si" is followed by the **indicative**.

Examples:	**Si llueve,** me quedo en casa.	*If it rains, I'm staying home.*
	Me quedaré en casa **si llueve.**	*I will stay home if it rains.*

—If the verb in the main clause is a **command**, then "si" is also followed by the **present indicative**.

Example:	**Si llueve**, quédate en casa.	*If it rains, stay home.*

—**But**, if the verb in the main clause is in the **conditional**, then "si" is followed by the **past subjunctive**.

These "si" phrases express a situation that is contrary to reality.

Examples: **Si lloviera,** me quedaría en casa.**

If it were raining (but it's not), I would stay home.

Si hubiera llovido, me habría quedado en casa.
If it had rained (but it didn't), I would have stayed home.

*Occasionally, you will find "si" followed by a past tense in indicative.
Example: No sabían si llovía porque no había ventanas donde trabajaban.
They didn't know if it was raining because there were no windows where they were working.
Sentences like this give information. They do not express a situation contrary to fact.

**Some speakers will use the past subjunctive in both clauses.
Example: Si lloviera, me quedara en casa.

To review the future and conditional tenses (indicative), see pp.178-181.
For exercises on "si," skip ahead to pp.182-186.
For *"como si,"* see p.190.

The Future and The Conditional

- **Overview**

  The future and conditional tenses are closely related in both form and function.
  In English, the future is made with the helping verb "will" (I will do it.)
  And the conditional is made with the helping verb "would" (I would do it.)*

  The future tense is used to express the future.
  The conditional tense expresses the future from a point in the past.
      (Use the conditional to put a future expression into the past.)

  Examples:

Future:	Él dice que ella irá.	*He says that she will go.*
Conditional:	Él dijo que ella iría.	*He said that she would go.*

  The conditional is also used to say what would happen under certain circumstances or conditions.

Example:	Yo lo haría.	*I would do it.*

  Both tenses in Spanish are also used to express conjecture:
  the future tense is used for conjecture in the present; and the conditional, for the past.

  Examples:

Future:	Será la medianoche.	*It's probably midnight.*
Conditional:	Sería la medianoche.	*It was probably midnight.*

  > * If *would* expresses a customary action (as in "Every summer we would visit our grandparents."),
  > the conditional tense is not used. To express a customary action, use the imperfect tense:
  > *Todos los veranos visitábamos a nuestros abuelos.*

  Note: In English we have the option to use the construction "going to (do something) to talk about the future. Spanish has the same option *(ir + a + infinitive)*. Latin American Spanish and American English use these constructions in the same way.

  Examples:

  I'm going to do it.   *Voy a hacerlo.*   (*Ir* + *a* + an infinitive.)

  The imperfect tense is used for the past tense of this expression:

  I was going to do it.   *Iba a hacerlo.*   (*Ir* + *a* + an infinitive.)

The Future and The Conditional

- **How to form the future and conditional tenses.**

  Both tenses are formed by adding endings to the infinitive.
  A number of verbs have irregular stems.
  These irregular stems are the same for both tenses.

	future	conditional
yo	-é	-ía
tú	-ás	-ías
él, ella, Ud.	-á	-ía
nosotros, nosotras	-emos	-íamos
ellos, ellas, Uds.	-án	-ían

Examples:

future: hablaré hablarás hablará hablaremos hablarán
conditional: comería comerías comería comeríamos comerían

Irregular Verb Stems

caber............cabr-   poner............pondr-   decir.............dir-
haber............habr-   salir...............saldr-   hacer............har-
poder............podr-   tener............tendr-
querer............querr-   valer............valdr-
saber............sabr-   venir............vendr-

Examples:

future: sabré sabrás sabrá sabremos sabrán
conditional: diría dirías diría diríamos dirían

A. Conjugate the following verbs in the future tense.

infinitive	yo	tú	él, ella, Ud.	nosotros, nosotras	ellos, ellas, Uds.
1. hablar	hablaré	hablarás	hablará	hablaremos	hablarán
2. pensar					
3. vivir					
4. divertirse					
5. tener					
6. hacer					
7. dar					
8. ser					
9. estar					
10. ir					

B. Conjugate the following verbs in the conditional tense.

infinitive	yo	tú	él, ella, Ud.	nosotros, nosotras	ellos, ellas, Uds.
1. hablar	hablaría	hablarías	hablaría	hablaríamos	hablarían
2. estudiar					
3. leer					
4. perderse					
5. poder					
6. querer					
7. dar					
8. ser					
9. estar					
10. haber					

C. What tense are the following verbs?

F   future
C   conditional
PS past subjunctive
O   other

_____1. hablaras   _____11. pensaré

_____2. quisiera   _____12. pudiera

_____3. comía   _____13. puse

_____4. estudiase   _____14. viva

_____5. creeríamos   _____15. mirara

_____6. daremos   _____16. verás

_____7. fueran   _____17. parecería

_____8. pediremos   _____18. se llamaba

_____9. podría   _____19. toque

_____10. pondría   _____20. escribirían

D. Change the following sentences from future to conditional.
Translate both sentences.

1. Trabajaré en el jardín. _____

_____

2. Ella navegará en la red *(surf the net)*. _____

_____

3. ¿Me acompañarás? _____

_____

4. ¿No te perderás? _____

_____

5. Valdrán la pena. _____

_____

6. Saldremos con ellos. _____

_____

E. The sentences below contain "si" + a verb in the indicative.
   There are four parts to this exercise:
   a. Change the verb that follows "si" to the past subjunctive—make any other necessary changes.
   b. Translate the new sentence.
   c. Then change both verbs in the new sentence to perfect tenses.
   d. Translate the new sentence.

Example: Si ella se da prisa, podemos salir a cenar antes de la obra *(play).*

a. *Si ella se diera prisa, podríamos salir a cenar antes de la obra.*

b. *If she hurried, we could go out to eat before the play.*

c. *Si ella se hubiéra dado prisa, habríamos podido salir a cenar antes de la obra.*

d. *If she had hurried, we could have gone out to eat before the play.*

1. Iremos por tren si tenemos tiempo.

   a._____

   b._____

   c._____

   d._____

2. Te lo diré si no me gusta la película.

   a._____

   b._____

   c._____

   d._____

3. Si encuentro tu libro en mi carro, te llamo.

   a._____

   b._____

   c._____

   d._____

4. Podemos esquiar este fin de semana si nieva.

   a._____

   b._____

   c._____

   d._____

5. Si hay mucho tráfico, tomaremos otra ruta.

    a._____

    b._____

    c._____

    d._____

6. Si Uds. llegan tarde, no me preocuparé.

    a._____

    b._____

    c._____

    d._____

7. Si ellos navegan la red, verán algunos sitios web *(websites)* interesantes.

    a._____

    b._____

    c._____

    d._____

8. Si hace sol, daremos un paseo en el parque.

    a._____

    b._____

    c._____

    d._____

F. Translate the following sentences using the past subjunctive:

1. If they were hungry, they would order a pizza.

    _____

2. I wouldn't stay here, if I were you.

    _____

3. If we had seen them before the party, we would have invited them.

    _____

4. They would have sung if you *(Uds.)* had asked them.

    _____

G. Complete the following sentences.

1. Si hiciera mucho calor_____

2. Me darían el dinero si _____

3. Si hubiera tiempo _____

4. Iríamos de vacaciones a España si _____

H. Translate the following (not all will use the past subjunctive).

Some notes on vocabulary: to get married = *casarse*
                                           to marry her = *casarse con ella*
                                           to be married to her = *estar casado con ella*
                                           to be happy = *ser feliz*

1. If he asks you *(tú)*, advise him *(aconsejar)* to get married.

   _____

2. If he had met her first, they would have gotten married.

   _____

3. If he were married to her, he would be happy.

   _____

4. If he had married her, he would have been happy.

   _____

5. If he marries her, he will be happy.

   _____

I. Write about what you would do if you won the lottery.
   Use at least 4 verbs in the conditional.

   _____

   _____

   _____

   _____

   _____

   _____

J. If you were in a position of great power, what would you do?
    State what the position would be and use at least 4 verbs in the conditional.

_____

_____

_____

_____

_____

_____

_____

K. Consider some of the decisions and happenstances of your life.
    What would your life be like if you'd made different decisions and/or things had happened differently.
    Use at least 5 verbs in the past subjunctive.

_____

_____

_____

_____

_____

_____

_____

_____

_____

L. Choose an event in history and write about what you would have seen or done.
   Use at least 4 sentences with "si" and with the verbs in past perfect subjunctive and conditional perfect.
   Example:

   Si yo **hubiera vivido** en España durante la época de Isabel y Fernando, creo que **habría estado** entusiasmada con los viajes de Cristóbal Colón.

   (If I had lived in Spain during the time of Isabel and Fernando, I think I would have been excited about the trips of Christopher Columbus.)

   Or

   Write about what would have happened if an important event had not happened as it did.
   Use at least 4 sentences with "si" with the verbs in past perfect subjunctive and conditional perfect.
   Example:

   Si Colón no **hubiera llegado** al Nuevo Mundo, otro país europeo lo **habría descubierto** y ahora no se hablaría español en este hemisferio.

   (If Columbus had never made it to the New World, another European country would have discovered it and now Spanish would not be spoken in this hemisphere.)

   _____

   _____

   _____

   _____

   _____

   _____

   _____

   _____

   _____

The Answer Key for this chapter begins on p.255.

#13 Verbs of Influence: A Shortcut —The Past Tense
(See p.97.)

- A number of verbs of influence/volition commonly bypass the subjunctive and instead use an indirect object pronoun and an infinitive. This can be done in all the indicative tenses: future, preterite, conditional, imperfect, present perfect, etc.

The indirect object pronouns are: *me, te, le, nos, les*.

Examples:

Les hago **cerrar** la puerta con llave.	*I have **them lock** the door.*
Les hice **cerrar** la puerta con llave.	*I had **them lock** the door.*
A mi hijo* **le** prohibo **fumar**.	*I forbid **(him)** my son **to smoke**.*
A mi hijo* **le** prohibía **fumar**.	*I used to forbid **(him)** my son **to smoke**.*

*"A mi hijo" clarifies, or emphasizes, who "le" is.

- Common verbs used in this way:

aconsejar...*to advise*	mandar ......*to order*	prohibir ....*to forbid, prohibit*
dejar** ....*to let, allow*	pedir ....*to request, ask*	recomendar ...*to recommend*
hacer ....*to have (done)*	permitir ......*to permit*	sugerir ....*to suggest*

Some other verbs used this way:

animar a (*to encourage*)	impedir (*to prevent*)	proponer (*to propose*)
convencer (*to convince*)	obligar a (*to make, to force*)	rogar (*to beg, plead*)
disuadir de (*to talk out of*)	ordenar (*to order*)	suplicar (*to ask, pray, plead*)
exigir (*to demand*)	persuadir a (*to persuade*)	urgir (*to urge*)

**Dejar takes a direct object pronoun: No la dejé fumar....*I didn't let her smoke.*

A. Write the indirect object pronoun (*me, te, le, nos, les*) that corresponds to the following subjects.

1. yo _____

2. tú y yo_____

3. el empleado _____

4. la empleada _____

5. los empleados _____

6. nosotros _____

7. las niñas _____

8. el comité _____

B. Translate the following sentences.

1. Mi profesor me aconsejó practicar más. _____

_____

2. ¿No te dejarían manejar su carro? _____

3. A mi hermanita yo no le permitía usar mis cosas. _____

_____

4. Les hice pintar la casa. _____

5 Ella nos ha sugerido tomar un taxi._____

6. Les prohibiré hacer eso. _____

C. Change the sentences below into sentences that use the subjunctive (3 are in present, 3 in past). Translate the sentences—each pair of sentences will mean the same thing.)

Example: Les mandé quitarse los zapatos lodosos.

Mandé que se quitaran los zapatos lodosos.
I ordered them to take off their muddy shoes.

1. Mi profesor me aconseja practicar más.

_____

_____

2. ¿No te dejarían manejar su carro?

_____

_____

3. A mi hermanita no le permitía usar mis cosas.

_____

_____

4. Les hice pintar la casa.

_____

_____

5 El patrón *(boss)* nos ha pedido trabajar tarde.

_____

_____

6. Ya les hemos mandado volver mañana.

_____

_____

D. Translate the following sentences in 2 ways: with the subjunctive and with an infinitive.

Example: I always had them check the oil.

Subjunctive___*Siempre hacía que revisaran el aceite.*

Infinitive_____*Siempre les hacía revisar el aceite.*

1.   They didn't let *(dejar)* us travel alone.

Subjunctive _____

Infinitive_____

2. They did not allow their employees to make personal calls.

Subjunctive _____

Infinitive_____

3. Had you *(tú)* recommended that he call me?

Subjunctive _____

Infinitive_____

> ## #14 Indirect Commands (See p.99.)
> There are no indirect commands with the past subjunctive.

A. Review ways to use the subjunctive.

Use 2 verbs of influence/volition in sentences, one with present subjunctive, one with past subjunctive.

1. _____

2. _____

Use 2 verbs of emotion in sentences, one with present subjunctive, one with past subjunctive.

3. _____

4. _____

Use 2 impersonal expressions in sentences, one with present subjunctive, one with past subjunctive.

5. _____

6. _____

Use 2 expressions of doubt or negation in sentences, one with present subjunctive, one with past subjunctive.

7. _____

8. _____

Use a compound verb in the past subjunctive.

9. _____

Use "para que" in 2 sentences, one with present subjunctive, one with past subjunctive.

10. _____

11. _____

Use a conjunction from p.145 in a past tense.

12. _____

Use "aunque" in 2 sentences: one with subjunctive (past or present) and one with only the indicative.

13. _____

14. _____

Use 2 sentences with hypothetical/non-existent people or objects: one with the present subjunctive and one with the past subjunctive.

15. _____

16. _____

Write 2 sentences with "si."

17. _____

18. _____

Write an indirect command.

19. _____

Como Si

- *Como si* (as if) is always followed by the past subjunctive because it is making a comparison that is figurative and contrary to fact.

  Examples:

  Me miró **como si** yo **estuviera** loca.   *He looked at me as if I were crazy.*

  Gastas dinero **como si creciera** en los árboles.   *You spend money as if it grew on trees.*

  No te preocupes. Los cuidaré **como si fueran** mis propios hijos.   *Don't worry. I'll take care of them as if they were my own children.*

- The other part of the sentence is often in a past or present tense, sometimes it's a command or the future tense, but any tense and/or mode can be used.

A. Complete the following sentences.

1. Él se comporta como si _____

2. Bailan como si _____

3. No me trates como si _____

4 Tú conduces como si _____

5. El elefante levantó el tronco como si _____

6. _____ como si flotaran en el aire.

7. _____ como si no nos hubiera visto,

8. El niño _____ como si _____

9. Ese árbol _____ como si _____

10. _____ como si _____

#15 The "-Ever"s —The Past Tense
(See p.103.)

- "Que" + the subjunctive is generally used in dependent clauses after the expressions below in all tenses because they almost always talk about something indefinite:

  1. cualquier (+ noun) ....*whatever, whichever (noun)*
  2. cualquiera ....*whatever, whichever*
  3. quienquiera ....*whoever, whomever*
  4. (a)dondequiera ....*(to) wherever*
  5. cuandoquiera.........................*whenever*
  6. por (+ adjective or adverb) ....*however (adjective or adverb)*

  Note: *Cualesquiera* and *quienesquiera* are the plural forms of *cualquiera* and *quienquiera*.

Examples with the past subjunctive (the main clause is usually in the conditional):

Viviría dondequiera que **encontrara** empleo.
He would live wherever he found work.

Yo escucharía a quienquiera que **supiera** algo sobre esto.
I would listen to whomever knew something about this.

Irían a los conciertos de ese conjunto cuandoquiera y adondequiera que **fueran**.
They would go to that group's concerts whenever and wherever they might be.

Por difícil que **hubiera sido**, lo habríamos hecho.
However difficult it might have been, we would have done it.

- Subjunctive + *lo que* + subjunctive

  Examples:

Present	haga lo que haga	*whatever you do, no matter what one does*
Past	hicieran lo que hicieran	*whatever they did, no matter what they did*

- [*El, la, los, las* + noun] + *que* + verb   or   *lo que* + verb

  These phrases can be in indicative (if it's information) or subjunctive (if it's not specific).

  Examples:

  Present
  Vamos a la película que tú **quieres**.   *Let's go the movie you want (a specific film).*
  Vamos a la película que tú **quieras**.   *Let's go to whichever movie you want (indefinite).*

  Past
  Eso es **lo que ella quería**.   *That is what she wanted (information).*
  Ella hacía l**o que quisiera.**   *She did whatever she wanted (not specific).*

- Occasionally, especially in the past tense, dependent clauses with the "-ever"s give information, and so use the indicative.

  Examples:

  Ese niño rompía cualquier juguete que **recibía**.
  That child used to break any toy that he received.

  El soldado iba adondequiera que lo **mandaban**.
  The soldier went wherever they sent him.

A. Translate the following sentences.

1. Digan lo que digan, no les creeremos.

_____

2. Dijeran lo que dijeran, no les habríamos creído.

_____

3. Por barato que fuera, no deberías haberlo comprado.

_____

4. Ellos irían de vacaciones adondequiera que hiciera sol y hubiera playa.

_____

5. Veríamos cualquier película que te interesara.

_____

6. No comprendí lo que significaba.

_____

7. Cuando salíamos a cenar, quienquiera que pagaba seleccionaba el restaurante.

_____

8. Juan hizo exactamente lo que le dio la gana.   (dar la gana = _to feel like_)

_____

9. Juan siempre hacía lo que le diera la gana.

_____

10. Por despacio y claro que hablara, ellos no me comprenderían.

_____

B. Translate the following sentences.

1. The police would find him wherever he might go / no matter where he went.

_____

2. Whoever knew her, admired her.

_____

3. Whatever house they might buy, they would make attractive and comfortable.

_____

4. No matter how much they might work, their money wouldn't be enough to pay their bills.
   (_no alcanzar para_)

_____

_____

#16 Expressions of Possibility (Single Clause) —Past Tense
(See p.107.)

- **Indicative**—the following expressions of possibility are used only with the indicative:

  a lo mejor ....*perhaps, probably*
  mejor que ....*it's better that, it's best that*
  menos mal que ....*at least, it's not so bad that*
  qué + [adjective / adverb / noun] + que......*how interesting (adj.), how quickly (adv.), what a problem (noun), etc.*

  Examples:

A lo mejor les **gustó**.	*They probably liked it.*
Menos mal que nos **gustó**.	*At least we liked it.*
Qué suerte que nos **gustó**.	*How lucky that we liked it.*

  Note: If any of the above expressions are restructured as impersonal expressions (see p.37), they are followed by the subjunctive. Example: Fue mejor que lo supieran.— It was better that they knew.

- **Subjunctive**—the following expressions of possibility are used only with the subjunctive:

  posiblemente ....*possibly*
  podría ser que...................*it could be, possibly*

  Examples:

Posiblemente lo **supieran**.	*Possibly they knew (it).*
Podría ser que lo **supieran**.	*It could be that they knew (it).*

- **Subjunctive** or **indicative**—the following expressions of possibility may be used with either:

  tal vez...............................*perhaps, maybe*
  quizá / quizás....................*perhaps, maybe*

  The use of indicative with these expressions shows more certainty; subjunctive shows more doubt.

  Examples:

Tal vez **vinieron**.	*Maybe they came.*	*(I think they did.)*
Tal vez **vinieran**.	*Perhaps they came.*	*(But I doubt it.)*

A. For each of the following, write the letters of the phrases that can complete the sentences. There will be more than one answer for each phrase.

Tal vez _____

Quizás _____

Podría ser que _____

A lo mejor_____

Qué sorpresa que _____

Fue sorprendente que _____

Posiblemente_____

Quizá _____

a. no podían ayudar

b. no pudieran ayudar

c. Juan se mudó lejos

d. Juan se mudara lejos

e. se casaron en junio

f. se casaran en junio

A. Review
Solve the crossword on p.195. (Translate the words in bold according to the context of the sentences.)

Horizontal

6. No puedo creer que _____ la tele. (I can't believe that they're **still watching** TV.) / **7.** he used to see

8. Ojalá que ____(I hope it fits.) / **11.** oil / **13.** ghost / **15.** store / **18.** garlic / **19.** east / **20.** not comedy

22. Nos alegramos de que él _____ mejor. (We're glad that he **is** better.)

24. grade / **26.** already / **32.** A menos que él _____ con más cuidado, va a tener un accidente.
    (Unless he **drives** more carefully, he's going to have an accident.)

33. Aunque _____ aquí, no lo sabría. (Even if it **were** here, I wouldn't know it.)

35. Si _____, habríamos esquiado. (If it **had snowed**, we would have skied.)

39. Me quedaré hasta que _____ listos. (I will stay until they **are** ready.) / **40.** that / **41.** arch / **43.** tooth

45. Aunque me gusta el pescado, no lo _____ a menudo. (Although I like fish, I don't **eat** it often.)

47. Tengan cuidado adondequiera que _____. (Be careful wherever you **go**.)

48. _____ Perón / **49.** tall / **51.** Me llamaron cuando lo _____. (They called me when they **received** it.)

54. No había casas en ese barrio que _____ feas. (There were no houses in that neighborhood that **were** ugly.)

55. report / **57.** Dudan que él lo _____. (They doubt that he **understands** it.)

58. Entraron sin que yo _____. (They came in without me **knowing**.) / **60.** power

62. No creía que _____ tanto. (I didn't believe that it **rained** so much.) / **64.** nothing

65. Tal vez _____. (Maybe they **will help** [I think so]).

67. Era mentira que _____ problemas. (It was a lie that **there were** problems.) / **68.** small amount

71. pause / **72.** ¿_____ ayudarme? (**Could you help** me?) / **74.** he ties

76. Les pedí que _____ a tiempo. (I asked them to **arrive** on time.) / **77.** healthy

78. Buscaba alguien que _____ lavaplatos. (I was looking for someone who **repaired** dishwashers.)

81. money / **83.** my / **84.** payment

85. No los dejó _____ al fútbol en la calle. (She didn't let them **play** soccer in the street.)

88. Yo _____ aprender eso. (**I would like** to learn that.) / **89.** cough / **90.** lightning / **92.** soup dish, tureen

93. Hablaron más alto para que los _____. (They talked louder so that we **could hear** them.)

Vertical

1. Si _____, ponte las botas. (If it **snows**, put on your boots.)

2. Fue evidente que ella _____ mucho. (It was evident that she **had spent** a lot.) / 3. party / 4. park

5. Dudaba que él lo _____. (I doubted that he **understood** it.) / 9. box / 10. bread

12. Aunque me gustaba el pescado, no lo _____ a menudo. (Although I liked fish, I didn't **eat** it often.)

13. fame / 14. negative / 15. Es bueno que Ud. _____ un buen empleo. (It's good that you **have** a good job.)

16. between / 17. from / 21. Tal vez _____. (Maybe they will **help** [but it's unlikely]).

23. Fue bueno que Uds. _____ un buen empleo. (It was good that you all **had** a good job.)

25. ¿Tenía miedo de que _____? (Were you afraid that they **had gotten hurt**?)

27. Creo que _____ una buena idea. (I believe that it **is** a good idea.)

28. Si _____, esquiaríamos. (If it **snowed**, we would ski.)

29. Es verdad que _____ problemas. (It's true that **there are** problems.)

30. death / **31.** floor / **33.** Me quedaba hasta que _____ listos. (I stayed until they **were** ready.)

34. tone / **36.** wheel / **37.** ship / **38.** sale / **42.** Quizá _____ en bicicleta. (Perhaps they **rode** bikes [but it's unlikely]).

44. the / **45.** with / **46.** crazy / **50.** north / **52.** daughter-in-law / **53.** eye

55. Llámenme cuando lo _____. (Call me when you **receive** it.) / **56.** background, bottom / **59.** noise

61. wing / **63.** Quiero que _____ a tiempo. (I want you to **arrive** on time.)

65. Véndelo a quienquiera que _____ tu precio. (Sell it to whoever **accepts** your price.) / **66.** years

68. bridge / **69.** hunt / **70.** Aunque esté aquí, no la _____. (Although it may be here, I don't **see** it.)

71. Ahorran dinero _____ a la universidad. (They're saving money **in order to attend** college.) / **72.** pool

73. where / **74.** soul / **75.** water

78. ¿Cuándo me _____ la lavadora? (When **will you repair** my washing machine?)

79. per / **80.** Hablen más alto para que los _____. (Talk louder so that we can **hear** you.)

82. red / **83.** sea / **84.** fish / **86.** uses / **87.** strange / **91.** already

Solution on p.196.

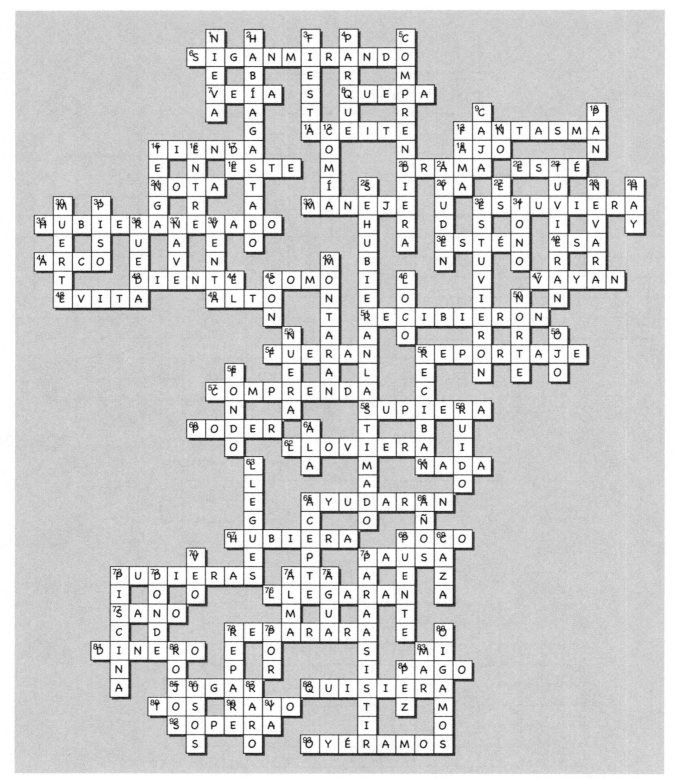

Solution to the puzzle on p. 196.

Answer Key

Nuts & Bolts: Grammar Terms

p.4

A. 1. C / 2. C / 3. P / 4. P / 5. P / 6. C / 7. P / 8. P

B. (El señor Sólis) es mi vecino. Vive en la casa amarilla. (Su esposa) trabaja mucho
                  él

en su jardín. (Ella) siempre me saluda, y de vez en cuando hablamos por unos
                                                            nosotras
                                                            or nosotros

momentos. Pero a él nunca lo veo. (Ella) dice que (su esposo) trabaja siempre.
                        yo

Además, (él) viaja mucho por su trabajo. (Su trabajo) es muy importante para él.

C. 1. Espero (que) (mis amigos vengan pronto).
       I hope my friends come soon.

2. Ellos admiran a las personas (que) (son inteligentes y sinceras).
   They admire people who are intelligent and sincere.

3. La oficina (donde) (trabajamos) está en el piso 20.
   The office where we work is on the 20th floor.

4. Mi compañero de casa nunca se acuerda de cerrar las ventanas (cuando) (llueve).

5. ¿Te gustó la cena (que) (ellos prepararon)?
   Did you like the dinner they made/prepared?

p.5

D. Answers will vary. Make sure that you have included a connecting word in each sentence.
   Here are some possible answers:

1. Me gusta ir de compras cuando tengo dinero.
   I like to go shopping when I have money.

2. Mis amigos quieren ir de vacaciones adonde puedan hacer esnórkel.
   My friends want to go on vacation where they can go snorkeling.

3. Este es el carro que quisiera tener.
   This is the car that I would like to have / own.

4. Ella juega tenis con una amiga que es muy competitiva.
   She plays tennis with a friend who's very competitive.

How to Form the Present Subjunctive: Regular Verbs

p.9

A. √ 1. viva / ___ 2. conozco / ___ 3. dormimos / ___ 4. jugamos / ___ 5. escribes / √ 6. preguntes
√ 7. ayude / √ 8. vengan / √ 9. durmamos / ___ 10. compra / ___ 11. invita / √ 12. cante

p.10
B.

yo, indic.	yo, subj.
1. hablo	hable
2. bailo	baile
3. paso	pase
4. dejo	deje
5. tomo	tome
6. me llamo	me llame
7. me quedo	me quede

yo, indic.	yo, subj.
8. encuentro	encuentre
9. pienso	piense
10. como	coma
11. creo	crea
12. quiero	quiera
13. pierdo	pierda
14. vivo	viva

yo, indic.	yo, subj.
15. asisto	asista
16. sigo	siga
17. salgo	salga
18. pongo	ponga
19. veo	vea
20. conozco	conozca

p.11
C.

infinitive	yo	tú	él, ella, Ud.	nosotros/as	ellos, ellas, Uds.
2. ayudar	ayude	ayudes	ayude	ayudemos	ayuden
3. comprar	compre	compres	compre	compremos	compren
4. estudiar	estudie	estudies	estudie	estudiemos	estudien
5. quedarse	me quede	te quedes	se quede	nos quedemos	se queden
6. escuchar	escuche	escuches	escuche	escuchemos	escuchen
7. usar	use	uses	use	usemos	usen
8. cocinar	cocine	cocines	cocine	cocinemos	cocinen
9. comer	coma	comas	coma	comamos	coman
10. comprender	comprenda	comprendas	comprenda	comprendamos	comprendan
11. vender	venda	vendas	venda	vendamos	vendan
12. leer	lea	leas	lea	leamos	lean
13. vivir	viva	vivas	viva	vivamos	vivan
14. dividir	divida	dividas	divida	dividamos	dividan
15. destruir	destruya	destruyas	destruya	destruyamos	destruyan
16. caerse	me caiga	te caigas	se caiga	nos caigamos	se caigan
17. ver	vea	veas	vea	veamos	vean
18. conocer	conozca	conozcas	conozca	conozcamos	conozcan
19. tener	tenga	tengas	tenga	tengamos	tengan
20. hacer	haga	hagas	haga	hagamos	hagan

How to Form the Present Subjunctive: Stem Changes

p.12

A.

infinitive	yo	tú	él, ella, Ud.	nosotros/as	ellos, ellas, Uds.
1. encontrar	encuentre	encuentres	encuentre	encontremos	encuentren
2. cerrar	cierre	cierres	cierre	cerremos	cierren
3. querer	quiera	quieras	quiera	queramos	quieran
4. poder	pueda	puedas	pueda	podamos	puedan
5. perder	pierda	pierdas	pierda	perdamos	pierdan
6. volver	vuelva	vuelvas	vuelva	volvamos	vuelvan
7. morir	muera	mueras	muera	muramos	mueran
8. seguir	siga	sigas	siga	sigamos	sigan

B.

infinitive	yo	tú	él, ella, Ud.	nosotros/as	ellos, ellas, Uds.
1. nadar	nade	nades	nade	nademos	naden
2. construir	construya	construyas	construya	construyamos	construyan
3. mostrar	muestre	muestres	muestre	mostremos	muestren
4. preparar	prepare	prepares	prepare	preparemos	preparen
5. pedir	pida	pidas	pida	pidamos	pidan
6. servir	sirva	sirvas	sirva	sirvamos	sirvan
7. pelear	pelee	pelees	pelee	peleemos	peleen
8. abrir	abra	abras	abra	abramos	abran

p.13

C. 1. salga / 2. se caiga / 3. terminemos / 4. puedas / 5. ayuden / 6. duerman / 7. tenga / 8. veas

D. 1. Ojalá que ellos no se pierdan.   I hope they don't get lost.

    2. Ojalá que nos veamos pronto.   I hope we see each other soon.

    3. Ojalá que no te pongas nervioso.   I hope you don't get nervous.

    4. Ojalá que venda mi carro.   I hope I sell my car.

    5. Ojalá que mi equipo gane.   I hope my team wins.

    6. Ojalá que tu abuela no muera.   I hope your grandmother doesn't die.

    Note: "Let's hope," "God willing," "God grant that," etc., can be substituted for " I hope."

How to Form the Present Subjunctive: Irregular Verbs

p.14

A.

infinitive	yo	tú	él, ella, Ud.	nosotros, nosotras	ellos, ellas, Uds.
1. ser	sea	seas	sea	seamos	sean
2. estar	esté	estés	esté	estemos	estén
3. ir	vaya	vayas	vaya	vayamos	vayan
4. dar	dé	des	dé	demos	den
5. haber	haya	hayas	haya	hayamos	hayan
6. saber	sepa	sepas	sepa	sepamos	sepan

p.15

B. 1. den / 2. estés / 3. seamos / 4. sepa / 5. haya / 6. vaya

C. 1. Ojalá que ellos no estén enfermos.   I hope they aren't sick.
    2. Ojalá que sepamos las respuestas.   I hope we know / will know the answers.
    3. Ojalá que María les dé las gracias por las flores.   I hope María thanks / will thank them for the flowers.
    4. Ojalá que sea rico algún día.   I hope I'll be rich someday.
    5. Ojalá que tú vayas despacio.   I hope you go / will go slowly.
    6. Ojalá que haya una fiesta.   I hope there is / will be a party.

    Note: "Let's hope," "God willing," "God grant that," etc., can be substituted for " I hope."

Spelling Adjustments

p.16

A.

infinitive	yo	tú	él, ella, Ud.	nosotros, nosotras	ellos, ellas, Uds.
1. buscar	busque	busques	busque	busquemos	busquen
2. pagar	pague	pagues	pague	paguemos	paguen
3. sacar	saque	saques	saque	saquemos	saquen
4. empezar*	empiece	empieces	empiece	empecemos	empiecen
5. practicar	practique	practiques	practique	practiquemos	practiquen
6. regar*	riegue	riegues	riegue	reguemos	rieguen

Empezar and *regar* are stem-change verbs.

B. 1. llegue / 2. organice / 3. saques / 4. juguemos / 5. empiece / 6. toque / 7. busquen / 8. paguen

p.17

C. 1. estés / 2. busque / 3. juguemos / 4. abra / 5. cierre / 6. den / 7. vea / 8. sepa / 9. escuchen
    10. hagamos / 11. oiga / 12. sirvan / 13. te diviertas / 14. seamos / 15. mires / 16. vote

#1 Influence / Volition

p.21

A. 1. quiero 　　　　 4. escribe 　　　 7. lees 　　　 10. decimos

　　 2. (salgan) 　　　 5. hablamos 　　 8. (leas) 　　 11. salir

　　 3. (esté) 　　　　 6. ojalá 　　　　 9. (digamos) 　 12. (tenga)

B. 1. <u>Queremos</u> |que| (haya) paz en el mundo.

　　 2. El general <u>mandará</u> |que| los soldados (ataquen)

　　 3. <u>Sugiero</u> |que| lo (llames)

　　 4. <u>Dicen</u> |que| yo (venga)

　　 5. ¿<u>Aconsejas</u> |que| (estudiemos) más ciencias?

p.22

C. aconsejamos ....we advise

　　 deseamos ....we wish

　　 dicen............................they tell

　　 espera ....she hopes / expects

　　 exige............................he demands

　　 insisto ....I insist

　　 manda ....he orders

　　 necesito ....I need

　　 obligan.........................they force / oblige

　　 permiten.......................do you all permit / allow?

　　 pide ....is she asking?

　　 prefieren ....they prefer

　　 prohibe ....do you forbid / prohibit?

　　 propone ....it proposes

　　 queremos ....we want

　　 requieren ....they require

　　 ruego ....I beg

　　 sugieren.......................they suggest

p.24

E. Answers will vary. Here are some possibilities:

　　 aconsejar, decir, desear, esperar, exigir, insistir, mandar, necesitar, obligar, pedir,

　　 permitir, preferir, prohibir, proponer, querer, requerir, rogar, sugerir, suplicar

F. Answers will vary. Here are some examples:

　　 Voy a pedir que me den un aumento. 　　　　　　 *I'm going to ask them for a raise.*

　　 Juan propone que invirtamos en su negocio. 　　 *Juan proposes that we invest in his business.*

　　 Sugerimos que lo pienses bien. 　　　　　　　　 *We suggest you think it over.*

　　 El profesor exige que los estudiantes 　　　　　 *The teacher demands that the students arrive on time.*
　　 　　 lleguen a tiempo.

　　 Sus padres prohiben que se casen. 　　　　　　 *Their parents forbid them to marry.*

p.24

G. Answers will vary. Some examples:

No deseo leer ese libro.

Prefieren quedarse en un hotel más económico.

Juan dice que necesita más tiempo para terminar.

I don't wish / want to read that book.

They prefer to stay in a more economical hotel.

Juan says that he needs more time to finish.

p.25

H. 1. ¿Quieres que yo ponga la mesa?
2. Ella no permitirá que sus hijos / niños esquíen solos.
3. Él quiere ir a la fiesta pero tiene que trabajar.
4. La escuela recomienda que cada estudiante tenga su propia computadora.
5. Ella necesita salir temprano.
6. Pediremos que nos llamen mañana.
7. Espero viajar este verano.
8. Sugieren que hagamos una reservación / reserva.
9. Díganle (a ella) que me llame.
10. La compañía requiere que sus empleados tomen una prueba / pruebas de detección de drogas.
11. ¿Prefiere hacerlo Ud. o prefiere que lo haga yo? / que yo lo haga?
12. La familia desea verte.

p.26

I. ___ 1. She says that her son is going to arrive tomorrow.
___ 2. Are you saying that they are lying?
√ 3. The teacher tells her students to study for the test.

√ 4. I'm telling you to turn down the volume.
√ 5. Don't tell him to do that.
___ 6. They say that they liked the movie.

p.27

J. Answers will vary. Some examples:

Abuela Ana

Mando que te dediques a tus estudios.
(I order you to devote yourself to your studies.)

Insisto en que no pierdas tiempo en tonterías.
(I insist you not waste time on foolishness.)

Prohibo que te emborraches.
(I forbid you to get drunk.)

Abuela Beatriz

Sugiero que te diviertas pero que no te distraigas
demasiado. *(I suggest that you enjoy yourself
but that you don't get too distracted.)*

Recomiendo que prestes atención a tus profesores.
(I recommend that you pay attention to your professors.)

Espero que aproveches tus oportunidades.
(I hope you take advantage of your opportunities.)

K. Answers will vary. Some examples:

Sala:

No quiero que dejes ropa sucia en la sala.   *(I don't want you to leave dirty clothes in the living room.)*

Sugiero que pases la aspiradora y que quites el polvo de los muebles de vez en cuando.
(I suggest you vacuum and dust the furniture once in a while.)

Pido que apagues la calefacción y las luces antes de salir de la casa.
(I ask that you turn off the heat and lights before leaving the house.)

Cocina:

Exigo que laves tus platos.   *(I demand you wash your dishes.)*

Ruego que no comas mi comida.   *(I beg you not to eat my food.)*

Deseo que limpies la estufa.   *(I want you to clean the stove.)*

Baño:

Prefiero que no dejes toallas mojadas en el suelo del baño. *(I prefer you not leave wet towels on the bathroom floor.)*

Propongo que tomemos turnos para limpiar el inodoro.   *(I propose that we take turns cleaning the toilet.)*

Insisto en que dejes limpia la bañera después de bañarte.   *(I insist that you leave the bathtub clean after you bathe.)*

#2 Emotion

p.29

A. 1. Nos <u>enoja</u> [que] siempre (llegues) tarde.

2. La doctora se <u>preocupa</u> [que] su paciente no se (mejore.)

3. Me <u>inquieta</u> [que] ellos (fracasen.)

4. ¿<u>Estás</u> emocionada [que] él se (gradúe?)

5. Los niños <u>tienen</u> miedo de [que] su perro (esté) perdido.

p.30

B. **Answers will vary. Some possibilities:**

alegrarse	entristecerse	odiar
arrepentirse	estar alegre, asustado,	ponerse emocionado, enojado,
asustarse	avergonzado, contento,	nervioso, triste, etc.*
dar(le) asco, miedo,	emocionado, molesto,	preocuparse
vergüenza, etc.	orgulloso, sorprendido, etc.*	sentir
emocionarse	fastidiar(le)	sorprenderse
encantar(le)	gustar(le)	temer
enfadarse	lamentar	tener miedo
enojarse	molestar(le)	volverse loco

These adjectives agree with the subject. Ex.: asustado / asustada / asustados / asustadas.

C. 1. El taxista se inquieta de que el precio de gasolina suba.   *The taxi driver worries that the price of gas will go up.*
2. Los niños están alegres de que haya una fiesta de cumpleaños.   *The children are glad that there is / will be a birthday party.*
3. A María le encanta salir a bailar.   *María loves to go out dancing.*
4. Estamos contentos de que puedas visitarnos.   *We're happy that you can / will be able to visit us.*
5. Lamento que estén enfermos.   *I'm sorry that they're sick.*
6. ¿Tienes miedo de que no vengan?   *Are you afraid that they aren't coming / won't come?*

When To Use "*De*"

In sentences #1, #2, #4 and #6 above, "de" has been added before "que."

If in a simple sentence an expression of emotion uses a preposition + noun, then in a sentence with subjunctive, "de" is used before "que."

Examples:

expression of emotion	simple sentence with prep.	sentence with subjunctive
preocuparse **por**	Me preocupo **por** mi hermano.	Me preocupo **de** que él **esté** mal.
tener miedo **a**	Tiene miedo **a** las serpientes.	Tiene miedo **de** que **sean** venenosas.
alegrarse **de/por/con**	Nos alegramos **por** ti.	Nos alegramos **de** que te **cases**.
estar triste ***de/por/con***	Están tristes **con** el mal tiempo.	Están tristes **de** que **llueva** tanto.
molestar(le) (no prep.)	Les molesta el tráfico. (no prep.)	Les molesta que **haya** mucho tráfico. (no ***de***)
alegrar(le) (no prep.)	¿Te alegra la noticia? (no prep.)	¿Te alegra que **vengan** a visitar? (no ***de***)
lamentar (no prep.)	Lamento el error. (no prep.)	Lamento que el error **cause** problemas. (no ***de***)

NOTE: Some speakers drop the "*de*" in the sentences with subjunctive.

    This tendency seems to be increasingly common.

    Examples: Me preocupo que él **esté** mal.   Tiene miedo que **sean** venenosas.
                    Nos alegramos que te **cases**.   Están tristes que **llueva** tanto.

NOTE: This book and answer key will sometimes use the "de" and sometimes omit it.

p.31

D. 1. No me gusta que viajes solo / sola.

2. Ella está orgullosa de que sus hijos / niños saquen buenas notas.

3. Los estudiantes se preocupan de que / están preocupados que
   el profesor les dé un examen / una prueba mañana.

4. Odiamos que Uds. vivan así.

5. El tiene vergüenza / está avergonzado admitirlo.

6. ¿No estás feliz / alegre / contento(a) de que no llueva?

7. Tienen miedo de decirle la verdad.

8. No estén tristes de que se acabe.

9. Lo siento que te duela la cabeza / tengas dolor de cabeza.

10. Están furiosos que salga mal.

p.32

E. 1. The employee is irritated / annoyed that they don't pay / aren't paying him more.
   The employee is irritated / annoyed that they won't pay him more.

2. Are you happy that they help / are helping you?
   Are you happy that they're going to help you?

3. My friend complains / is complaining that the trip costs / is costing a lot.
   My friend complains / is complaining that the trip will cost a lot.

4. We are glad / happy that they are successful.
   We are glad / happy that they will be successful.

5. I love that there is live music.
   I love that there will be live music.

p.33

F. Answers will vary. Some possibilities:

1. Me sorprende que estés de vacaciones en México.

2. Me alegro de que se diviertan.

3. Estoy envidiosa de que haga buen tiempo, porque hace mucho frío aquí.

4. Me da pena que haya mucha contaminación allí, y siento que tengas los ojos irritados.

5. Estoy contenta(o) de que conozcan lugares interesantes.

6. Estoy emocionada(o) de que vayan a conocer / que conozcan el Museo Nacional de Antropología.
   Es magnífico.

7. Estoy alegre de que nos veamos pronto. ¿Quieres que yo te recoja en el aeropuerto?

G. Answers will vary. See p.231 for sample sentences.

H. Answers will vary. See p.231 for sample sentences.

#3 Impersonal Expressions

p.37

A. 1. <u>Es horrible</u> que me (digas) eso.

2. <u>Es fantástico</u> que nos (visiten)**

3. <u>Es verdad</u> que un carro como ése cuesta un dineral.

4. ¿<u>Es necesario</u> que (salgamos) ahora?

5. <u>Es increíble</u> que (existan) los OVNIs.

6. <u>Es preciso</u> pagar por adelantado.

p.38

B. Answers will vary. Some possibilities:

Es aconsejable	Es fantástico	Es malo	Es preciso	Es triste
Es agradable	Es feo	Es mentira	Es preocupante	No es cierto
Es bueno	Es horrible	Es misterioso	Es sorprendente	No es importante
Es curioso	Es interesante			

C. Answers will vary. Some possibilities: es verdad, es evidente, no es mentira, es cierto, es claro

D. Answers will vary. Some possibilities:

1. Es triste que su hijo esté enfermo.
2. Es bueno que no haya mucho tráfico ahora.
3. Es impresionante que María estudie para ser abogada.
4. Es cierto que Caracas es la capital de Venezuela.
5. Es interesante que vendan carros eléctricos.
6. Es fantástico que la guerra termine.
7. No es aconsejable que ellos beban mucho.
8. Es difícil que hagamos ejercicio todos los días.
9. Es increíble que tú veas fantasmas.
10. No es mentira que tengo miedo a las serpientes.

p.39

E. 1. Es divertido esquiar.

2. Es peligroso que los niños jueguen en la calle.
3. No es correcto que lo dejen solo.
4. Es verdad que él sabe manejar / conducir. Pero no es verdad que maneje / conduzca bien.
5. Es maravilloso que te cases.
6. Es increíble que cueste tanto.

F. Answers will vary. See p.231 for sample sentences.

p.40

G. Answers will vary. Some possibilities:

Es feo que ellos se comporten así.　　　　*It's awful that they behave like that.*

Es agradable que no llueva　　　　　　　*It's pleasant that it's not raining*
　y que podamos comer en el patio.　　　　*and we can eat on the patio.*

Es preciso que Uds. terminen a tiempo.　　*It's necessary that you all finish on time.*

No es imposible que haya una huelga.　　　*It's not impossible that there will be a strike.*

Es emocionante que nos den una fiesta.　　*It's exciting that they're giving us a party.*

H. Answers will vary.

#4 Doubt and Negation

p.41

A. _√_ 1. Es verdad que mañana es jueves.

_√_ 2. No niego que él es guapo.

_X_ 3. No creen que existan los extraterrestres.

_X_ 4. Dudamos que él sea de confianza.

_√_ 5. Es que la tierra sí es plana.

_√_ 6. Creo que salimos a las 9:00.

p.42

B. Answers will vary. Some possibilities:

dudar,   es dudoso,   es mentira,   negar,   no creer,   no es cierto,

no es que,   no estar seguro/a(s),   no es verdad

C. creer,   es cierto,   es que,   estar seguro/a(s),   es verdad,

no dudar,   no es mentira,   no negar,   parece

D. 1. El no cree que sea verdad.

2. Dudan que ella sepa cocinar paella.

3. No creo que él maneje / conduzca bien.

4. No estamos seguros de que vengan a la fiesta.

5. Ella no cree que debamos trabajar allí.

E. Answers will vary. Some possibilities:

Dudo que haya algún problema.   *I doubt that there's any problem.*

María no cree que eso sea buena idea.   *María doesn't think that that's a good idea.*

No es verdad que ese plomero cobre mucho.   *It's not true that that plumber charges a lot.*

F. Answers will vary. Some possibilities:

No dudamos que se esfuerzan.   *We don't doubt that they are making an effort.*

Creo que debes hacerlo.   *I think you should do it.*

Es cierto que cuesta mucho.   *It's true that it costs a lot.*

p.43

G. 1. No es verdad que mañana sea jueves.

2. Niego que él sea guapo.

3. Creen que los extraterrestres existen.

Creen que no existen los extraterrestres.

4. No dudamos que él es de confianza.

5. No es que la tierra sea plana.

6. No creo que salgamos a las 9.

p.44

H. **Answers will vary. Some possibilities:**

Sara:
- No creo que sea el mejor día.
  Es verdad que hay más dinero, pero también hay más personas y más seguridad.
  > *(I don't think it's the best day. It's true that there's more money, but there are also more people and more security.)*

- Dudo que podamos robar tanto. Es posible que consigamos $250.000.
  > *(I doubt that we can steal so much. It's possible that we'll get $250,000.)*

- Es ridículo que pongan el dinero en los bolsillos. Es imposible que quepa.
  > *(It's ridiculous to put the money in your pockets. It's impossible that it will fit.)*

- No quiero que usen armas. Tengo miedo de que alguien se lastime.
  Además es un disparate que pienses llevar granadas.
  > *(I don't want you to use weapons. I'm afraid someone will get hurt.*
  > *Besides, it's absurd that you're planning on carrying grenades.)*

- Me asombra que no tomes el guardia en serio.   *(I'm amazed that you're not taking the guard seriously.)*
  Les aconsejo que tengan cuidado de él.   *(I advise you to be careful of him.)*

- No creo que las barbas sean una buena idea.   *(I don't think the beards are a good idea.)*
  Es bueno que se disfracen, pero recomiendo que lleven gorras y máscaras.
  > *(It's good to disguise yourselves, but I recommend that you wear caps and masks.)*

- Creo que podré abirles la caja.   *(I think I'll be able to open the safe for you.)*

- No es verdad que puedan escaparse en bicicleta con tanto dinero.
  > *(It's not true that you can escape by bicycle with so much money.)*

- Espero que no hagas tal locura. Es preciso no llamar la atención.
  > *(I hope you don't do anything so crazy. It's necessary to not attract attention.)*

- No niego que me gustan los carros deportivos, pero creo que compraré algo menos llamativo.
  > *(I don't deny that I like sports cars, but I think I'll buy something less conspicuous.)*

pp.44-45

I. **Answers will vary. See p.231 for sample sentences.**

p.45

J. **Answers will vary. Some possibilities:**

Creo que Dios existe. / No creo que Dios exista.
I believe God exists. / I don't believe that God exists.

Creo que los seres humanos son esencialmente buenos. / No creo que sean esencialmente buenos.
I believe human beings are essentially good. / I don't believe that they are essentially good.

Creo que hay vida en otros planetas. / No creo que haya vida en otros planetas.
I believe that there is life on other planets. / I don't believe that there's life on other planets.

#5 Compound Verbs

p.50

A. 1. hablar / 2. comer / 3. vivir / 4. hacer / 5. leer / 6. dar / 7. dormir / 8. ver / 9. venir / 10. perder

B.
1. hablando / hablado
2. corriendo / corrido
3. saliendo / salido
4. leyendo / leído
5. durmiendo / dormido
6. haciendo / hecho
7. practicando / practicado
8. viendo / visto
9. muriendo / muerto
10. escribiendo / escrito
11. tomando / tomado
12. llegando / llegado
13. continuando / continuado
14. siendo / sido
15. escuchando / escuchado
16. jugando / jugado

p.51

C.

Estar	yo	tú	él, ella, Ud.	nosotros / nosotras	ellos, ellas, Uds.
present indicative	estoy	estás	está	estamos	están
present subjunctive	esté	estés	esté	estemos	estén

Seguir	yo	tú	él, ella, Ud.	nosotros / nosotras	ellos, ellas, Uds.
present indicative	sigo	sigues	sigue	seguimos	siguen
present subjunctive	siga	sigas	siga	sigamos	sigan

Haber	yo	tú	él, ella, Ud.	nosotros / nosotras	ellos, ellas, Uds.
present indicative	he	has	ha	hemos	han
present subjunctive	haya	hayas	haya	hayamos	hayan

D.
1. No lo **ha** hecho.
2. No lo **han** hecho.
3. No lo **hemos** hecho.
4. No lo **han** hecho.
5. No lo **he** hecho.
6. No lo **has** hecho.
7. No lo **han** hecho.
8. No lo **han** hecho.
9. **Estás** escuchándola.
10. **Estamos** escuchándola.
11. **Están** escuchándola.
12. **Están** escuchándola.
13. **Estoy** escuchándola.
14. **Está** escuchándola.
15. **Está** escuchándola.
16. **Estamos** escuchándola.

p.52

E.
1. sigo esperando   I keep waiting / hoping
2. hemos mirado   we have looked / watched
3. él había tocado   he had touched / played
4. se habrá roto   it will have broken / it has probably broken
5. andan diciendo   they go around saying
6. has dicho   you have said / told
7. Ud. ha vivido   you have lived
8. estaba divirtiéndome   I was having a good time / enjoying myself
    me estaba divirtiendo

F.
1. estoy escuchando   he escuchado
2. él sigue gritando   él ha gritado
3. estaban / estuvieron viniendo   habían venido
4. ella estará dando   ella habrá dado
5. estamos escribiendo   hemos escrito
6. está haciendo   ha hecho
7. siguen reuniéndose   se han reunido
    se siguen reuniendo
8. estamos divirtiéndonos   nos hemos divertido
    nos estamos divirtiendo

p.53

G.
1. Dudo que nuestro hijo (haya) terminado.   *I doubt that our son has finished.*
2. Ojalá que no se nos (haya) acabado la leche.   *I hope that we haven't run out of milk.*
3. Es feo que (siga) lloviendo.   *It's awful / yucky that it keeps raining.*
4. Estamos impresionados que (hayas) pasado la tarde limpiando tu cuarto.   *We are impressed that you've spent the afternoon cleaning your room.*
5. María espera que Juan (esté) escuchando.   *María hopes that Juan is listening.*
6. El maestro no está convencido de que los alumnos (hayan) (estado) estudiando.   *The teacher is not convinced that the students have been studying.*

p.54

H. **Answers will vary. Some possibilities:**

1. estén jugando al béisbol

    Me sorprende que los niños estén jugando al béisbol en este tiempo.
    I'm surprised that the children are playing baseball in this weather.

2. sigamos esperando

    Es ridículo que sigamos esperando que llamen.
    It's ridiculous that we keep waiting for them to call.

3. haya salido para México

    Dudo que él haya salido para México.
    I doubt that he's left for Mexico.

4. hayas pedido un café

    Espero que hayas pedido un café.
    I hope you've ordered coffee.

5. haya comprado un carro nuevo

    El no cree que yo haya comprado un carro nuevo.
    He doesn't believe that I've bought a new car.

I. 1. Me molesta que sigan llamando.

2. Tenemos miedo de que se hayan perdido.

3. Ella cree que él está hablando por teléfono.

4. No creen que tú lo hayas hecho.

p.56

K. **Answers will vary. Some possibilities:**

1. Es emocionante que María haya dado a luz a gemelos.

2. Dudo que Juan esté buscando un nuevo empleo.

3. No es sorprendente que María haya recibido un aumento.

4. Es una lástima que a Juan se le haya roto la pierna.

5. Es bueno que María siga ofreciéndose como voluntaria.

6. Me alegro que Juan haya estado ayudando a sus padres.

7. No es verdad que María se haya negado a pagar sus impuestos.

8. Es triste que Juan y María se hayan divorciado.

p.57

L. **Answers will vary. See p.231 for sample sentences.**

#6 Intended Purpose

p.59

A. 1. Juan trabaja mucho (para) mantener a su familia.

2. Mi tía me manda dinero (a fin de que) yo les compre regalos a los niños.

3. Les escribimos (de modo que) sepan la buena noticia.

4. Nos encanta esta canción. Voy a subir el volumen (para que) la oigamos mejor.

5. ¿Quieres que yo te lleve al aeropuerto (de manera que) no tengas que pagar el estacionamiento?

6. Van a plantar los rosales aquí (para que) reciban suficiente sol.

p.60

B. **Answers will vary. In sentences 1, 2, 4, 5 any of the following can be used:**
para que / a fin de que / de modo que / de manera que.
But in sentences 3 and 6, only "para" can be used.

1. Van a casa de Sara de modo que ella pueda ayudarlos / que ella los ayude con sus tareas.

2. Recojo a mis vecinos en el aeropuerto esta noche para que no tengan que tomar un taxi.

3. No salen mucho para ahorrar dinero.

4. Se lo explica / Está explicándoselo a fin de que Uds. comprendan.

5. Sus padres insisten en que él estudie todos los días para que saque buenas notas.

6. ¿Vas a México para estudiar o para visitar amigos?

C. 1. Hacen ejercicio para ser sanos y fuertes. *They exercise in order to be healthy and strong.*

2. Sus padres le van a prestar dinero para que ella compre un carro.
Her parents are going to lend her money so that she can buy a car.

3. Ella toma aspirina para bajar su fiebre. *She takes aspirin to lower her fever.*

4. Llamamos para confirmar la cita. *We're calling to confirm the appointment.*

5. Él mantiene bien su carro para que dure mucho tiempo.
He takes good care of his car so that it will last a long time.

6. Corremos para alcanzar el autobús a tiempo. *We're running in order to reach the bus on time.*

7 Él practica fútbol mucho para que su equipo gane. *He practices soccer a lot so his team will win.*

8. Él practica fútbol mucho para recibir una beca. *He practices soccer a lot to get a scholarship.*

p.61

D. Answers will vary. Some possibilities:

1. Voy al supermercado por los ingredientes **para que** tú puedas hacer un pastel.
   I'm going to the supermarket for the ingredients so that you can make a cake.

2. Ellos se levantan temprano **para** ayudar con todos los quehaceres.
   They get up early in order to help with the chores.

3. Ella trabaja mucho en su jardín **de modo que** esté bonito.
   She works a lot in her garden so that it looks nice.

4. Él mantiene su carro con cuidado **a fin de que** corra bien.
   He maintains his car carefully so that it runs well.

5. Deben cambiar la ley **de manera que** sea más justa.
   They should change the law so that it's fairer.

E. Answers will vary. See p.231 for sample sentences.

p.62

F. Answers will vary. Some examples:

Esta tarde mi esposo va a una librería para mirar unos libros de informática.

This afternoon my husband is going to a bookstore to look at computer books.

Mañana voy a echar una tarjeta al correo de modo que mi sobrina la reciba el día de su cumpleaños.

Tomorrow I'm going to put a card in the mail so that my niece gets it on her birthday.

Si nieva el fin de semana, será necesario quitar la nieve de la acera
para que la gente pueda pasar y de manera que nadie se caiga.

*If it snows on the weekend, it will be necessary to shovel the snow from the sidewalk
so that people can pass / get by and no one falls down.*

La semana que viene, la gobernadora va a visitar el sitio del desastre
para consultar con el alcalde y a fin de que la gente se anime.

*Next week the governor is going to visit the disaster site in order to consult with the
mayor and so that the people are encouraged / cheered up.*

#7 Contingencies

p.63

A. 1. Van a jugar al béisbol a menos que llueva   unless it rains

2. Hasta que ella se gradúe va a vivir con sus padres.   Until she graduates

3. Nadie puede entrar en la casa sin que yo lo sepa.   without me knowing it

4. Antes de que salgas, quiero que limpies tu cuarto.   Before you leave / go out

5. Su hijo puede usar el carro siempre que pida permiso   as long as / provided that he asks permission

6. En caso de que la jefa no esté haga el favor de dejar el informe con la recepcionista.   In case the boss is not in

p.64

B. a menos que ....unless

antes de que ....before

así que ....as soon as

con tal de que ....provided that

después de que..................after

en caso de que ....in case that

en cuanto ....as soon as

hasta que ....until

luego que ....as soon as, after

mientras que ....while, as long as

siempre que ....provided that, as long as

sin que ....without

tan pronto como................as soon as

p.65

C. 1. No me iré <u>a menos que</u> quieras que me vaya.   I won't go / leave unless you want me to (go / leave).

2. No me iré <u>mientras que</u> no quieras que me vaya.   I won't go / leave as long as you don't want me to (go).

3. No me iré <u>sin que</u> quieras que me vaya.   I won't go / leave without you wanting me to (go).

4. Me iré <u>tan pronto como</u> quieras.   I will go / leave as soon as you want.

5. No me iré <u>siempre que</u> no quieras que me vaya.   I won't go / leave as long as you don't want me to (go).

6. No me iré <u>hasta que</u> quieras que me vaya.   I won't go / leave until you want me to (go).

7. No me iré <u>antes de que</u> quieras que me vaya.   I won't go / leave before you want me to (go).

8. Me iré <u>con tal de que</u> quieras que me vaya.   I will go / leave provided that you want me to (go).

9. Me iré <u>después de que</u> me digas que me vaya.   I will go / leave after you tell me to (go).

10. Me iré <u>en cuanto</u> me digas que me vaya.   I will go / leave as soon as you tell me to (go).

11. Me iré <u>así que</u> me digas que me vaya.   I will go / leave as soon as you tell me to (go.)

12. No me iré <u>en caso de que</u> me necesites.   I will not go / leave in case you need me.

13. Me iré <u>luego que</u> nos despidamos.   I will go / leave as soon as / after we say goodbye.

p.66

D. 1.   Se lo diré en cuanto / tan pronto como / así que yo lo vea.

2.   Él nos acompañará / irá con nosotros al cine con tal de que / siempre que paguemos nosotros.

3.   Antes de que se enojen / se enfaden / se pongan enojados, escúchennos.

4.   A menos que ellos estudien, no van a salir bien en el examen / la prueba.

5.   Lleva / Llévate tu paraguas en caso de que llueva.

E. Answers will vary. Some possibilities:

1.   Iré al parque en cuanto deje de llover.
      I'll go to the park as soon as it stops raining.

2.   Nuestros amigos van de vacaciones a Europa con tal de que obtengan suficientes días de vacaciones.
      Our friends are going on vacation to Europe providing that they get enough vacation days.

3.   Queremos comprarlo siempre que sea bueno el precio.
      We want to buy it as long as the price is good.

4.   Vamos a quedarnos en un hotel en la playa a menos que no podamos reservar una habitación con vista al mar.
      We're going to stay in a hotel at the beach unless we can't reserve a room with an ocean view.

5.   Queremos vivir en el centro mientras (que) haya un apartamento económico cerca de nuestro trabajo.
      We want to live downtown as long as there's an affordable apartment near our work.

6.   Uds. deben quedarse hasta que terminen.
      You should stay until you finish.

7.   Claro. Te llamo en cuanto llegue a casa.
      Of course. I'll call you as soon as I get home.

8.   Juan trabajará unas horas antes de que su familia salga de vacaciones.
      Juan will work a few hours before his family leaves on vacation.

p.67

F.   Answers will vary. See p.231 for sample sentences.

p.68

G. Jorge: Oye, estoy enamorado de otra. Me voy.   *Listen, I'm in love with another woman. I'm leaving.*

Ana: No. Nadie se va a menos que lo mande. Y yo no lo mando.
    No. Nobody leaves unless I order it. And I don' t (order it).

Jorge: No somos felices. Es mejor que me vaya antes de que nos odiemos.
    We're not happy. It's better that I leave before we hate each other.

Ana: No quiero que te vayas hasta que nos odiemos. No me dejes.
    I don't want you to leave until we hate each other. Don't leave me.

Ana: Además, no debes abandonarme hasta que nazca la criatura.
    Besides, you shouldn't abandon me until the baby is born.

Jorge: Llámame después de que des a luz para que yo pueda conocer a mi hijo.
    Call me after you give birth so that I can meet / know my son.

Jorge: Te prometo mandar dinero para mantener a mi hijo siempre que nos dejes en paz a mí
y a mi nueva mujer.
    I promise to send you money to support my son as long as you leave my new wife and me alone.

Ana: Nunca los dejaré en paz ni a ti ni a la fulana esa hasta que yo esté muerta.
    I will never leave either you or that slut / so-and-so alone until I'm dead.

Ana: En serio. Y antes de que yo permita que veas a tu hijo, te mato.
    Seriously. And before I allow you to see your son, I'll kill you.

Jorge: No seas así. Tan pronto como seas razonable, cumpliré con mis responsabilidades.
    Don't be like that. As soon as you're reasonable, I will fulfill my responsibilities.

Ana: Seré razonable así que renuncies a esa mujer. *I will be reasonable as soon as you give up that woman.*

Ana: Podemos ser felices de nuevo con tal de que abandones a la fulana esa.
    We can be happy again provided that you abandon that slut / so-and-so.

Jorge: Nunca, jamás. Pero no quiero irme sin que me prometas ser razonable.
    Never ever. But I don't want to leave without you promising to be reasonable.

Ana: Quédate entonces.   *Stay then.*

Jorge: No. Adiós, Ana.   *No. Goodbye, Ana.*

H. A sample dialogue: Hijo y Madre

H: Mamá, ¿me das las llaves para que yo pueda ir a la bibilioteca?
    Mom, will you give the keys so that I can go to the library?

M: Te las doy siempre que llenes el depósito de gasolina. No queda suficiente para ir a la bibilioteca.
    I'll give them to you as long as you fill the gas tank. There's not enough left to go to the library.

H: Lo lleno con tal de que me des el dinero.   *I'll fill it provided that you give me some money.*

M: No tengo efectivo. Papá puede dártelo mañana después de que le presentes el recibo.
    I don't have any cash. Dad can give it to you tomorrow after you give him the receipt.

H: Pero no tengo dinero. ¿Quieres prestarme tu tarjeta de crédito de modo que yo pueda ir a la gasolinera?
    But I don't have any money. Do you want to lend me your credit card so that I can go to the gas station?

M: Te la presto en cuanto su hermana me la devuelva.   *I'll lend it to you as soon as your sister returns it to me.*

Se la di esta mañana para que esta tarde ella compre unas cosas para su clase.
    I gave it to her this morning in order for her to buy some things for her class.

H: ¿Cuándo debe llegar ella a casa?   *When should she get home?*

M: No llegará hasta que haga sus compras.   *She won't arrive until she makes her purchases.*

H: ¿Entonces no puedo usar el carro a menos que regrese con la tarjeta de crédito? ¡Qué lata!
    Then I can't use the car unless she returns with the credit card? What a pain!

M: ¿Por qué no la llamas de manera que ella sepa que la esperas?
    Why don't you call her so that she knows that you're waiting for her?

#8 Cuando

p.69

A. 1. <u>C</u> When / whenever my friends hear music, they dance.
2. <u>C</u> I take my laptop when / whenever I travel.
3. <u>F</u> When you go to college, buy me a tee shirt.
4. <u>C</u> We invite him to dinner when / whenever we make paella.
5. <u>F</u> My friend will pick me up at the airport when I call her.
6. <u>F</u> When their daughter turns 15, they will give her a big party.

p.70

B. 1. e / 2. a / 3. f / 4. c / 5. g / 6. h / 7. d / 8. b

1. Cuando él habla, debes escuchar.   *When / whenever he talks, you should listen.*
2. Les escribiré cuando me den su dirección.   *I will write them when they give me their address.*
3. Vamos de compras cuando tenemos dinero y tiempo libre.
   We go shopping when / whenever we have money and free time.
4. Cuando veas a Mercedes, salúdala de mi parte.   *When you see Mercedes, say hello to her for me.*
5. Cuando terminen el curso sobre la Guerra Civil, Uds. comprenderán mejor esa época.
   When you finish the course on the Civil War, you will understand that era better.
6. José se pone de mal humor cuando llueve mucho.
   Jose gets in a bad mood when / whenever it rains a lot.
7. Llámame cuando llegues a casa.   *Call me when you get home.*
8. Cuando vamos al cine, nos gusta salir a comer antes.
   When / whenever we go to the movies, we like to go out to eat before.

p.71

C. 1. ¿Usa / utiliza Ud. mantequilla cuando hace galletas?
2. Él siempre paga cuando vamos al cine.
3. Ella siempre se quita los zapatos cuando llega a casa.
4. Cuando él estudia, sale bien en los exámenes.
5. No siempre contestan cuando suena el teléfono.
   No siempre contestan el teléfono cuando suena.

D. 1. Cuando Ud. haga las galletas para la fiesta, no use / utilice mantequilla.
2. Él pagará cuando vayamos al cine mañana.
3. Cuando ella llegue al aeropuerto, nos llamará.
4. Cuando Uds. estudien para el examen, háganlo en la biblioteca.
5. Cuando el teléfono suene, (yo) lo contestaré.
6. Cuando vayas a España, visita los museos de arte.

p.72

E. 1. Cuando viajamos, el vecino cuida (a) nuestro perro.
2. Él espera comprar un carro cuando consiga / obtenga un trabajo / empleo / puesto.
3. Se enojarán / se enfadarán / se pondrán enojados / se pondrán enfadados cuando él les diga la noticia.
4. Se preocupan cuando (yo) no llamo.
5. Ella siempre trae flores cuando nos visita.
6. Cuando Ud. llegue a la esquina, dé vuelta / doble a la izquierda.

p.72

F. Answers will vary. See pp.231-232 for sample sentences.

p.73

G. Answers will vary. Some possibilities:

1. Veré a mis amigos en dos semanas cuando vengan a visitar.
   I will see my friends in two weeks when they come to visit.

2. Corren en el parque cuando hace buen tiempo.
   They run in the park when the weather is nice.

3. Por lo general voy de compras cuando mi ropa está gastada.
   I usually go shopping when my clothes are worn out.

4. Iré de compras cuando se abra el centro comercial.
   I will go shopping when the mall opens.

5. Siempre alquilamos un carro cuando visitamos a mi mamá en la Florida.
   We always rent a car when we visit my mother in Florida.

6. Va a viajar al Perú cuando haya ahorrado suficiente dinero.
   She will visit Perú when she has saved enough money.

7. Quiero salir cuando todo esté listo, siempre que sea antes de que comience la hora punta.
   I want to leave when everything is ready, as long as it's before rush hour begins.

8. Como no, señora. La llamo cuando tenga los resultados.
   Of course, ma'am. I'll call you when I have the results.

H. Answers will vary. An example:

Para llegar a mi casa, tome Ud. el autobús hasta mi barrio.
To get to my house, take the bus to my neighborhood.

Cuando vea la biblioteca, baje del autobús.
When you see the library, get off the bus.

Camine dos cuadras hacia el sur y doble a la izquierda en la calle 10.
Walk two blocks south and turn left at 10th St.

Siga derecho. Cuando pase la escuela, mire a su derecha. Verá mi casa en la esquina.
Continue straight. When you pass the school, look to your right. You will see my house on the corner.

Cuando llame a la puerta, mi perro ladrará mucho, pero no es tan feroz. No tenga miedo.
When you knock on the door, my dog will bark a lot, but he's not so ferocious. Don't be afraid.

#9 Aunque

p.75

A. 1. Aunque llueve mucho, me gusta el clima (de) aquí.

2. Vamos al cine todos los fines de semana aunque es caro.

3. Aunque ella saca buenas notas, le es difícil / es difícil para ella / le cuesta mucho.

4. Nos visitan raras veces / rara vez / con poca frecuencia, aunque no viven lejos.

p.76

B. 1. Aunque salgan temprano mañana, no llegarán hasta la noche.

2. Aunque sea hermoso / bello allí, prefieren quedarse en casa este fin de semana.

3. Aunque los misterios / las novelas de misterio sean / puedan ser interesantes, sólo / solamente leemos la ciencia ficción.

4. Él nunca responde aunque sepa la respuesta.

C. 1. Él desea / quiere tener un perro aunque viaja mucho.

2. Ella tiene un gato aunque tiene alergias.

3. Aunque se enojen / se enfaden / se pongan enojados / enfadados, tienes que decirles la verdad.

4. Aunque Uds. estén ocupados, llámennos por favor / hagan el favor de llamarnos.

5. El deseará / querrá manejar / conducir aunque haya mucho tráfico.

6. Aunque no conozco su casa / no he ido a su casa antes, la encontraré.

p.77

D. Answers will vary. See pp.231-232 for sample sentences.

p.78

E. 1. voy — *When I go downtown, I like to have lunch in a restaurant.*

2. esté — *We're going to work in the garden tomorrow even though it's raining.*

3. manejan — *Although they always drive too fast, they have not had any accidents.*

4. ha — *Even though he's looked a lot, he hasn't found a job.*

5. viajes — *When you travel to Colombia, buy me a CD of cumbias.*

6. están — *When they are nervous, they don't eat.*

7. cuesten — *I don't know how much the tickets for the concert will cost, but I will buy them even if / even though they cost $100.*

8. es — *Even though he's my friend, sometimes he drives me crazy.*
Note: *It's also common to say: Aunque sea mi amigo...: He may be my friend but.... (Use "es" for the puzzle.)*

9. lee — *When she reads novels, she always starts by reading the end.*

10. lea — *But I'm going to recommend that she not do that when she reads this mystery.*

p.79

F. 1. voy   2. esté   3. manejan   4. ha   5. viajes   6. están   7. cuesten   8. es   9. lee   10. lea

p.79

G. Answers will vary. Some possibilities:

1. Vas a acompañarme al cine, ¿verdad?

   Sí, voy, aunque debo quedarme en casa y preparar mi declaración de impuestos.
   Yes, although I should stay home and do my taxes.

2. ¿Crees lo que él dice?

   Sí. Aunque no me caiga bien, se lo creo.
   Yes. Although I may not like him, I believe him.

3. ¿Crees que podamos superar esta situación?

   Sí, creo que podemos superarla aunque cueste mucho.
   Yes, I think we can overcome / get through it although it may be difficult.

p.80

H.

El pueblo está emocionado que el presidente / la presidenta visite la semana que viene
aunque conlleva dificultades.

*The town is excited that the president will visit next week, **although it entails** difficulties.*

Aunque seamos un pueblo pequeño, sabemos responder a los problemas. Un problema es el tráfico.

***Although we may** be a small town, we know how to address the problems. One problem is traffic.*

Aunque siempre **hay** muchos problemas de tráfico dondequiera que el presidente /la presidenta vaya,
tenemos una solución.

***Although there are** always traffic problems wherever the president goes, we have a solution.*

Aunque algunas personas se quejen, hemos decidido cerrar todas las calles a carros, incluso al del
presidente /de la presidenta.

***Although some people may complain**, we've decided to close all the streets to cars, including the president's.*

Aunque sea una solución rara, para que el presidente / la presidenta no tenga que caminar y para
que todos puedan verlo/la entrar al pueblo, hemos aquilado un elefante.

***Although it may be** a strange solution, so that the president does not have to walk and so that everyone can see
him / her enter the town, we've rented an elephant.*

Andará en él desde el aeropuerto al centro, y **aunque esté lloviendo**, el presidente / la presidenta
estará bien porque montará bajo un palio encima del elefante.

*He / she will go on it from the airport to downtown, **even if it's raining**, the president will be fine
because he / she will ride under a canopy on top of the elephant.*

Cuando él / ella llegue al centro, habrá una fiesta con discursos, presentaciones y música.

When he / she arrives downtown, there will be a party with speeches, presentations and music.

Aunque el presidente / la presidenta visite 5.000 pueblos durante su mandato, creemos que
siempre recordará nuestro pueblito.

***Even if the president visits** 5,000 towns during his / her term, we think that he / she will always remember
our little town.*

#10 Non-existent People and Objects

p.81

A.

 __X__ 1. No hay (nadie) aquí que <u>conozca</u> Bolivia.

 There's nobody here who's been to Bolivia.

 _____ 2. Sólo hay (dos de mis vecinos) que no <u>tienen</u> perros.

 There are only two of my neighbors who don't have dogs.

 __X__ 3. No existe (ninguna universidad) en este estado que <u>dé</u> cursos de maya.

 Not a single / Not one / No university exists in this state that gives classes on Mayan / Mayan classes.

 __X__ 4. No tenemos (computadora) que <u>funcione</u>.

 We don't have a computer that works.

p.82

B. 1. No hay nadie en la oficina que hable ruso.

 2. No tengo ningún libro que explique la historia mexicana.

 3. No conozco a nadie que trabaje allí.

 4. Ellos desean / quieren comprar una casa en este barrio pero
    no pueden encontrar una que tenga cuatro recámaras / alcobas / dormitorios.

C. 1. No existe un equipo que **tenga** mejores jugadores.

 2. Compro el carro que no **usa** mucha gasolina.

 3. No hay nadie en su familia que se **haya graduado** de la universidad.

 4. Ella nunca ha escrito un / ningún libro que **sea** aburrido.

 5. Compramos pantalones, pero no zapatos.

p.83

D. Answers will vary. See pp.231-232 for sample sentences.

p.84

E.

I hate school. I don't have a single teacher who isn't / any teachers who aren't boring. There's not a single class that is / there are no classes that are worthwhile. There are no dishes in the cafeteria that don't turn my stomach / that aren't disgusting. I don't know anyone who understands me.

Answers will vary. An example:

Queremos un buen carro que sea económico, y estoy molesta que no podamos encontrar ninguno. No hay un ningún carro nuevo que cueste menos de $20.000, y los híbridos y los eléctricos cuestan aun más. No hay ninguno que sea cómodo, que tenga aire acondicionado y que también obtenga más de 35 millas por galón. Además mi color favorito es morado, y no existe ninguno que sea morado.

We want a good car that's economical, and I'm irritated that we can't find one. There is no new car that costs less than $20,000, and hybrids and electric ones cost even more. There isn't a single one that's comfortable, has air conditioning and also gets more than 35 miles per gallon. In addition, my favorite color is purple and none / not one exists that's purple.

Negatives

p.85

A. 1. nunca   2. nada   3. ningún   4. nadie   5. de ninguna manera

6. no   7. ni....ni   8. tampoco   9. ninguna parte

p.86

B.

   Note: **In the following sentences, the word order given is not the only possibility.**
   Negative elements can appear in any order, but one negative must precede the verb.

1. No quiero ver ninguna película con ese actor.

2. No tengo ninguna razón para llamarlo.

3. Esperamos que tú tampoco le digas nada a él.
   or   Esperamos que tú no le digas nada a él tampoco.

4. Nunca fue a ninguna parte con nadie.
   or   No fue nunca a ninguna parte con nadie.

5. De ninguna manera dijo eso ella.
   or   Ella no dijo eso de ninguna manera.

6. No quieren visitar ni a Ud. ni a mí.

7. Me alegro de que no hayas perdido nada.

C.

   Note: **In the following sentences, the word order given is not the only possibility.**
   Negative elements can appear in any order, but one negative must precede the verb.

1. No, no he conocido nunca a nadie famoso.	*No, I've never met anyone famous.*
No, nunca he conocido a ninguna persona famosa.	*No, I've never met anyone famous.*
2. No dejaron nada.	*They didn't leave anything.*
3. No, no es importante que nadie sepa nada sobre esto.	*No, it's not important that anyone knows anything about this.*
4. No te lo diré nunca (jamás).	*I will never tell you [it].*
Jamás / Nunca te lo diré.	*I will never tell you [it].*
5. No queremos ni éstos ni ésos.	*We don't want either these or those.*
No queremos ninguno de los libros.	*We don't want any of the books.*
No queremos ningún libro.	*We don't want any book.*
6. No los he llevado a ninguna parte.	*I haven't taken them anywhere.*

#11 Hypothetical People & Objects

p.88

A.

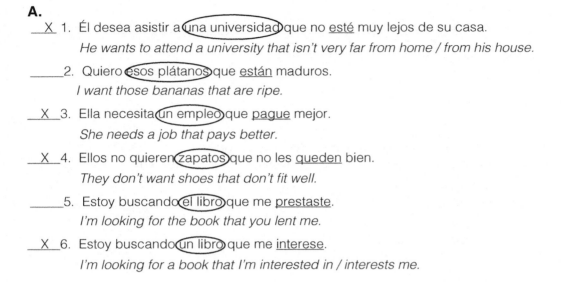

__X__ 1. Él desea asistir a una universidad que no <u>esté</u> muy lejos de su casa.
He wants to attend a university that isn't very far from home / from his house.

_____2. Quiero esos plátanos que <u>están</u> maduros.
I want those bananas that are ripe.

__X__3. Ella necesita un empleo que <u>pague</u> mejor.
She needs a job that pays better.

__X__4. Ellos no quieren zapatos que no les <u>queden</u> bien.
They don't want shoes that don't fit well.

_____5. Estoy buscando el libro que me <u>prestaste</u>.
I'm looking for the book that you lent me.

__X__6. Estoy buscando un libro que me <u>interese</u>.
I'm looking for a book that I'm interested in / interests me.

p.89

B. 1. Necesitan un intérprete que **hable** inglés, español y maya.

  2. ¿Venden juguetes que **sean** seguros?

  3. Deseo / Quiero ver una película que a ti te **guste** también.

  4. Ella busca un perro adulto / maduro que **necesite** un hogar y que no **sea** muy grande.

C. 1. El equipo desea / quiere jugadores que **sepan** jugar bien.

  2. Compro un carro / coche que no **usa** / **utiliza** mucha gasolina. Lo recojo mañana.

  3. Vamos a una película que nos **haga** reír.

  4. Buscan una niñera que **maneje** / **conduzca** y que **pueda** trabajar en las noches / de noche.

  5. Deseo / Quiero hablar con la persona que **escribió** esto.

p.91

E. Answers will vary. See pp.231-232 for sample sentences.

p.92

F. Examples:

Soy una extraterrestre sensible y atractiva que lleva cinco años en su bello planeta. Quiero practicar las lenguas humanas y comprender mejor sus costumbres. En mi tiempo libre me gusta conjugar verbos y criar pulpos.

I am a sensitive and attractive extraterrestrial who has been on your beautiful planet for five years. I want to practice human languages and better understand your customs. In my free time I like to conjugate verbs and raise octopuses.

Busco un hombre que **sea** curioso y libre de prejuicios. Quiero un compañero que **sepa** muchos idiomas y que **hable** despacio y claramente. Prefiero un hombre a quien no le **guste** comer mariscos y a quien le **encante** caminar en la playa y mirar las estrellas.

I'm looking for a man who's curious and open-minded. I want a companion who knows many languages and who speaks slowly and clearly. I prefer a man who does not like to eat seafood and who loves to walk on the beach and look at the stars.

p.93

G. An example:

Sueño con una casita que **esté** en uno de los pueblitos blancos de España. Quiero una casa pequeña que **tenga** un patio amplio y pintoresco. Prefiero una casa que **dé** a una plaza o mejor que **tenga** una vista al mar. El pueblo debe ser un lugar que **sea** tranquilo y en el que no **haya** mucho tráfico.

I dream about a little house that's in one of the white villages of Spain. I want a small house that has a large and picturesque patio. I prefer a house that faces onto a plaza or better yet that has a view of the sea. The town should be a place that's peaceful and in which there's not a lot of traffic.

H. An example:

La hija de José y Sonia: Eugenia es una niña muy inteligente. Sabe tocar tres instrumentos. Es muy creativa. Tiene miedo a la oscuridad y sufre de pesadillas—entonces grita y muerde. Pero de día es tranquila y cariñosa.

José and Sonia's daughter: Eugenia is a very intelligent child. She knows how to play three instruments. She's very creative. She's afraid of the dark and suffers from nightmares—then she screams and bites. But by day she is calm and affectionate.

Buscan una niñera que **sea** responsable y comprensiva. Necesitan una persona que **sepa** manejar para llevar a Eugenia a sus clases de música. Es preciso que tengan una niñera paciente que **pueda** responder a los temores de la niña. La niñera perfecta es alguien que **aprecie** sus buenas calidades y que **se mantenga** en calma cuando ella da una rabieta.

They are looking for a nanny who is responsible and understanding. They need a person who knows how to drive in order to take Eugenia to her music classes. It's necessary to have a patient nanny who can deal with the child's fears. The perfect nanny is someone who appreciates her good qualities and keeps calm when she throws a tantrum.

#12 "Si" Clauses

p.95

A.

1. Don't do heavy exercise if it's hot out / the weather's hot.

2. If there is a lot of traffic, we're going to take a different / another route.

3. If you (all) arrive late tonight, please don't call me until morning.

4. We will go by train if we have (the) time.

B.

1. Si tienes hambre, pide / ordena una pizza.

2. Voy a quedarme aquí, si (a Uds.) no les importa.

3. Si (a Ud.) no le gusta el hotel, dígame.

4. Si los vemos antes de la fiesta, los invitaremos.

p.96

C. Answers will vary. Some possibilities:

1. Si hace mucho calor, prefiero no trabajar afuera.

   If it's hot out, I prefer to not work outside.

2. Dámelo si tú no lo quieres.

   Give it to me if you don't want it.

3. Si hay tiempo mañana, vete a la tienda por comestibles.

   If there's time tomorrow, go to the store for groceries.

4. Irán de vacaciones a España si bajan los precios.

   They will go on vacation to Spain if the prices come down.

D. An example:

María va a preparar pescado, pero si no hay pescado fresco en el mercado ese día, hará lasaña.
María is going to make fish, but if there isn't any fresh fish in the market that day, she'll make lasagne.

Si Juan decide no traer a una amiga, María piensa invitar a su vecina Sonia.
If Juan decides not to bring a date, María plans to invite her neighbor Sonia.

María quiere servir un buen vino español si puede encontrar uno que no sea muy caro.
María wants to serve a good Spanish wine if she can find one that's not too expensive.

Si los vinos españoles son muy caros, buscará uno argentino.
If the Spanish wines are too expensive, she'll look for an Argentine one.

Para postre va a preparar un pastel de chocolate, pero si el pastel no sale bien, servirá helado.
For dessert she's going to make a chocolate cake, but if the cake doesn't turn out, she'll serve ice cream.

#13 Verbs of Influence—A Shortcut

p.97

A. 1. me   2. nos   3. le   4. le   5. les   6. nos   7. les   8. le

B.

1. My teacher advises me to practice more.
2. Don't you let him drive your car?
3. I don't let / allow / permit my sister to use my things.
4. I will have them paint the house.
5. Do you suggest we take a taxi?

p.98

C.

1. Mi profesor aconseja que yo practique más.
2. ¿No dejas que él maneje tu carro?
3. No permito que mi hermana use mis cosas.
4. Haré que pinten la casa.
5. ¿Sugieres que tomemos un taxi?

D.

1. No permiten que viajemos solos.
   No nos permiten viajar solos.

2. Prohiben que sus empleados hagan llamadas personales.
   Les prohiben a sus empleados hacer llamadas personales.

3. ¿Recomienda (Ud.) que (yo) la llame?
   ¿Me recomienda (Ud.) llamarla?

#14 Indirect Commands

p.99

A. 1. Have a good time! / May you have a good time!
2. Don't fall!
3. Let's leave / go out together!
4. Have your parents call us!
5. Let / Have her clean her own room!
6. Let / Have the employees smoke outside!

p.100

B. 1. ¡Diviértanse!   *Have fun!*
2. ¡No te caigas!   *Don't fall!*
3. ¡Salgamos juntos!   *Let's leave / go out together!*

C. 1. —No hay autobús a esa hora.
    "There isn't a bus at that hour."
    —Entonces, ¡que caminen!
    "Then let / have them walk!"

2. —Nos vamos.
    "We're going / leaving."
    —Bueno. ¡Que lo pasen bien!
    "OK. Have a good time!"

3. —Sacaron muy malas notas.
    "They got very bad grades."
    —¡Que estudien más!
    "Have them study more!"

4. —No puedo terminar a tiempo.
    "I can't finish on time."
    —Pues, ¡que te ayude él!
    "Well, have him help you!"

p.101

D. Answers will vary. Some possibilities:

1. No es mi turno para poner la mesa.
    It's not my turn to set the table.
    ¡Que la pongas tú!
    You set it!

2. No es bueno que ella haga tanto.
    It's not good that she's doing so much.
    ¡Que la ayuden ellos!
    Have them help her!

3. ¿Estás diciéndome mentiras?
    Are you telling me lies.
    ¡Que seas sincero conmigo!
    Be honest with me!

4. ¿Por qué tienes tanta prisa?
    Why are you in such a hurry?
    ¡Que vayas más despacio!
    Slow down!

E. Answers will vary. Some possibilities:

1. —¡Ay! ¡Casi me caí!
    "Oh! I almost fell!"
    —¡Que tenga(s) más cuidado!
    "Be more careful!"

2. —La boda va a ser afuera.
    "The wedding is going to be outside."
    —¡Que no llueva!
    "Let it not rain!"

3. —No tengo bastante dinero.
    "I don't have enough money."
    —¡Que pidas un aumento!
    "Ask for a raise."

4. —Ya me voy.
    "I'm leaving / going."
    —¡Que te vaya bien!
    "May it go well with you! / Fare-thee-well!"

p.102

F. Answers will vary. See pp.231-232 for sample sentences.

#15 The "-Ever"s

p.104

A. 1. Whatever / no matter what it costs, it's worth it.
2. However cheap / no matter how cheap it may be, don't buy it.
3. Any mother would say the same (thing).
4. Wherever / no matter where he takes his car, they won't be able to repair it.
5. We will see any / whichever movie you all are interested in.
6. Whatever!
7. Whoever pays, (is the one who) decides.
8. "Which of these shirts do you prefer?" "Whichever / any of them. It's all the same to me."
9. Juan will do whatever he feels like.
10. However / no matter how slowly and clearly I speak, they never understand me.

p.105

B. 1. La policía lo encontrará adondequiera que él vaya.   2. Quienquiera que la conozca, la admira.
3. Por mucho que trabajen, su dinero no alcanza para pagar sus cuentas.
4. Cualquier casa que compren, la harán atractiva y confortable.

C. Answers will vary. An example:

María:	¿Adónde quieres ir de vacaciones?
Juan:	Adondequiera, mientras que no sea muy caro.
María:	El precio de un crucero incluye todo—comida, alojamiento y transporte. ¿Qué te parece?
Juan:	Lo que quieras. ¿Pero no es caro?
María:	Depende de adónde vamos.
Juan:	¿No hay algo más económico?
María:	Pues, supongo que podríamos ir de camping. ¿Adónde te interesa ir? ¿A la playa, a la sierra, o al desierto?
Juan:	Cualquiera de los tres—me da igual.
María:	Por indeciso que seas, hay que planear. Hay que hacer reservaciones aun para sitios de camping. Por ejemplo, ¿cuándo podemos ir?
Juan:	Cuandoquiera. Tú decides y avísame nomás.

María:	*Where do you want to go on vacation?*
Juan:	*Wherever, as long as it's not too expensive.*
María:	*The price of a cruise includes everything—food, lodging, transportation. What do you think?*
Juan:	*Whatever you want. But isn't it expensive?*
María:	*It depends on where we go.*
Juan:	*Isn't there something cheaper?*
María:	*Well, I suppose we could go camping. Where are you interested in going? To the beach, the mountains or the desert?*
Juan:	*Any of the three. It's all the same to me.*
María:	*However indecisive you may be, one has to plan. You have to make reservations even for campsites. For example, when can we go?*
Juan:	*Whenever. You decide and let me know.*

p.106

D.

cualquier niño ....any / whichever child / boy	dondequiera ....wherever
diga lo que diga .....whatever you /he/she/it may say ......no matter what you /he/she/it says	cuandoquiera ....whenever
	por feo que canten ...however / no matter how ugly / awful they may sing
cualquiera ....whatever / whichever	
lo que sea...............whatever	por fácil que sea.......however / no matter how easy it is / may be
cualesquiera...........whichever ones	
lo que quieras ....whatever you (may) want	quienquiera ....whoever / whomever

#16 Expressions of Possibility (Single Clause)

p.108

A. Tal vez ....a. through f.

    Quizás ....a. through f.

    Puede ser que ....b., d., f.

    A lo mejor ....a., c., e.

    Qué sorpresa que ....a., c., e.

    Es sorprendente que ....b., d., f.

    Posiblemente ....b., d., f.

    Quizá ....a. through f.

Sample sentences

with verbs of influence/volition:
Ella quiere que su hermana la visite.
Él prefiere que su hijo estudie para ser médico.
La ley requiere que todos usemos cinturones
    de seguridad.

She wants her sister to visit her.
He prefers that his son study to be a doctor.
The law requires that we all use seat belts.

with verbs of emotion:
Él se preocupa de que su esposa esté muy enferma.
Me molesta que los vecinos hagan mucho ruido.
Estamos nerviosos de que nadie asista a la conferencia.
Estoy emocionada de que salgamos mañana
    para Madrid.
Me sorprende que ellos digan eso.

He's worried that his wife is very ill.
It bothers me that the neighbors make a lot of noise.
We're nervous that no one will attend the lecture.
I'm excited that we're leaving for Madrid tomorrow.

It surprises me that they say that.

with impersonal expressions:
Es feo que ellos se comporten así.
Es agradable que no llueva
    y que podamos comer en el patio.
Es preciso que Uds. terminen a tiempo.
No es imposible que haya una huelga.
Es emocionante que nos den una fiesta.

It's awful that they behave like this.
It's pleasant that it's not raining
    and that we can eat on the patio.
It's necessary for you all to finish on time.
It's not impossible that there will be a strike.
It's exciting that they are giving us a party.

with verbs of doubt/negation:
Dudo que haya algún problema.
María no cree que eso sea buena idea.
No es verdad que esta tienda cobre más
    que aquélla.

I doubt that there's any problem.
María doesn't think that that's a good idea.
It's not true that this store charges more than that one.

with verbs that assert a truth:
No dudamos que se esfuerzan.
Creo que debes hacerlo.
Es cierto que cuesta mucho.

We don't doubt that they are making an effort.
I think you should do it.
It's true that it costs a lot.

with a compound verbs (in subjunctive}:
No me gusta que esté lloviendo.
Me alegro de que no haya nevado mucho este invierno.

I don't like that it's raining.
I'm glad that it hasn't snowed much this winter.

with "para," "para que" or other expressions of intended purpose:
Voy al supermercado por los ingredientes
    para que tú puedas hacer el pastel.
Ellos se levantan temprano para hacer todos
    sus quehaceres.
Ella trabaja mucho en su jardín de modo que esté bonito.
Él mantiene su carro con cuidado de forma que corra bien.
Queremos salir bien en el examen
    a fin de que el profesor nos dé una buena nota.
Deben cambiar la ley de manera que sea más justa.

I'm going to the supermarket for the ingredients
    so that you can make the cake.
They get up early to do all their chores.

She works a lot in her garden so that it looks nice.
He maintains his car carefully so that it runs well.
We want to do well on the test
    so that the teacher gives us a good grade.
They should change the law so that it is fairer.

with conjunctions that introduce contingencies:
Ella va a leer hasta que lleguen.
Antes de que lo compres, enséñamelo.
Sabré por quién votar en cuanto termine el debate.

She is going to read until they arrive.
Before you buy it, show it to me.
I will know who to vote for as soon as the debate is over.

Sample sentences continue on p. 232.

Sample sentences, cont.

with "cuando":

"Cuando" with indicative...

Cuando **sirven** pizza, también sirven cerveza. — *When they serve pizza, they also serve beer.*

Cuando **hace** buen tiempo, — *When the weather's nice,*
    es bueno echar una siesta en la hamaca. — *it's good to take a nap in the hammock.*

Cuando el equipo **juega** en su ciudad, suelen ganar. — *When the team plays at home, they tend to win.*

Cuando uno se lastima la espalda, lo mejor es guardar cama. — *When one hurts one's back, bed rest is best.*

"Cuando" with subjunctive:

Cuando vengan los niños esta tarde, sírvales Ud. pizza. — *When the children come this afternoon, serve them pizza.*

Él cortará el césped mañana o pasado mañana — *He'll mow the lawn tomorrow or the day after*
    cuando **haga** buen tiempo. — *when the weather is good.*

Espero que el equipo gane — *I hope the team wins when it plays in the championship.*
    cuando **juegue** en el campeonato.

La invitaré a la fiesta cuando la vea. — *I will invite her to the party when I see her.*

with "aunque":

"Aunque" with indicative...

Aunque ella tiene gripe, se niega a guardar cama. — *Although she has the flu, she refuses to stay in bed.*

La invitaré a la fiesta aunque no creo que venga. — *I will invite her to the party, although I don't think she'll come.*

"Aunque" with subjunctive...

Aunque tu hermano sepa reparar carros, — *Although your brother may know how to fix cars,*
    prefiero ir a un taller. — *I prefer to go to a shop.*

No van a comprarlo aunque sea una ganga. — *They aren't going to buy it even though it may be a bargain.*

about a person or object that doesn't exist:

No se ha encontrado ninguna medicina que pueda curar esa enfermedad.
    No medicine has been found that can cure that illness.

Actualmente, no hay artista que compare con Picasso.
    Currently, there is no artist who compares with Picasso.

about a hypothetical person or object:

Ella desea vivir en una casa que esté ubicada en la copa de un árbol.
    She wants to live in a house that's located in a treetop.

Buscan novias que sean inteligentes, guapas y ricas.
    They are looking for girlfriends who are smart, attractive and rich.

in the present tense with "si":

Si quieren desayunarse, sírveles café con leche y pan dulce.
    If they want to eat breakfast, serve them coffee with milk and a sweet roll.

Ella ganará si todos votan.
    She will win if everyone votes.

an indirect command:

¡Que pague Juan la cuenta!   *Let Juan pay the bill.*

¡Que te diviertas!   *Have a good time!*

How to Form the Past Subjunctive

p.113

A.

infinitive	ellos, preterite	yo, past subjunctive
1. hablar	hablaron	hablara
2. bailar	bailaron	bailara
3. pasar	pasaron	pasara
4. dejar	dejaron	dejara
5. tomar	tomaron	tomara
6. llevarse	se llevaron	me llevara
7. perderse	se perdieron	me perdiera
8. encontrar	encontraron	encontrara
9. pensar	pensaron	pensara
10. comer	comieron	comiera
11. creer	creyeron	creyera
12. querer	quisieron	quisiera
13. ir, ser	fueron	fuera
14. vivir	vivieron	viviera
15. asistir	asistieron	asistiera
16. seguir	siguieron	siguiera
17. salir	salieron	saliera
18. poner	pusieron	pusiera
19. ver	vieron	viera
20. conocer	conocieron	conociera

p.114

B.

infinitive	yo,	tú	él, ella, Ud.	nosotros, nosotras	ellos, ellas, Uds.
1. hablar	hablara	hablaras	hablara	habláramos	hablaran
2. invitar	invitara	invitaras	invitara	invitáramos	invitaran
3. pensar	pensara	pensaras	pensara	pensáramos	pensaran
4. comprender	comprendiera	comprendieras	comprendiera	comprendiéramos	comprendieran
5. comer	comiera	comieras	comiera	comiéramos	comieran
6. poder	pudiera	pudieras	pudiera	pudiéramos	pudieran
7. vivir	viviera	vivieras	viviera	viviéramos	vivieran
8. ser, ir	fuera	fueras	fuera	fuéramos	fueran
9. estar	estuviera	estuvieras	estuviera	estuviéramos	estuvieran
10. tener	tuviera	tuvieras	tuviera	tuviéramos	tuvieran
11. vender	vendiera	vendieras	vendiera	vendiéramos	vendieran
12. leer	leyera	leyeras	leyera	leyéramos	leyeran
13. hacer	hiciera	hicieras	hiciera	hiciéramos	hicieran
14. decir	dijera	dijeras	dijera	dijéramos	dijeran
15. dar	diera	dieras	diera	diéramos	dieran
16. caerse	se cayera	te cayeras	se cayera	nos cayéramos	se cayeran
17. ver	viera	vieras	viera	viéramos	vieran
18. conocer	conociera	conocieras	conociera	conociéramos	conocieran
19. saber	supiera	supieras	supiera	supiéramos	supieran
20. querer	quisiera	quisieras	quisiera	quisiéramos	quisieran
21. volver	volviera	volvieras	volviera	volviéramos	volvieran
22. seguir	siguiera	siguieras	siguiera	siguiéramos	siguieran
23. haber	hubiera	hubieras	hubiera	hubiéramos	hubieran
24. servir	sirviera	sirvieras	sirviera	sirviéramos	sirvieran
25. morir	muriera	murieras	muriera	muriéramos	murieran

p.115

C.

_X_ 1. viva   _X_ 7. ayudáramos

____ 2. conocíamos   _X_ 8. vengan

____ 3. dormimos   ____ 9. ayudamos

____ 4. jugaré   ____ 10. compra

_X_ 5. escribieras   ____ 11. invitaste

_X_ 6. preguntases   _X_ 12. cantaras

D.

1. diera	2. estuviera	3. fuéramos	4. pudieras
5. viviera	6. durmieran	7. tuviera	8. hubiera

p.116

E.

1. estuvieras	5. cerrara	9. escucharan	13. te divirtieras
2. buscara	6. dieran	10. hiciéramos	14. fuéramos
3. jugáramos	7. viera	11. oyera	15. miraras
4. abriera	8. supiera	12. sirvieran	16. lloviera

p.117

F.

1. Ojalá que yo comprendiera esto.	*I wish / If only I understood this.*
2. Ojalá que llegáramos a tiempo.	*I wish / If only we arrived on time.*
3. Ojalá que no te pusieras tan nervioso.	*I wish / If only you didn't so get nervous.*
4. Ojalá que yo supiera las respuestas.	*I wish / If only I knew the answers.*
5. Ojalá que mis hijos estudiaran más.	*I wish / If only my kids / children studied more.*
6. Ojalá que el bebé durmiera toda la noche.	*I wish / If only the baby slept all night.*
7. Ojalá que hubiera una fiesta.	*I wish / If only there were a party.*
8. Ojalá que ellos ganaran la lotería.	*I wish / If only they won the lottery.*
9. Ojalá que sacaras buenas notas en tus clases.	*I wish / If only you got good grades in your classes.*
10. Ojalá que él bailara mejor.	*I wish / If only he danced better.*

Preterite and Imperfect

p.124

A.

1. quise / quería

2. ¿mandaste? / ¿mandabas?

3. sugirió / sugería

4. dijimos / decíamos

5. insistieron / insistían

6. me alegré / me alegraba

7. ¿estuviste triste? / ¿estabas triste?

8. le molestó / le molestaba

9. tuvimos miedo / teníamos miedo

10. se preocuparon / se preocupaban

11. fue bueno / era bueno

12. fue increíble / era increíble

13. dudé / dudaba

14. ¿no creíste? / ¿no creías?

15. no quiso decir / no quería decir

16. negamos / negábamos

17. no creí / no creía

18. no estuvieron seguros / no estaban seguros

#1. Influence/Volition
#2. Emotion
#3. Impersonal Expressions
#4. Doubt and Negation

p.126 **Note:** The choice between preterite and imperfect may depend on your interpretation of the sentence's context.

A.

1. Queríamos que hubiera paz en el mundo. — *We wanted there to be peace in the world.*
2. El general mandó que los soldados atacaran. — *The general ordered the soldiers to attack.*
3. Sugerí que lo llamaras. — *I suggested that you call him.*
4. Dijeron que yo viniera. — *They told me to come.*
5. ¿Aconsejaste que estudiaran más ciencias? — *Did you advise them to study more sciences?*
6. Nos enojaba que siempre llegaras tarde. — *It made us mad that you always arrived late.*
7. La doctora se preocupaba de que su paciente no se mejorara. — *The doctor (was) worried that her patient would not get better / was not getting better.*
8. El empleado estaba molesto que no le pagaran más. — *The employee was irritated that they did not pay him more.*
9. ¿Estabas emocionada de que ellos se casaran? — *Were you excited that they got / were going to get married?*
10. Los niños tenían miedo de que su perro estuviera perdido. — *The children were afraid that their dog was lost.*
11. Fue horrible que me dijeras eso. — *It was terrible that you said that to me.*
12. Fue fantástico que nos visitaran. — *It was wonderful that they visited us.*

p.127

B.

1. El taxista se inquietó / inquietaba que el precio de la gasolina subiera. — *The taxi driver (was) worried that the price of gas would go up.*
2. Los niños estaban / estuvieron alegres de que hubiera una fiesta de cumpleaños. — *The children were happy that there was / would be a birthday party.*
3. A Luz María le encantaba salir a bailar. — *Luz María loved going out to dance / to go dancing.*
4. Estábamos contentos que pudieras visitarnos. — *We were happy that you could visit us.*
5. Lamenté / lamentaba / sentí / sentía que estuvieran enfermos. — *I was sorry that they were sick.*
6. ¿Tenías miedo de que no vinieran? — *Were you afraid that they didn't / wouldn't come?*
7. Mi amigo se quejó de que el viaje costara mucho. — *My friend complained that the trip cost so much.*
8. Me encantó / encantaba que hubiera música en vivo. — *I loved that there was live music.*

p.128

C.

1. ¿Querías / quisiste que yo pusiera la mesa?
2. Ella no permitió / permitía que sus hijos esquiaran solos.
3. Él quería ir a la fiesta pero tuvo / tenía que trabajar.
4. La escuela recomendó que los estudiantes tuvieran su propia computadora.
5. Ella necesitó / necesitaba salir temprano.
6. Pedimos que nos llamaran el martes.
7. Sugirieron que hiciéramos una reserva/reservación.
8. La compañía /empresa requería / requirió que sus empleados tomaran pruebas / una prueba de detección de drogas.
9. La familia deseaba / quería verlo.
10. No me gustó / gustaba que viajaras solo/sola.
11. Ella estaba / estuvo orgullosa de que sus hijos sacaran buenas notas.
12. La clase se preocupaba / se preocupó / estaba preocupada / estuvo preocupada que el profesor / la profesora / el maestro / la maestra les /le diera un examen / una prueba.
13. Él tenía vergüenza / tuvo vergüenza / estaba avergonzado de / estuvo avergonzado admitirlo.

Cont. on p. 238.

p.129 C. cont.

14. ¿No te alegrabas / estabas contento/a de que no lloviera?
15. Tenían miedo de decirle la verdad.
16. Sentía / Lamentaba / sentí / lamenté que tuvieras un dolor de cabeza / te doliera la cabeza.
17. Estaban / estuvieron furiosos/as de que saliera mal.
18. Era / Fue peligroso que los niños jugaran en la calle.
19. No fue / era correcto que ellos lo dejaran solo.
20. Fue / Era verdad que él sabía conducir / manejar.
    Pero no fue / era verdad que él condujera / manejara bien.
21. Fue / Era increíble que costara tanto.
22. Él no creía / creyó que fuera verdad.
23. Dudaban / Dudaron que ella supiera cocinar paella.
24. No estábamos / estuvimos seguros/as de que vinieran a la fiesta.
25. Ella no creía / pensaba que debiéramos trabajar allí.
26. Era / Fue triste que se acabara.

p.130

D., E., F., G. Answers will vary. See pp.262-264 for examples.

p.131

H. Answers will vary. An example:

Juan: Yo creo que Chile va a ganar la Copa Mundial.
María: Estás loco. Es imposible que Chile **gane**.
Juan: No me gusta que **hables** así. Recomiendo que **tengas** la mente abierta.
María: No es que yo **quiera** que Chile **pierda**, pero hay muchos equipos que son mejores.
Juan: No creo que **haya** otro equipo que **se esfuerce** tanto.
María: Al contrario, considera los equipos de España, México, Argentina, Italia, y muchos otros.
Juan: Pues, de todos modos, espero que Chile derrote a esos equipos.
María: Y yo espero que no **quedes** muy desilusionado, porque es muy improbable que tu sueño **se realice**.

Juan: *I think Chile is going to win the World Soccer Cup.*
María: *You're crazy. It's imposible that Chile will win.*
Juan: *I don't like you to talk like that. I recommend that you have an open mind.*
María: *It's not that I want Chile to lose, but there are many teams that are better.*
Juan: *I don't think there is any team that makes a greater effort.*
María: *On the contrary, consider the teams of Spain, Mexico, Argentina, Italy and many others.*
Juan: *Well, anyway, I hope Chile defeats those teams.*
María: *And I hope you aren't too disappointed, because it's very unlikely that your dream will come true.*

I. Answers will vary. An example:

Yo dije que yo creía que Chile iba a ganar la Copa Mundial.
María dijo que yo estaba loco, que era imposible que Chile **ganara**.
Yo respondí que no me gustó que ella **hablara** así. Recomendé que ella **tuviera** la mente abierta.
Ella dijo que no era que ella **quisiera** que Chile **perdiera**, pero que había muchos equipos que eran mejores.
Yo dije que yo no creía que **hubiera** otro equipo que **se esforzara** tanto.
María dijo que yo debía considerar los equipos de España, México, Argentina, Italia, y muchos otros.
Entonces yo dije que yo esperaba que Chile **derrotara** a esos equipos.
Y María dijo que ella esperaba que yo no **quedara** muy desilusionado, porque era muy improbable que mi sueño **se realizara**.

Cont. on p. 239.

p.131

I., cont. from p.238.

I said that I thought that Chile was going to win the World Soccer Cup.
María said that I was crazy, that it was imposible that Chile would win.
I answered that I didn't like her to talk like that. I recommended that she have an open mind.
She said that it wasn't that she wanted Chile to lose but that there were many teams that were better.
I said that I didn't think there were any teams that made a greater effort / tried harder.
María said that I should consider the teams of Spain, Mexico, Argentina, Italy and many others.
Then I said that I hoped Chile would defeat those teams.
And María said that she hoped that I wouldn't end up too disappointed, because it was very unlikely that my dream would come true.

p.132

J. Answers will vary. An example:

María: ¿Recuerdas cuando celebramos nuestro aniversario en el Café XX?
　　　 Me gustó que me **invitaras** a cenar allí.
Juan: ¡El Café XX! No me gustó nada. Me sorprendió que los platos **fueran** tan pequeños
　　　 y que todo **saliera** tan caro.
María: No dudo que fue caro, pero me encantó que el ambiente **fuera** tan romántico y que la comida
　　　 estuviera tan rica (aunque los platos sí eran pequeños).
　　　 ¿Por qué no vamos allí este fin de semana?
Juan: Pues, me alegro que te **gustara**, pero no quiero cenar allí de nuevo.

María:　Do you remember when we celebrated our anniversary at Café XX?
　　　　 I liked that you invited me to have dinner there.
Juan:　 ¡Café XX! I didn't like it at all. It surprised me that the servings were so small and that it turned out to be so expensive.
María:　I don't doubt that it was expensive, but I loved that the atmosphere was so romantic and that the food was so delicious (although the servings were small.)
　　　　 Why don't we go there this weekend?
Juan:　 Well, I'm glad that you liked it, but I don't want to eat dinner there again.

p.133

Nota: Ojalá

A.

　　1. I hope she helps / will help them with their homework.
　　2. I hope they've already arrived without any problem and are now at their hotel.
　　3. I wish he didn't / If only he wouldn't say such things.
　　4. I wish / If only I hadn't told my sister-in-law that.
　　5. I hope he gets / will get good grades.
　　6. If only / I wish it weren't true.

B.

　　1. Ojalá que yo hubiera terminado.
　　2. Ojalá que comience / empiece pronto.
　　3. Ojalá que hubiéramos salido más temprano.
　　4. Ojalá que no llueva mañana.
　　5. Ojalá que que no hiciera tanto calor.
　　6. Ojalá que hayan votado.

p.134

C. Answers will vary.

#5 Compound Verbs—The Past Tense

p.135

A.

	haber	**estar**	**seguir**
yo	hubiera	estuviera	siguiera
tú	hubieras	estuvieras	siguieras
él, ella, Ud.	hubiera	estuviera	siguiera
nosotros, nosotras	hubiéramos	estuviéramos	siguiéramos
ellos, ellas, Uds.	hubieran	estuvieran	siguieran

p.136

B.

1. Dudaban / Dudaron que su hijo hubiera terminado.
   They doubted that their son had finished.
2. Me sorprendió que se nos hubiera acabado la leche.
   It surprised me that we had run out of milk.
3. Fue / Era feo que siguiera lloviendo.
   It was awful that it kept raining.
4. Estuvimos / Estábamos impresionados de que hubieras pasado la tarde limpiando tu cuarto.
   We were impressed that you had spent the afternoon cleaning your room.
5. María esperaba / esperó que Juan estuviera escuchando.
   María hoped that Juan was listening.
6. El maestro no estaba / estuvo convencido de que los alumnos hubieran estado estudiando.
   The teacher was not convinced that the students had been studying.

p.137

C. Answers will vary.
Some possibilities:

1. estuvieran jugando al béisbol
   Me alegraba de que los niños estuvieran jugando al béisbol.
   I was glad that the children were playing baseball.
2. siguiéramos esperando
   Él insistió que siguiéramos esperando.
   He insisted that we keep waiting.
3. hubieras salido para México
   Ellos no creían que hubieras salido para México.
   They didn't believe that you had left for México.
4. hubiera pedido un café
   Ojalá que yo hubiera pedido un café y no una cerveza.
   If only I'd ordered coffee and not a beer.
5. hubieran comprado un carro nuevo
   El estudiante esperaba que sus padres le hubieran comprado un carro nuevo.
   The student hoped that his parents had bought him a new car.

p.138

D.

1. Me molestaba que siguieran llamando.

2. Teníamos / Tuvimos miedo de que se hubieran perdido.

3. Ella creyó / creía que él estaba hablando por teléfono.

4. No creyeron / creían que tú lo hubieras hecho.

E. Answers will vary.
   Some possibilities:

1. Nos sorprendió de que María hubiera dado a luz a gemelos.

2. No creían que Juan estuviera buscando un nuevo empleo.

3. Fue bueno que María hubiera recibido un aumento.

4. Fue una lástima que a Juan se le hubiera roto la pierna.

5. Yo recomendé que María siguiera ofreciéndose como voluntaria.

6. Fue una mentira que Juan hubiera estado ayudando a sus padres.

7. Fue increíble que María se hubiera negado a pagar sus impuestos.

8. La familia estaba triste de que Juan y María se hubieran divorciado.

p.139

F. Answers will vary. See pp.262-264 for sample sentences.

#6. Intended Purpose—The Past Tense

p.141

A.

1. Juan trabajó / trabajaba mucho para mantener a su familia.
Juan worked / used to work a lot to support his family.

2. Mi tía me mandó / mandaba dinero a fin de que yo les comprara regalos a los niños.
My aunt sent / would send / used to send me money for me to buy presents for the children.

3. Les escribimos de modo que supieran la buena noticia.
We wrote them so that they would know the good news.

4. Porque nos encantaba esta canción, siempre subía el volumen para que la oyéramos mejor.
Because we liked this song, I always turned up / used to turn up / would turn up the volume so that we could hear it better.

5. Querían / quisieron que yo los llevara al aeropuerto de manera que no tuvieran que pagar el estacionamiento.
They wanted / used to want me to take them to the airport so that they wouldn't have to pay for parking.

6. Iban a plantar los rosales allí de forma que recibieran suficiente sol.
They were going to plant rose bushes there so that they would get enough sun.

p.142

B. Answers will vary:

"so that" can be translated as: *para que, de modo que, de forma que, a fin de que,* or *de manera que.*

1. Iban (a ir) a la casa de Sara para que ella los ayudara / pudiera ayudarlos con su(s) tarea(s).

2. Recogí a mis hijos en la escuela ayer para que no tuvieran que caminar a casa en la lluvia.

3. No salieron / salían mucho para ahorrar dinero.

4. Se lo explicó (a Uds.) de forma que (Uds.) lo comprendieran / entendieran.

5. Sus padres insistían en que él estudiara todos los días a fin de que sacara buenas notas.

6. ¿Fuiste a México para estudiar o para visitar amigos?

C. Answers will vary.

Some examples:

1. Le di a mi amigo $100 para que comprara las entradas al concierto.
I gave my friend $100 for him to buy the tickets to the concert.

2. Ellos salieron a las 5:00 para llegar a tiempo.
They left at 5:00 to arrive on time.

3. Sus padres sacrificaron mucho para que él asistiera a la universidad.
His parents made lots of sacrifices so that he could attend university.

4. Debías de hablar más fuerte de modo que todos pudiéramos oírte.
You should have talked louder so that we could all hear you.

5. Habríamos preferido que ellos se quedaran en un hotel a fin de que estuvieran más cómodos.
We would have preferred that they stay in a hotel so that they would be more comfortable.

6. Ella sacó la maleza de manera que las verduras crecieran mejor.
She weeded so that the vegetables would grow better.

p.143

D. **Answers will vary.**
    See pp.262-264 for sample sentences.

p.144

E. An example:

El més pasado mi club de libros se reunió en mi casa para cenar y discutir el libro. Mi familia ayudó a limpiar la casa para que yo pudiera dedicarme a cocinar. Cenamos en la terraza para disfrutar del buen tiempo. En la reunión, una de las personas del grupo trajo críticas del libro e información sobre el autor a fin de que pudiéramos discutir el libro más a fondo. Otra persona presentó una variedad de libros de modo que escogiéramos el próximo libro para leer. El marido de otra socia estaba muy enfermo, por eso ella no asistió de manera que él no estuviera solo. Aunque la extrañamos, lo pasamos muy bien.

Last month my book club met at my house to have dinner and discuss the book. My family helped clean the house so that I could spend my time cooking. We ate dinner on the deck in order to enjoy the good weather. In the meeting, one of the people of the group brought reviews of the book and information about the author so that we could discuss the book in more depth. Another person presented a variety of books so that we could choose the next book to read. Another member's husband was very ill, so she didn't attend so that he wouldn't be alone. Although we missed her, we had a good time.

#7. Contingencies / Anticipated Actions
#8. Cuando

p.147

A.

1. estudiaré / estudiaría ....I will study / I would study
2. haremos / haríamos ....we will make or do / we would make or do
3. ¿irás? / ¿irías?...will you go? / would you go?
4. ella comprenderá / ella comprendería............she will understand / she would understand

5. vamos a dar / íbamos a dar ....we are going to give / we were going to give
6. ellas van a llegar / ellas iban a llegar..............they are going to arrive / they were going to arrive
7. ¿vas a organizar? / ¿ibas a organizar?............are you going to organize? / were you going to organize?
8. él va a morir / él iba a morir ....he's going to die / he was going to die

9. él pide   pidió / pedía ....he asked for / he used to ask for, he was asking for
10. hacemos   hicimos / hacíamos   we made or did / we used to make or do, we were making or doing
11. ellos van   fueron / iban ....they went / they used to go, they were going
12. comes   comiste / comías ....you ate / you used to eat, you were eating

13. pregunten   preguntaran
14. salgamos   saliéramos
15. sepas   supieras
16. Ud.lea   leyera

17. llueve   llovió / llovía
18. haga sol   hiciera sol
19. vamos a volar   íbamos a volar
20. viajaré   viajaría
21. él tiene   tuvo / tenía
22. compras   compraste / comprabas
23. venderemos   venderíamos
24. voy a dormir   iba a dormir

p.148

B.

1. No iría a la fiesta a menos que me invitaran.
    I wouldn't go to the party unless they invited me.

2. Dábamos un paseo en el parque todos los domingos con tal de que no lloviera.
    We used to go / would go / went for a walk in the park every Sunday provided it didn't rain.

3. Montaba mi bicicleta antes de que hubiera mucho tráfico.
    I would ride / was riding / rode my bicycle before there was much traffic.
    Monté mi bicicleta antes de que hubiera mucho tráfico.
    I rode my bicycle before there was much traffic.

4. En caso de que mi equipo ganara el campeonato, tenía / tuve lista una buena botella de champán.
    In case my team won the championship, I had / got a good bottle of champagne ready.

5. Nunca pude / podía visitarla sin que ella me repitiera esa misma historia.
    I never managed to / never could visit her without her repeating that same story to me.

6. Íbamos a comprar una casa antes de que subieran los precios de nuevo.
    We were going to buy a house before the prices went up again.

7. Me imaginaba que estaban trabajando en la computadora a menos que tuvieran que cuidar a los niños.
    I imagined they were working on the computer unless they had to take care of the children.

p.149

C.

1. Ella sabía lo que yo pensaba / estaba pensando sin que yo **dijera** palabra.
2. Comimos antes de que **llegaran.**
3. ¿Ibas a avisarme antes de que yo **saliera**?
4. Dejaban un plato de galletas en la mesa en caso de que los niños **tuvieran** hambre.
5. A menos que le **dieran** un aumento de sueldo, él no iba a poder comprar un carro.
6. Yo habría invertido en esa empresa / compañía con tal de que Ud. **hubiera invertido** en ella también.

D.

   1. F   2. A/C   3. A/C   4. F   5. F   6. A/C

p.151

E.

1. Se lo dije luego que / tan pronto como / en cuanto / así que lo vi.
2. ¿Usó Ud. mantequilla cuando hizo estas galletas?
3. Él nos acompañaba al cine siempre que lo invitábamos.
4. Bailamos hasta que la orquesta dejó de tocar.
5. Él siempre pagaba cuando salíamos a comer.
6. Sus padres lo dejaron / le permitieron usar el carro después de que cumplió 16 y (que) obtuvo / consiguió / tuvo su licencia.
7. Ella siempre se quitaba los zapatos cuando llegaba a casa.
8. Luego que / Tan pronto como / En cuanto / Así que ella consiguió / obtuvo / tuvo el tatuaje, nos lo enseñó /mostró.

p.152

F.

1. Yo pensaba / planeaba decírselo en cuanto / luego que / tan pronto como / así que lo **viera**.
2. Yo quería ver esa película cuando **saliera**.
3. Él prometió que ellos nos llevarían al cine siempre que **visitáramos**.
4. Ella nos dijo que llamaría cuando **llegara** al aeropuerto.
5. Íbamos a bailar hasta que **saliera** el sol / **amaneciera**.
6. Sus padres dijeron / decían que él podría usar el carro después de que **cumpliera** 16 y que **obtuviera / consiguiera / tuviera** su licencia.
7. Nos dieron su dirección en caso de que **quisiéramos** visitarlos.
8. Ella recomendó que visitaras los museos de arte cuando **fueras** a España.
9. Cruzamos / atravesamos las montañas / la sierra antes de que **nevara**.
10. Yo iba a abrir el paquete así que / en cuanto / luego que / tan pronto como **llegara**.

p.153

G. Answers will vary. Some possibilities:

1. Fue al parque antes de que nevara.

   He went to the park before it snowed.

2. Sí, iban a a hacer un viaje a Europa en cuanto hubieran ahorrado suficiente dinero.
   Yes, they were going to take a trip to Europe as soon as they had saved enough money.

   Sí, iban a a hacer un viaje a Europa a menos que se enfermaran sus padres.
   Yes, they were going to take a trip to Europe unless their parents got sick.

3. Sí, pensábamos hacerlo con tal de que ella nos dijera el tipo que prefería.

   Yes, we planned to do so provided that she told us what kind she preferred.

4. Me quedé en un hotel cercano en caso de que ellos me necesitaran.

   I stayed in a nearby hotel in case they needed me.

5. Queríamos vivir en la playa a menos que no tuviéramos suficiente dinero para comprar una casa.
   We wanted to live at the beach unless we didn't have enough money to buy a house.

   Queríamos vivir en el centro hasta que nos jubiláramos.
   We wanted to live downtown until we retired. (a future event, we hadn't retired yet.)

   Queríamos vivir en París con tal de que ganáramos la lotería.
   We wanted to live in Paris provided we won the lottery.

6. Quería salir así que se partiera el pastel.

   I wanted to leave as soon as they cut the cake. (They hadn't cut it yet.)

7. No Iba a decírtelo antes de que terminaras.

   I wasn't going to tell you before you finished.

   Iba a decírtelo cuando te viera.
   I was going to tell you when I saw you.

8. Sí, les daban regalitos cuando visitaban sin que los niños se los pidieran.
   Yes, they gave them little presents when they visited without the children asking (them) for them.

H. Answers will vary. Some possibilities:

1. Fue en cuanto terminó la escuela.

   He went as soon as school was out.

2. Sí, hIcieron un viaje cuando era su aniversario.
   Yes, they took a trip when it was their anniversary.

3. Sí, se la compramos luego que se abrió la tienda.
   Yes, we bought it for her as soon as the store opened.

4. Me quedé en casa de unos amigos hasta que alquilé un departamento.
   I stayed with friends until I rented an apartment.

5. Vivíamos con mis padres mientras mi esposo estudiaba en la universidad.
   We lived with my parents while my husband was in college.

6. Sí, la llamé tan pronto como saliste.
   Yes, I called her as soon as you left.

p.154

I.

1. Antes de que Uds. **hicieran** su viaje, ¿hicieron reservaciones / reservas?
2. Hicimos reservaciones / reservas tan pronto como / en cuanto / luego que / así que él **confirmó** las fechas de sus vacaciones.
3. Esperaba comprar un carro cuando él **consiguiera** / **obtuviera** / **tuviera** un empleo / puesto / trabajo.
4. Así que / Tan pronto como / En cuanto / Luego que el taller les **reparó** la llanta, siguieron / continuaron con su viaje.
5. Más personas inocentes morirían / gente inocente moriría / a menos que la guerra **terminara**.
6. Se preocuparon cuando no **llamé** / **telefoneé**.
7. Tenía miedo / temía que se enojaran / se enfadaran cuando les **dijera** la noticia.
8. Cociné el pavo / guajolote hasta que **se doró**.
9. Él iba a llamar / telefonear en cuanto / tan pronto como / luego que / así que **llegáramos**, pero no había cobertura.
10. Ella quería trabajar en el jardín hasta que se **pusiera** el sol.
11. Ella trabajó en el jardín hasta que se **puso** el sol.
12. Cuidaba su perro cuando viajababan siempre que **fuera** por menos de una semana.

Extra Practice with "Cuando"

p.155

J.

1. Siempre cerraba la puerta con llave cuando salía de casa.
2. Cuando mis amigos oían música, bailaban.
3. La semana pasada cuando viajé, llevé mi computadora portátil.
4. Cuando fuiste a la universidad, ¿me compraste una camiseta?
5. Siempre lo invitábamos a cenar cuando preparábamos paella.
6. Anoche mi amiga me recogió en el aeropuerto cuando yo la llamé.
7. El año pasado, cuando su hija cumplió 15, le dieron una gran fiesta.
8. Yo lavaba el carro cuando estaba sucio.

K. Answers will vary. Some examples:

1. Los vi cuando estaba en el centro. —**Fact**: *I saw them when I was downtown.*
2. Corrían en el parque cuando hacía buen tiempo. —**Fact**: *They ran in the park when the weather was good.*
3. Yo iba a ir de compras cuando cambiara mi cheque —**Contingency***: *I was going to go shopping when / as soon as I cashed my check.*
4. Fui de compras cuando cambié mi cheque. —**Fact**: *I went shopping when I cashed my check.*
5. Alquilábamos un carro cuando viajábamos. —**Fact**: *We would rent a car when we traveled.*
6. Pensaba viajar a Chile cuando se jubilara. —**Cont.***: *She planned to travel to Chile when she retired.*
7. Quería salir cuando ellos estuvieran listos. —**Cont.***: *I wanted to leave when they were ready.*

   Note: It's possible to answer this as a fact—with the indicative.
   Example: Quería salir cuando él dijo eso. *I wanted to leave when he said that.*

8. Sí, iba a llamarte cuando tuviera todos los datos. — **Cont.***: *Yes, I was going to call you when I had all the facts.*

   * Contingency, Anticipated Event.

p.157

M. Answers will vary. See pp.262-264 for sample sentences.

pp.158-159

N.

Jorge dijo que estaba enamorado de otra y que se iba.
Jorge said that he was in love with another woman and that he was leaving.

Ana dijo que nadie iba a irse / se iría a menos que ella lo mandara.
Ana said that nobody was going to leave / would leave unless she ordered it.

Ana dijo que ella no mandó / mandaba que se fuera.
She said she didn't order / wasn't ordering him to go.

Jorge dijo que ellos no eran felices.
Jorge said that they were not happy.

Jorge dijo que era mejor que él se fuera antes de que se odiaran.
Jorge said that it was better that he leave before they hated each other.

Ana dijo que no quería que él se fuera hasta que se odiaran.
Ana said that she didn't want him to leave until they hated each other.

Ana le dijo que no la dejara.*
Ana told him not to leave her.

Ana dijo que él no debía abandonarla hasta que naciera la criatura.
Ana said that he shouldn't abandon her until the baby was born.

Jorge le dijo que lo llamara* después de que diera a luz para que él pudiera conocer a su hijo.
Jorge told her to call him after she gave birth so that he could know his son.

Jorge dijo que él prometía mandar dinero para mantener a su hijo siempre que Ana dejara en paz a él y a su nueva mujer.
Jorge said that he promised to send money to support his son as long as Ana left him and his new woman / wife alone.

Ana dijo que ella nunca los dejaría en paz ni a él ni a la fulana esa hasta que estuviera muerta.
Ana said that she would never leave either him or that slut alone until she was dead.

Ana dijo que lo mataría antes de permitir que él viera a su hijo.
Ana dijo que lo mataría antes de permitirle ver a su hijo.
Ana dijo que lo mataría antes de que ella permitiera que él viera a su hijo.
Ana dijo que lo mataría antes de que ella le permitiera ver a su hijo.
Ana said that she would kill him before she let him see his son.

Jorge le dijo que no fuera* así.
Jorge told her not to be like that.

Jorge dijo que tan pronto como ella fuera razonable, cumpliría con sus responsabilidades.
Jorge told her that as soon as she was reasonable, he would fulfill his responsibilities.

Ana dijo que ella sería razonable así que él renunciara a esa mujer.
Ana said that she would be reasonable as soon as he gave up that woman.

Ana dijo que ellos podrían ser felices de nuevo con tal de que él abandonara a la fulana esa.
Ana said that they could be happy again provided that he abandoned that slut.

Jorge dijo que no quería irse sin que ella le prometiera ser razonable.
Jorge said that he didn't want to leave without her promising him to be reasonable.

Ana le dijo que se quedara* entonces.
Ana told him to stay then.

Jorge dijo—Adiós, Ana.
Jorge said, "Goodbye, Ana."

> * *Decir* **can be used to report a conversation or to express a command. (See p.26.)**
> **In this sentence,** *decir* **is used as a verb of influence.**

p.160

O. **Answers will vary. Here's an example:**

El hijo le preguntó a su madre si ella le daría las llaves del carro para que él pudiera ir a la bibilioteca.
The son asked his mother if she would give him the car keys so that he could go to the library.

La madre le dijo que se las daría con tal de que él llenara el depósito de gasolina porque no quedaba suficiente para llegar a la bibilioteca.
The mother told him that she would give them to him provided that he filled the gas tank because there wasn't enough left to get to the library.

El hijo le dijo a su mamá que lo llenaría con tal de que le diera el dinero.
The son told his mom that he would fill it provided that she gave him some money.

La madre le dijo que no tenía efectivo. Dijo que Papá podía dárselo al siguiente día después de que le presentara el recibo.
The mother told him that she didn't have any cash. She said that Dad could give it to him the next day after he gave him the receipt.

El hijo le dijo a su mamá que él no tenía dinero. Le pidió que ella le prestara su tarjeta de crédito de modo que él pudiera ir a la gasolinera.
The son told his mom that he didn't have any money. He asked her to lend him her credit card so that he could go to the gas station.

La madre le dijo que se la prestaría en cuanto su hermana se la devolviera. Dijo que se la había dado esa mañana para que en la tarde ella comprara unas cosas para su clase.
The mother said that she would lend it to him as soon as his sister returned it to her. She said that she had given it to her that morning so that in the afternoon she could buy some things for her class.

El hijo le preguntó a su mamá cuándo ella debía llegar a casa.
The son asked his mother when she should get home.

La madre le dijo que no llegaría hasta que hiciera sus compras.
The mother said that she wouldn't arrive until she made her purchases.

El hijo le dijo a su mamá que entonces no podía usar el carro a menos que su hermana regresara con la tarjeta de crédito.
The son told his mother that then he couldn't use the car unless his sister returned with the credit card.

La madre le dijo que la llamara de manera que ella supiera que la esperaba.
The mother told him to call her so that she knew that he was waiting for her.

#9. Aunque

p.164

A.

1. Aunque llovía mucho, lo pasamos bien.
2. Íbamos al cine todos los fines de semana, aunque era caro.
3. Aunque ella aprobó la clase / el curso, le fue difícil / fue difícil para ella / le costó mucho (trabajo).
4. Sólo nos visitaron un par de veces, aunque no vivían lejos.

B.

1. Aunque (Uds.) salieran a las cinco de la mañana, no llegarían hasta la noche.
2. Aunque no tuviera trabajo que hacer, yo preferiría quedarme en casa este fin de semana.
3. Aunque me hubieran ofrecido el trabajo / el empleo / el puesto, yo no lo habría aceptado.
4. No pondríamos / plantaríamos una huerta aunque tuviéramos el espacio.

p.165

C.

1. Ellos querían tener un perro aunque **viajaban** mucho.
2. Ella tiene un gato aunque **tiene** alergias.
3. Aunque se **enojen** / se **enfaden**, tienes que decirles la verdad.
4. Nos llamaría aunque **estuviera** ocupada.
5. Él quería manejar aunque **había** mucho tráfico.
6. Él querría manejar aunque **hubiera** mucho tráfico.
7. Aunque lo **supiera**, no se lo diría.
8. Lo compramos aunque **costó** mucho.
9. Lo compraremos aunque **cueste** mucho.
10. Lo compraríamos aunque **costara** mucho.

p.166

**D. See pp.231-232 for present tense sample sentences.
See pp.262-264 for present and past tense examples.**

p.167

E.

1. Cuando **iba** al centro, me gustaba almorzar en un restaurante.
   When I went / would go / used to go downtown, I liked / used to like to have lunch in a restaurant.
2. Vamos a trabajar en el jardín mañana, aunque **esté** lloviendo.
   We're going to work in the garden tomorrow, even if it's raining / although it may be raining.
3. Aunque ellos siempre **han** manejado demasiado rápido, nunca han tenido ningún accidente.
   Although they have always driven too fast, they have never had a single accident.
4. Aunque él **hubiera** buscado mucho, no habría encontrado un empleo.
   Even if he had looked a lot, he wouldn't have found a job.
5. Cuando tú **viajes** a Colombia, cómprame algo.
   When you travel to Colombia, buy me something.
6. Cuando ellos **estaban** nerviosos, no comían.
   When they were nervous, they didn't / wouldn't eat.
7. Él habría comprado los boletos para el concierto aunque **hubieran** costado $500.
   He would have bought the tickets for the concert even if they had cost $500.
8. Aunque él **era** mi amigo, a veces me volvía loco.
   Although he was my friend, sometimes he drove me crazy.
9. Cuando ella **lee** novelas, siempre empieza leyendo el final.
   When she reads novels, she always starts by reading the end.
10. Al darle ese misterio a ella, le hice prometer que no haría eso cuando lo **leyera**.
    When I gave her that mystery, I made her promise that she would not do that when she read it.

p.168

F. Answers will vary. Some possibilities:

1. Lo acompañaste al cine. ¿Verdad?   *(You went with him to the movies, right?)*

   Sí, lo acompañé aunque tenía que levantarme temprano el siguiente día.

   Yes, I went with him even though I had to get up early the next day.

2. ¿Creíste lo que él dijo?   *(Did you believe what he said?)*

   No, no lo creí aunque parecía que él hablaba muy en serio.

   No, I didn't believe it even though it seemed he was speaking in earnest.

3. ¿Creerías a ellos?   *(Would you believe them?)*

   No, no les creería aunque juraran sobre un montón de Biblias.

   No, I wouldn't believe them even if they swore on a stack of Bibles.

4. ¿Crees que podamos superar esta situación?   *(Do you think that we can overcome this situation?)*

   Sí, creo que podemos superarla aunque tú no lo creas.

   Yes, I think we can overcome it / get through it even though you don't believe it.

5. ¿Pudieron Uds. superar esa situación?   *(Were you able to overcome that situation?)*

   Sí pudimos superarla aunque costó mucho trabajo.

   Yes, we were able to overcome it although it was hard.

6. ¿Fuiste de compras ayer?   *(Did you go shopping yesterday?)*

   Sí, fui de compras aunque hacía sol y habría preferido estar afuera.

   Yes, I went shopping although it was sunny and I would have preferred to be outside.

7. ¿Van Uds. a la playa mañana?   *(Are you going to the beach tomorrow?)*

   No, no vamos mañana aunque nos reparen el carro para el mediodía.

   No, we're not going tomorrow even if they repair our car by noon.

8. ¿Te gustó la película?   *(Did you like the movie?)*

   Sí, me gustó aunque generalmente prefiero las películas de acción.

   Yes, I liked it although I usually prefer action movies.

p.168

G. Answers will vary. An example:

Pasamos mucho tiempo planeando nuestro viaje al Ecuador.
We spent a lot of time planning our trip to Ecuador.

Aunque planeamos mucho, el viaje no salió como pensábamos.
Although we planned a lot, the trip did not turn out how we thought.

Llegamos a Quito y **aunque nos gusta** el esquí nórdico y las excursiones en las montañas de nuestro estado, no estábamos preparados para la altitud en la capital.
We arrived in Quito and although we like cross-country skiing and hiking in the mountains of our state, we were not prepared for the altitude in the capital.

Aunque hubiéramos sabido que tendríamos dificultades, no sé cómo habríamos podido responder al problema.
Even if we had known that we would have trouble, I don't know how we would have been able to address the problem.

Aunque teníamos ganas de ver la ciudad y otros lugares en la Sierra, no salimos del hotel porque mi esposo estaba enfermo por la altitud.
Although we felt like seeing the city and other places in the mountain region, we didn't leave the hotel because my husband was sick because of the altitude.

Entonces tratamos de cambiar nuestros planes para ir a las Islas Galápagos.
So we tried to change our plans to go to the Galapagos Islands.

Pero **aunque teníamos** reservaciones para la siguiente semana, no podíamos cambiarlas porque todos los vuelos y barcos estaban completos.
But although we had reservations for the following week, we couldn't change them because all the flights and ships were full.

Entonces decidimos ir al *Oriente* para conocer la cuenca de Amazonas.
So we decided to go to Oriente *(Ecuador's jungle region) to see the Amazon Basin.*

No hubo problema. **Aunque nos hubiéramos presentado** en el aeropuerto al último momento, habríamos podido comprar pasajes porque el avión estaba medio vacío.
There was no problem. Even if we had showed up at the airport at the last moment we would have been able to buy tickets because the plane was half empty.

Aunque no era parte de nuestros planes originales, lo pasamos muy bien en el Oriente.
Although it wasn't part of our original plans, we had a very good time in the Oriente (the jungle region).

#10. Non-existent People and Objects
#11. Hypothetical People and Objects

p.170

A.

1. No había nadie allí que conociera Bolivia.
   There was nobody there who'd been to Bolivia.
2. Sólo había dos de mis vecinos que no tenían perros.
   There were only two of my neighbors who did not have dogs.
3. No existía ninguna universidad en este estado que diera cursos de maya.
   Not a single / Not one / No university existed in this state that gave classes on Mayan / Mayan classes.
4. No teníamos impresora que funcionara.
   We didn't have a printer that worked.
5. Él deseaba asistir a una universidad que no estuviera muy lejos de su pueblo.
   He wanted / wished to attend a university that wasn't very far from his town.
6. Quería esos plátanos que estaban más maduros.
   I wanted those bananas that were riper.
7. Ella necesitaba un empleo que pagara mejor.
   She needed a job that paid / would pay better.
8. Ellos nunca compraban zapatos que no les quedaran bien.
   They never bought shoes that didn't fit them well.
9. Estaba / Estuve buscando el libro que me prestaste.
   I was looking for the book that you lent me.
10. Estaba / Estuve buscando un libro que me interesara.
    I was looking for a book that was interesting to me / that I found interesting.

p.171

B.

1. No había nadie en la oficina que pudiera hablar ruso.
2. No tenía ningún libro que explicara claramente la historia mexicana.
3. No conocía a nadie que trabajara allí.
4. Trataron de comprar una casa en este barrio, pero no pudieron encontrar una que tuviera cuatro recámaras / dormitorios / alcobas / habitaciones.

C.

1. No existía un equipo que tuviera mejores jugadores.
2. Compré un carro que no usaba mucha gasolina.
3. No había nadie en su familia que se hubiera graduado de la universidad.
4. Ella nunca había escrito un / ningún libro que fuera aburrido.
5. Compramos pantalones, pero no zapatos.

p.172

D.

1. Necesitaban / Necesitaron un intérprete que pudiera hablar inglés y francés.
2. ¿Vendían / Estaban vendiendo juguetes que fueran peligrosos?
3. Yo quería ver una película que a ti te gustara también.
4. Ella buscaba un perro adulto que necesitara un hogar y que no fuera muy grande.

E.

1. El equipo quería jugadores que supieran jugar bien.
2. Vimos una película que nos hizo reír.
3. Buscaban una niñera que pudiera manejar / conducir y trabajar de noche / en las noches.
4. Quería / Quise hablar con la persona que escribió esto.

p.173

F. See pp.231-232 for present tense sample sentences.   /   See pp.262-264 for present and past tense examples.

p.174

G.

Cuando yo era estudiante odiaba la escuela.
No tenía ningún profesor que no fuera aburrido.
No había ninguna clase que valiera la pena.
No había plato en la cafetería que no me diera asco.
No conocía a nadie que me comprendiera.

An example:

Queríamos un buen carro que fuera económico, y yo estaba molesta que no pudiéramos encontrar ninguno. No había un carro nuevo que costara menos de $20.000, y los híbridos y los eléctricos costaban aun más. No había ninguno que fuera cómodo, que tuviera aire acondicionado y que también obtuviera más de 35 millas por galón. Además mi color favorito es morado, y no existía ninguno que fuera de ese color.

We wanted a good car that was economical, and I was irritated that we couldn't find one. There was no new car that cost less than $20,000, and hybrids and electric ones cost even more. There wasn't a single one that was comfortable, had air conditioning and also got more than 35 miles per gallon. In addition, my favorite color is purple and none existed that was that color.

p.175

H. Some examples:

1. Quería una pareja que **fuera** rico y que **tuviera** un carro deportivo.
2. Quería una pareja que **fuera** alto, moreno y guapo.
3. Quería una pareja que **fuera** una estrella de rock.
4. Quería una pareja a quien **le gustara** viajar.
5. Quería una pareja que **cocinara** muy bien y a quien también **le gustara** limpiar la casa.
6. Quería una pareja que **hablara** muchos idiomas.
7. Quería una pareja que **bailara** tango y salsa.
8. Quería una pareja a quien **le encantaran** los paseos por la playa.
9. Quería una pareja que **quisiera** tener un gato y un perro.
10. Quería una pareja que **tuviera** un buen sentido de humor.

I. An example:

Cuando era niño soñaba con ser vaquero y vivir en Montana. Deseaba tener un caballo que **fuera** blanco con manchas negras y que **se llamara** Rayo. Quería tener un trabajo en el que yo **montara** mi caballo, **llevara** el ganado a un pueblo para venderlo, y en que yo **durmiera** bajo las estrellas.

When I was a boy I dreamt about being a cowboy in Montana. I dreamt about having a horse that was white with black spots and that was called Lightning. I wanted to have a job in which I rode my horse, drove the cattle to town to sell them and in which I slept under the stars.

p.176

J. An example:

La primera vez que quería alquilar un departamento, buscaba uno que **costara** menos de $125 por mes y que **estuviera** cerca de la universidad y del restaurante donde trabajaba. No me importaba que el apartamento **fuera** nuevo ni que **tuviera** un lavaplatos. Pero sí prefería un departamento amueblado que **permitiera** mascotas.

The first time I wanted to rent an apartment, I was looking for one that cost less than $125 a month and that was close to the university and to the restaurant where I worked. I didn't care if the apartment was new or that it had a dishwasher. But I did prefer a furnished apartment that allowed pets.

#12. "Si" Clauses

p.180

A.

infinitive	yo	tú	él, ella, Ud.	nosotros, nosotras	ellos, ellas, Uds.
1. hablar	hablaré	hablarás	hablará	hablaremos	hablarán
2. pensar	pensaré	pensarás	pensará	pensaremos	pensarán
3. vivir	viviré	vivirás	vivirá	viviremos	vivirán
4. divertirse	me divertiré	te divertirás	se divertirá	nos divertiremos	se divertirán
5. tener	tendré	tendrás	tendrá	tendremos	tendrán
6. hacer	haré	harás	hará	haremos	harán
7. dar	daré	darás	dará	daremos	darán
8. ser	seré	serás	será	seremos	serán
9. estar	estaré	estarás	estará	estaremos	estarán
10. ir	iré	irás	irá	iremos	irán

B.

infinitive	yo	tú	él, ella, Ud.	nosotros, nosotras	ellos, ellas, Uds.
1. hablar	hablaría	hablarías	hablaría	hablaríamos	hablarían
2. estudiar	estudiaría	estudiarías	estudiaría	estudiaríamos	estudiarían
3. leer	leería	leerías	leería	leeríamos	leerían
4. perderse	me perdería	te perderías	se perdería	nos perderíamos	se perderían
5. poder	podría	podrías	podría	podríamos	podrían
6. querer	querría	querrías	querría	querríamos	querrían
7. dar	daría	darías	daría	daríamos	darían
8. ser	sería	serías	sería	seríamos	serían
9. estar	estaría	estarías	estaría	estaríamos	estarían
10. haber	habría	habrías	habría	habríamos	habrían

p.181

C. **F-future / C-conditional / PS-past subjunctive / O-other**

1. PS	8. F	15. PS
2. PS	9. C	16. F
3. O (imperfect)	10. C	17. C
4. PS	11. F	18. O (imperfect)
5. C	12. PS	19. O (present subjunctive
6. F	13. O (preterite)	or command)
7. PS	14. O (present subjunctive	20. C
	or command)	

D.

1. Trabajaré en el jardín. .... *I will work in the garden.*
   Trabajaría en el jardín. .... *I would work in the garden.*

2. Navegará en la red. .... *She will surf the web.*
   Navegaría en la red. .... *She would surf the web.*

3. ¿Me acompañarás? .... *Will you go with me?*
   ¿Me acompañarías? .... *Would you go with me?*

4. ¿No te perderás? .... *Won't you get lost?*
   ¿No te perderías? .... *Wouldn't you get lost?*

5. Valdrán la pena. .... *They will be worth it / worthwhile.*
   Valdrían la pena. .... *They would be worth it / worthwhile.*

6. Saldremos con ellos .... *We will leave / go out with them.*
   Saldríamos con ellos. .... *We would leave / go out with them.*

pp.182-183

E.

Note: Your first new sentence talks about the present. Your second new sentence talks about the past. Both are contrary to reality.

1. Iremos por tren si tenemos tiempo.   *We will go by train if we have time.*
   Iríamos por tren si **tuviéramos** tiempo.   *We would go by train if we had time.*
   Habríamos ido por tren si **hubiéramos tenido** tiempo.   *We would have gone by train if we'd had time.*

2. Te diré si no me gusta la película.   *I will tell you if I don't like the movie.*
   Te **diría** si no me **gustara** la película.   *I would tell you if I didn't like the movie.*
   Te **habría dicho** si no me **hubiera gustado** la película.   *I would have told you if I hadn't liked the movie.*

3. Si encuentro tu libro en mi carro, te llamo.   *If I find your book in my car, I'll call you.*
   Si **encontrara** tu libro en mi carro, te **llamaría**.   *If I found your book in my car, I would call you.*
   Si **hubiera encontrado** tu libro en mi carro, te   *If I had found your book in my car, I would*
      habría llamado.   *have called you.*

4. Podemos esquiar este fin de semana si nieva.   *We can ski this weekend if it snows.*
   Podríamos esquiar este fin de semana si nevara.   *We could / would be able to ski this weekend*
                                                                if it snowed.

   Habríamos podido esquiar este fin de semana   *We could have skied this weekend if it had*
      si **hubiera nevado**.   *snowed.*

Cont. on p. 257.

5. Si hay mucho tráfico, tomaremos otra ruta.
   If there is a lot of traffic, we'll take a different route.
   Si **hubiera** mucho tráfico, **tomaríamos** otra ruta.
   If there were a lot of traffic, we would take a different route.
   Si **hubiera habido** mucho tráfico, **habríamos tomado** otra ruta.
   If there had been a lot of traffic, we would have taken a different route.

6. Si Uds. llegan tarde, no me preocuparé.
   If you (all) arrive late, I won't worry.
   Si Uds. **llegaran** tarde, no me **preocuparía**.
   If you (all) were to arrive late, I wouldn't worry.
   Si Uds. **hubieran llegado** tarde, no me **habría preocupado**.
   If you (all) had arrived late, I wouldn't have worried.

7. Si navegan la red, verán algunos sitios web interesantes.
   If they surf the web, they'll see some interesting websites.
   Si **navegaran** la red, **verían** algunos sitios web interesantes.
   If they surfed / were to surf the web, they would see some interesting websites.
   Si **hubieran navegado** la red, **habrían visto** algunos sitios web interesantes.
   If they had surfed the web, they would have seen some interesting websites.

8. Si hace sol, daremos un paseo en el parque.   *If it's sunny, we'll go for a walk in the park.*
   Si **hiciera** sol, **daríamos** un paseo en el parque.   *If it were sunny, we would go for a walk in the park.*
   Si **hubiera hecho** sol, **habríamos dado** un paseo en el parque.
   If it had been sunny, we would have gone for a walk in the park.

p.183

F.

1. Si tuvieran hambre, pedirían una pizza.
2. No me quedaría aquí si fuera yo tú / si yo fuera tú / si fuera tú yo
3. Si los hubiéramos visto antes de la fiesta, los habríamos invitado.
4. Ellos habrían cantado si Uds. se lo hubieran pedido.

p.184

G. Answers will vary. Some examples:

1. Si hiciera mucho calor pondríamos el aire acondicionado.
   If it were very hot we would turn on the air conditioning.
2. Me darían el dinero si yo lo necesitara.
   They would give me the money if I needed it.
3. Si hubiera tiempo ellos pasearían en bicicleta.
   If there were time they would go for a bike ride.
4. Iríamos de vacaciones a España si no tuviéramos miedo de volar.
   We would go on vacation to Spain if we weren't afraid of flying.

H.

1. Si te pregunta, aconséjale que no se case.
2. Si él la hubiera conocido primero, se habrían casado.
3. Si él estuviera casado con ella, sería feliz.
4. Si él se hubiera casado con ella, habría sido feliz.
5. Si él se casa con ella, será feliz.

p.184

I. **Answers will vary. An example:**

Si yo **ganara** la lotería, **viajaría** alrededor del mundo, les **pagaría** la universidad a mis parientes, **haría** renovar mi casa, **donaría** dinero a causas y organizaciones que me importaban. **Emplearía** un jardinero y una persona que limpiara la casa. No **compraría** mucho porque tengo todo lo necesario, pero cuando se **gastara** mi carro, me **compraría** uno eléctrico.

If I won the lottery, I would travel around the world, I would pay for college for my relatives, I would have my house renovated, I would donate money to causes and organizations that were important to me. I would hire a gardener and a person to clean the house. I would not buy much because I have all that's necessary, but when my car wore out, I would buy myself an electric one.

p.185

J. **Answers will vary. An example:**

Si yo fuera alcalde de mi ciudad, yo **pagaría** para que músicos de todo tipo tocaran en las puertas del aeropuerto. Yo **cerraría** todas las tiendas en los días de fiesta para que los empleados disfrutaran de las fiestas con sus familias. **Declararía** prohibido el uso de celulares y otros aparatos electrónicos personales en todo lugar público donde es prohibido fumar. Y **sería** mandatorio que cualquier muro de concreto de más de 144 pies cuadrados fuera pintado, preferiblemente con un mural.

If I were mayor of my city, I would pay so that all kinds of musicians would play at the boarding gates in the airport. I would close all the stores on holidays so that the employees could enjoy the holiday with their families. I would declare the use of cell phones and other personal electronic devices prohibited in any public place where smoking is prohibited. And it would be mandatory that any concrete wall of more than 144 square feet be painted, preferably with a mural.

K. **Answers will vary. An example:**

Si se **hubiera ofrecido** francés en mi colegio, probablemente yo nunca habría aprendido español.
If French had been offered at my high school, I probably would never have learned Spanish.

Si yo no **hubiera aprendido** español, a lo mejor no habría conocido Latinoamérica.
If I hadn't learned Spanish, perhaps I would not have gone to Latin America.

Si no **hubiera conocido** Latinoamérica, habría perdido la oportunidad de conocer a mucha buena gente y muchos lugares bellos.
If I hadn't gone to Latin America, I would have missed the opportunity of knowing many good people and seeing many beautiful places.

Si **hubiéramos comprado** una casa en otro barrio, no tendríamos tan buenos vecinos.
If we had bought a house in a different neighborhood, we wouldn't have such good neighbors.

Si el terremoto **hubiera sido** más fuerte, nuestra casa podría haber sido dañada.
If the earthquake had been stronger, our house could have been damaged.

L. **Answers will vary.**

#13 Verbs of Influence, a Shortcut

p.187

A.

1. me / 2. nos / 3. le / 4. le / 5. les / 6. nos / 7. les / 8. le

B. Translate the following sentences:

1. My teacher advised me to practice more.

2. Wouldn't they let you drive their car?

3. I didn't let my little sister use my things.

4. I had them paint the house.

5 She has suggested that we take a taxi.

6. I will forbid them to do that.

p.188

C.

1. Mi profesor me aconseja que yo practique más.   *My teacher advises me to practice more.*

2. ¿No dejarían que tú manejaras su carro?   *Wouldn't they let you drive their car?*

3. Yo no permitía que mi hermanita usara mis cosas.   *I didn't let my little sister use my things.*

4. Hice que pintaran la casa.   *I had them paint the house.*

5. El patrón ha pedido que trabajemos tarde.   *The boss has asked us to work late.*

6. Ya hemos mandado que vuelvan mañana.   *We've already ordered them to come back / return tomorrow.*

D.

1. Subjunctive: No dejaron / dejaban que viajáramos solos.

   Infinitive: No nos dejaron / dejaban viajar solos.

2. Subjunctive: No permitían / permitieron que sus empleados hicieran llamadas personales.

   Infinitive: No les permitían / permitieron a sus empleados hacer llamadas personales.

3. Subjunctive: ¿Habías recomendado que él me llamara?

   Infinitive: ¿Le habías recomendado llamarme?

#14 Indirect Commands

p.189

A. See pp.262-264 for present and past tense examples.

Como Si

p.190

A. **Answers will very. Some examples:**

1. Él se comporta como si **estuviera** en escena y **desempeñara** el papel estelar.

   He behaves as if he were on stage and playing the star role.

2. Bailan como si **tuvieran** 100 años.

   They dance as if they were 100 years old.

3. No me trates como si yo **fuera** una niña.

   Don't treat me as if I were a child.

4. Tú conduces como si no **hubiera** ningún otro carro en el camino.

   You drive as if there were no other cars on the road.

5. El elefante levantó el tronco como si no **pesara** nada.

   The elephant picked up the tree trunk as if it didn't weigh a thing.

6. Los novios entraron en la recepción como si **flotaran** en el aire.

   The bride and groom entered the reception as if they were floating on air.

7. Ella no nos saludó y nos dio la espalda como si no nos **hubiera visto**.

   She didn't greet us and turned her back to us as if she hadn't seen us.

8. El niño lloraba como si no **tuviera** ningún amigo en el mundo.

   The child was crying as if he didn't have a friend in the world.

9. Ese árbol se estrechaba hacia el cielo como si **intentara** abrazarlo.

   That tree stretched to the sky as if it were trying to embrace it.

10. Estaba lloviendo a cántaros día y noche como si jamás **volviera** a hacer sol.

    It was pouring down rain day and night as if it would never be sunny again.

#15. The "-Evers"

p.192

A.

1. Whatever they may say / Say what they may / No matter what they say, we won't believe them.

2. Whatever they might have said / Say what they might / No matter what they said, we wouldn't have believed them.

3. However cheap it might have been / No matter how cheap it was, you shouldn't have bought it.

4. They would go on vacation wherever / anywhere where it was sunny and there was a beach.

5. We would see whichever / whatever movie you were / might be interested in.

6. I didn't understand what it meant.

7. When we went / would go / used to go out for dinner / to eat dinner, whoever paid would choose the restaurant.

8. Juan did exactly what he felt like.

9. Juan always did whatever he felt like.

10. However / No matter how slowly and clearly I spoke, they wouldn't understand me.

B.

1. La policía lo encontraría / encontraría a él adondequiera que fuera.

2. Quienquiera que conocía a ella / la conociera, la admiraba.

3. Cualquier casa que compraran, la harían atractiva y cómoda / confortable.

4. Por mucho que trabajaran, su dinero no alcanzaría para pagar sus cuentas.

#16. Expressions of Possibility

p.193

A.

Tal vez............................a., b., c., d., e., f.

Quizás.............................a., b., c., d., e., f.

Podría ser que ....b., d., f.

A lo mejor........................a., c., e.

Qué sorpresa que............a., c., e.

fue sorprendente que .....b., d., f.

Posiblemente ....b., d., f.

Quizá ....a., b., c., d., e., f.

How to Use the Past Subjunctive: Sample Sentences

With verbs of influence/volition:
—present subjunctive
Ella quiere que su hermana la visite.
She wants her sister to visit her.

—past subjunctive
Ella quería que su hermana la visitara.
She wanted her sister to visit her.
Iba a pedir que me dieran un aumento.
I was going to ask them to give me a raise.
Juan propuso que invirtiéramos en su negocio.
Juan proposed that we invest in his business.
Sugerimos que él lo pensara bien.
We suggested that he think it over.
El profesor exigía que los estudiantes llegaran a tiempo.
The teacher demanded that the students arrive on time.
Sus padres prohibieron que se casaran.
Their parents forbid them to marry.

With verbs of emotion:
—present subjunctive
Me sorprende que ellos digan eso.
It surprises me that they say that.

—past subjunctive
Me sorprendió que ellos dijeran eso.
It surprised me that they said / would say that.
Él estaba preocupado de que su esposa estuviera muy enferma.
He was worried that his wife was very ill.
Me molestaba que los vecinos hicieran mucho ruido.
It bugged me that the neighbors made so much noise.
Estábamos nerviosos de que nadie asistiera a la conferencia.
We were nervous that nobody would attend the lecture.

With impersonal expressions:
—present subjunctive
Es emocionante que nos den una fiesta.
It's exciting that they are giving us a party.

—past subjunctive
Fue emocionante que nos dieran una fiesta.
It was exciting that they gave us a party.
Era feo que ellos se comportaran así.
It was awful that they behaved like that.
Era agradable que no lloviera y que pudiéramos comer en el patio.
It was pleasant that it didn't rain and that we were able to eat on the patio.
Fue preciso que Uds. terminaran a tiempo.
It was necessary that you (all) finish on time.

Sample sentences continue on pp.263.

With verbs of doubt/negation:
—present subjunctive

María no cree que eso sea buena idea.
> *María doesn't think that that's a good idea.*

—past subjunctive

Él no creía que fuera verdad.
> *He didn't believe that it was true.*

Dudaban que yo supiera hacerlo.
> *They doubted that I knew how to do it.*

No estábamos seguros de que vinieran a la fiesta.
> *We weren't sure that they would come to the party.*

No era verdad que esta tienda cobrara más que aquélla.
> *It wasn't true that this store charged more than that one.*

With a compound verb:
—present subjunctive

El dueño le dará al jugador un aumento para que siga jugando para su equipo.
> *The owner will give the player a raise so that he will keep playing for his team.*

Ella se alegra de que las flores en su jardín no se hayan marchitado en la onda de calor.
> *She's glad the flowers in her garden haven't shriveled up in the heat wave.*

—past subjunctive

El dueño le dio al jugador un aumento para que siguiera jugando para su equipo.
> *The owner gave the player a raise so that he would keep playing for his team.*

Ella se alegraba de que las flores en su jardín no se hubieran marchitado en la onda de calor.
> *She was glad the flowers in her garden hadn't shriveled up in the heat wave.*

With "para," "para que" and other expressions of intended purpose:
—present subjunctive

Voy a llamarlos para que no se preocupen.
> *I'm going to call them so that they don't / won't worry.*

—past subjunctive

Los llamé para que no se preocuparan.
> *I called them so that they wouldn't worry.*

Renovaron la antigua estación de tren para que sirviera como un museo y centro comunitario.
> *They renovated the old train station to serve as a museum and community center.*

Le di aspirinas a ella de modo que no le doliera la cabeza y pudiera acompañarnos al cine.
> *I gave her aspirins so that her head wouldn't hurt and she could go with us to the movies.*

With conjunctions that introduce contingencies:
—present

El equipo ganará en cuanto mejore su defensa.
> *The team will win as soon as it improves its defense.*

—past

Él cortaba el césped todos los fines de semana a menos que lloviera.
> *He mowed the lawn every weekend unless it rained.*

Ella trabajó para esa empresa hasta que se jubiló.
> *She worked for that company until she retired.*

Compramos útiles para la escuela antes de que terminaran las vacaciones.
> *We bought school supplies before vacation was over.*

Sample sentences continue on pp.264.

With "cuando":

—present subjunctive

Espero que mi equipo gane cuando
juegue mañana.
I hope my team wins when it plays tomorrow.

—past subjunctive

Pensaba plantar una huerta cuando
pasaran las heladas.
I was planning to plant a garden when the frosts ended.

—no subjunctive

Cuando **llueve** a cántaros,
me gusta leer al lado de la chimenea.
When it pours down rain, I like to read by the fireplace.

—no subjunctive

Cuando **recibí** el cheque, lo deposité.
When I received the check, I deposited it.

With "aunque":

—present subjunctive

Aunque sea un incendio pequeño, ellos necesitarán
ayuda para apagarlo.
Even if it's a small fire, they will need help to put it out.

—present subjunctive

Aunque fuera un incendio pequeño,
necesitarían ayuda para apagarlo.
Even if it were a small fire, they would need help to put it out.

—no subjunctive

Aunque es un incendio pequeño, necesitan
ayuda para apagarlo.
Although it's a small fire, they need help to put it out.

—no subjunctive

Aunque era un incendio pequeño, necesitaron
ayuda para apagarlo.
Although it was a small fire, they needed help to put it out.

About a hypothetical/non-specific person or object:

—present subjunctive

Buscan novias que sean inteligentes, guapas y ricas.
They are looking for girlfriends who are smart, attractive and rich.
Quiero ir de vacaciones adonde haga sol.
I want to go on vacation where it's sunny.

—past subjunctive

Yo buscaba un empleo que fuera más interesante.
I was looking for a job that was / would be more interesting.

About a person or object that doesn't exist:

—present subjunctive

No hay restaurante en mi pueblo que **sirva** comida tan rica como ésta.
There's no restaurant in my town that serves food as delicious as this.

—past subjunctive

No había ningún restaurante allí que **sirviera** comida guatemalteca.
There was no restaurant there that served Guatemalan food.

With "si":

—present tense (no subjunctive)

Ella piensa ir al trabajo en su bicicleta si no llueve.
She's planning to go to work on her bicycle if it doesn't rain.

—past subjunctive

Si él fuera al trabajo en su bicicleta, estaría en mejor forma.
If he rode his bicycle to work, he would be in better shape.

Indirect Commands:

—only present tense

¡Que Dios te bendiga!
May God bless you.

¡Que lo haga Juan!
Let Juan do it.

Index

aconsejar 97, 187
adondequiera 103,191
advise 97, 187
a fin de que 59, 141
after 63, 141
alegrar 29
allow 97, 187
a lo mejor 107, 193
a menos que 63, 141
andar 48
animar...97, 187
antes (de) que 63, 141
anticipated action...........................69, 145
así que 63, 141
ask 97, 187
asking for instructions 150
as long as 63, 141
asserting a truth 37
as soon as....................................63, 141
at least (it's not so bad that) 107, 193
aunque 75, 163
before 63, 141
beg. 97, 187
buscar...87, 169
clause, definition...................................7
comiese, comieses, comiese,
          comiésemos, comiesen 115
commands....................................69, 95, 99
commands, indirect 99
como si 190
compound verbs.....................................47
compound verbs, past tense 135
conditional tense 146, 163, 178, 179
conditional tense,
          Irregular verb stems 178, 179
conjugate, definition 7
conjunction, definition 7
conjunctions 63, 69, 75, 95, 163, 177
con tal (de) que 63, 141
contingencies 63, 145
convencer.....................................97, 187
convince 97, 187
coordinating tenses 121
could 118
courtesy expressions.............................118
creer 46
creer, In questions 46
creer, in statements 46
cualesquiera 103, 191
cualquiera.....................................103, 191
cualquier (+ noun) 103, 191

cuando 69, 141
cuandoquiera 103, 191
customary action...................................150
dar...15
debiera 118
decir 27
de forma que.....................................141
dejar 97, 187
demand 97, 187
de manera que 59, 141
de modo que..................................59, 141
de ninguna manera 85
de ningún modo 85
dependent clause, definition 7
desear...87, 169
después (de) que 63, 141
direct commands....................69, 95, 99
direct object pronouns...............48, 97, 187
disuadir de 97, 187
dondequiera 103, 191
doubt 41, 125
dudar..41
el hecho de que 43
el / la / los / las (noun) + verb 103
el que 43
emotion 29, 125
en caso de que 63, 141
encourage 97, 187
en cuanto 63, 141
es bueno..37
es evidente 37
es importante 37
esperar..21
es sorprendente 37
estar 15, 48
estar contento 29
estar triste 29
es triste 37
es verdad..37
even if 163
"-ever"s, the...............................103, 191
exigir 21, 97, 187
expressions of possibility,
          single clause 107, 133
forbid...97, 187
force 97, 187
forming:
     conditional tense, the 178, 179
     future tense, the 178, 179
     imperfect tense, the...................122
     participles 48, 49

forming, cont.
    past participles 49
    past subjunctive, the 111, 115
    present participles 48
    present subjunctive, the..........10, 13, 15
        irregular verbs 15
        regular verbs 10
        spelling adjustments.....................17
        stem-change verbs 13
    preterite tense, the 112, 122
future contingency 63, 69
future tense 69, 95, 146, 163, 178, 179
    irregular verb stems 178, 179
grammar terms 7
haber..15, 49
hacer..97, 187
han..53
has..53
hasta que..63, 141
have (something done)..................97, 187
he 53
helping verbs 47, 48, 49, 53
hemos...53
hiciese, hicieses, hiciese,
    hiciésemos, hiciesen....................115
however (+ adjective or adverb) 103, 191
how interesting, unfortunate,
        great, etc......107, 193
hypothetical objects........................87, 169
hypothetical people 87, 169
iba a + infinitive 146
immediate future.................................150
impedir..97, 187
imperative 5
Imperfect 146
    irregular verbs 122
    verb endings 122
Imperfect vs. preterite, summary 123
impersonal expressions.................37, 125
in case that 63, 141
independent clause, definition.................7
indicative 5
indicative, present tense......................150
Indirect commands 99, 189
indirect object pronouns 48, 97, 187
indirect object pronouns
        and the infinitive 187
infinitives 37, 97
Infinitive, definition....................................7
infinitive, with indirect object pronoun......187
influence / volition 21, 125

in no way, not any way...........................85
in order that 59, 141
in other words 107
insistir 21
instructions, asking for.........................150
intended purpose 59, 141
ir 15, 48
ir a + infinitive 146, 178
irregular verb stems
    conditional.................................178, 179
    future 178, 179
it could be 107, 193
it's best that 107, 193
it's better that...............................107, 193
it's hard to believe 43
it's not so bad that 107, 193
jamás...85
le, les 187
let..97, 99, 187
lo que
    (subjunctive + lo que + subjunctive) 103
lo que + verb 103, 191
luego que..63, 141
make, to force 97, 187
main clause, definition.............................7
mandar 21, 97, 187
maybe..107, 193
mejor que 107, 193
menos mal que 107, 193
me, te, le, nos, les 187
mientras que................................63, 141
mode...5
molestar 29
mood...5
nada...85
nadie...85
narrative past......................................150
necesitar 87, 169
negar..41
negation,....................................41, 125
negatives 85
neither...85
neither / nor 85
never..85
never ever 85
ni..85
ningún..85
ninguna...85
ninguna parte 85
ninguno...85
no 85

nobody 85
no creer 41, 46
no es cierto 41
no es mentira 37
no es que 41
no estar seguro de 41
none 85
no parece 41
non-existent objects 81, 169
non-existent people 81, 169
nor 85
not 85
not any 85
not anybody 85
not anything 85
not anywhere 85
not even 85
not ever 85
nothing 85
nowhere 85
nunca 85
obligar a 97, 187
odiar 29
ojalá 13, 133
ordenar 97, 187
order 97, 187
o sea que 107
para + an infinitive ....59 , 141
para que 59, 141
parece mentira que 43
participles. 47, 48, 49, 53
past participles 47, 49, 53
    forms 111
    irregular 49, 53
    other past subjunctive form, the 115
    pronoun placement 49
    spelling adjustments 49
    stem changes 49
    verb endings 111
perfect tenses 49, 53
perhaps 107, 193
permit 97, 187
permitir 97, 187
personal "a" 87, 169
persuade 97, 187
persuadir a 97, 187
phrase, definition 7
plead 97, 187
podría ser que 193
por (+ adjective or adverb) 103, 191
posiblemente 107, 193

possibly 107, 193
pray 97, 187
prefer 21
preferir 21
present participles 47, 48, 53
    spelling adjustments 48
    stem changes 48
present subjunctive, forms 10, 13, 15
    irregular verbs 15
    regular verbs 10
    spelling adjustments 17
    stem-change verbs 13
present tense indicative 150
present tense, meanings 150
preterite 146
preterite, "ellos" form 112
preterite, verb endings 122
preterite vs. imperfect, summary 123
prevent 97, 187
probably 107, 193
progressive tenses 47, 48
prohibir 97, 187
prohibit 97, 187
pronoun placement 48, 49
pronouns, direct object 48, 97, 187
pronouns, indirect object 48, 97, 187
pronouns, reflexive 48
proponer 97, 187
propose 97, 187
provided that 63, 141
pudiera 118
puede ser que 107
que 7, 21, 29, 37, 43, 125, 191
qué + [adjective /
    adverb / noun] + que 107, 193
querer 21, 87, 169
quienesquiera 103, 191
quienquiera 103, 191
quisiera 118
quizá / quizás 107, 193
recomendar 97, 187
recommend 97, 187
reflexive pronouns 48
rogar 97, 187
saber 15
seguir 48
sentence, definition 7
ser 15
ser + an adjective. 37
ser fantástico 37
should 118

"si" clauses 95, 177
siempre que 63, 141
simple verbs...47
single clause—
    expression of possibility..............107, 133
sin que 63, 141
so that..59, 141
spelling adujstments 17, 48, 112
stem-change verbs 112
subject, definition.....................................7
subjunctive +
    lo que + subjunctive....................103, 191
subordinate clause, definition 7
sugerir...21, 97, 187
suggest 21, 97, 187
suplicar...97, 187
talk out of 97, 187
tal vez 107, 193
tampoco...85
tan pronto como 63, 141
that is to say..107
the fact that...43
unless 63, 141
until 63, 141
urge...97, 187
urgir...97, 187
uses of the present tense 150
va a + infinitive 146
venir..48
verb, definition...7
verb endings for imperfect 122
verb endings for preterite 122
verbs, compound 47, 135
verbs, helping 48
verbs of influence: a shortcut.............97, 187
verbs, simple..47
verbs, stem-change 112
volition / influence 21, 125, 187
whatever 103, 191
when 141
whenever 103, 191
wherever 103, 191
whichever.......................................103, 191
while 63, 141
whoever 103, 191
without 63, 141
would like 118
would want..118

Author's Acknowledgements

This workbook is the result of many years of teaching adult students. Explanations and exercises have evolved over time and have been influenced by my professors, numerous textbooks, workshops at PNCFL, WAFLT and COFLT conferences, discussions with fellow teachers, and most of all by the needs of my students.

Thank you to all the students who worked through earlier versions of this book, finding endless typos and mistakes, pointing out confusions and indicating what parts needed to be expanded.

Thanks to early readers Sofia Basto, Meg Hayertz and Diane Andrikopoulos, and to proofreaders Nancy Battaglia, Susan Bishop, Susan Safford, Rochelle Silver and especially Angie Stambuk. I appreciate your time, the quality of your comments and your encouragement.

And I am grateful to Brian Jelgerhuis for his unconditional support and encouragement, and for his advice, design work and cover art.

About the Author

Leslie Hayertz holds a BA ed in Spanish from Central Washington University and an MA in Spanish from Middlebury College. She's worked in Quito, Ecuador, as a teacher and interpreter at the Instituto Nacional de Estadística y Censos, and has studied and traveled in Ecuador, Colombia, Central America, México and Spain. She was the founder of the Language Center in Port Townsend, WA, which offered classes in seven languages. When first arriving in Oregon, she worked as a bilingual farm secretary. She's since taught Spanish at community colleges in Oregon and for businesses such as Freightliner and Key Bank, as well as for county agencies in Clackamas County, Oregon. She is a playwright of one-act plays and the published author of reviews and short fiction. She currently teaches private Spanish classes in Portland, Oregon.

Printed in Great Britain
by Amazon